CLASSROOM MANAGEMENT

Proven strategies, tips, and techniques
for teachers in grades 5 - 9

**Includes 125 ready-to-use classroom activities
to improve discipline and student success**

by Brian Harris, B.A., M. Ed.

© 2012 by Brian Harris

All rights reserved. No part of this work may be reproduced
or transmitted in any form or by any means, electronic or
mechanical, including photocopying and recording, or by
any information storage or retrieval system, without
permission in writing from the publisher, except for the purchaser
of this book who can photocopy activities/handouts
for his/her classroom usage with students.

ISBN 978-1467961219

CGS Communications Inc.

www.highlyeffectiveteaching.com

TABLE OF CONTENTS

INTRODUCTION ... 5

A. TIPS + STRATEGIES FOR THE FIRST FEW WEEKS OF SCHOOL ... 13

   1. A Simple Beginning That Can Create Lasting Benefits 17

   2. Classroom Rules That Really Make A Difference 37

   3. Classroom Routines That Will Make Teaching Easier For You 71

   4. The Benefits Of Establishing A Positive Classroom Environment 107

B. HOW TO DEAL EFFECTIVELY WITH INAPPROPRIATE BEHAVIOR ... 139

   5. The Benefits Of Developing Empathetic Listening Skills 145

   6. Constructive Assertiveness 175

   7. How To Successfully Resolve Conflicts 199

   8. How To Teach Your Students Anger Management 231

   9. Specific Discipline Strategies 251

C. COMMON TRAITS OF HIGHLY EFFECTIVE TEACHERS ... 295

   10. How Your Teaching Methods Impact Classroom Management 297

   11. Looking After Yourself 313

BIBLIOGRAPHY ... 329

"Teachers generally believe that they are not only unprepared to deal with disruptive behaviour, but the amount of disruptive behaviour in their classes substantially interferes with their teaching."
Lowry, Sleet, Duncan, Powell, & Kolbe, 1995

"A journey of a thousand miles begins with a single step."
Chinese Proverb

INTRODUCTION

Imagine a classroom where students are hungry to learn. Imagine a classroom where students complete their work on time, where homework is never forgotten, and where students accomplish more instead of less. Imagine a classroom where students are positive and encouraging to each other as well as their teacher. Imagine a classroom where students are motivated to succeed. Imagine a classroom where teaching is a joy. Imagine.

A few years ago I was asked to present a workshop to a group of new teachers. The workshop was to occur one week before the new school year began. As an experienced teacher who had worked in almost every grade from 1 through to senior high school and as someone who had taught evening and summer professional courses to teachers for more than twenty years, I thought I had a pretty good idea of some things I would like to present to these "rookie" teachers. None-the-less it was important for me to better understand their needs rather than just assuming what I thought might benefit them. Through interviews with first year teachers and eventually with some soon-to-be teachers fresh out of college, I sought to learn what would be most helpful to the group I was going to be presenting to. In many ways, the results of those interviews followed by feedback from my actual work with new teachers (and along with my three decades of experience in education) led to the writing of this book.

So what was the number one request from these new teachers? Interestingly, their number one need was similar to what I also heard from experienced teachers as I worked with them in my evening courses or sat with them in staff rooms over many years. I suspect as a reader of this book, regardless of the number of years you have been a teacher, that you already know the single concern that is of greatest interest to educators, whether a beginner emerging from college or someone who is a veteran teacher. What is this one aspect of teaching that is most frequently bantered about in staff rooms, that sometimes leads to sleepless nights, that can cause stress to the point of being physically sick and in some cases result in a career change, that directly influences our ability to teach, and for some educators remains elusive for years? Yes, you are quite right if are thinking "discipline".

The word discipline might be defined as:
- training that corrects, molds or perfects
- control gained by obedience or training: orderly conduct
- a system of rules that govern conduct
- to train, especially in the area of self-control

While educators might frequently talk about discipline, the reality is that this is a term that is a part of something much larger that could be labeled as "classroom management". Without a properly managed classroom, effective teaching and learning cannot occur. Misbehavior and a lack of appropriate focus can not only become a great source of frustration for teachers, but can lead to disillusionment and apathy among those students who would really like to learn. The person most directly responsible for establishing a classroom environment most conducive to learning is the teacher.

> "The most important factor affecting student learning is the teacher. The results also show that the single factor that has the greatest relationship to improving education is to improve the effectiveness of teachers."
> S. Paul Wright, Sandra Horn, and William Sanders - 1997

Teaching our academic subjects, which is crucial to student success (more on this later in the book), is dependent on establishing an effective environment for learning. It could be said that classroom management provides the foundation for learning. Educational research confirms common sense that the amount of time "on task" in a classroom directly corresponds to academic success.

> "Research shows that on-task time correlates more powerfully with student achievement than does any other variable."
> University of California at Davis - 1978

How then do you increase the amount of time your students are actually engaged in your teaching of the curriculum which might also be rephrased as how do you decrease student misbehavior and inattentiveness? Is it really possible for a beginning teacher to master classroom management in a short period of time? After all, Geoff Colvin in his bestselling book "Talent Is Overrated - What Really Separates World-Class Performers from Everybody Else" clearly states that the research supports a high level of success in any endeavor requires thousands of hours of deliberate practice over many years. Thousands of hours over many years is simply too long for a beginning teacher to wait. Effective classroom management needs to begin on the first day of school. So how can this be done? Is there some way that a new teacher (or even an experienced teacher) can quickly learn classroom management techniques and strategies?

> "Success leaves clues"
> Anthony Robbins, Author of Unlimited Power

It has been often been stated that the fastest way to become successful is to find someone who has already achieved what you want to accomplish and then copy what they did. This "short-cut" to success becomes even more profound if the person who has achieved what you desire also agrees to become your mentor. This person can then provide the deliberate practice that Geoff Colvin found to be so important in his research. I believe the book you are now reading can help you to become a more effective classroom teacher, although I also think you would benefit from having a "master" teacher who could act as a mentor for you as you are attempting to learn and implement some of the principles in this book. As in any other learning, by putting the principles of this book into action you can begin to assess their value to help you as a teacher. While you may dream of having that perfect class, whatever that may be for you, action is required before results will occur.

In writing this book I was determined to discover the "clues" that lead to effective classroom management. Sometimes I found these clues in educational research. Other times I found these clues by observing and talking to effective teachers (and even learning from ineffective teachers). I also incorporated comments from both parents and students in considering techniques and strategies that can make a positive difference in classroom management. In addition, my findings were refined by my extensive classroom experiences as a teacher as well as my work in both administration and counseling in various schools.

While there is no magic wand that will solve all classroom concerns, I believe this book provides practical strategies and tips that can truly make a difference for teachers. Although I also believe that some of this content can make an immediate difference, I do think it is important to recognize that any type of achievement requires patience, persistence and preparation. In addition, I can't recommend strongly enough that the content of this book will be much more effective (and easier learned) if you pair yourself with a "master" teacher in your school who can guide and assist you.

This resource is different than most other books related to classroom management as it provides practical activities that you can use with your students. I have selected activities that I have either personally used or seen in action. Where you don't feel a specific activity might be appropriate for your students, then consider the principle behind the activity and attempt to design an activity for your students based on that principle. A basic approach that I am presenting throughout this book is that both you and your students can learn some strategies and techniques together related to classroom management. After all, if you go back to the definition of discipline that I mentioned earlier in this introduction, you will find the word "training" repeated several times. The activities in this book can help you as you train (or teach) your students appropriate classroom behavior and effective work habits.

There is a strong philosophical belief in this book that the foundation that you lay during the first few weeks of any school year or term can make a huge difference in classroom management throughout the remainder of the year. As such, it is important for you to realize that the time spent in establishing classroom routines, rules and procedures during those first few weeks can pay dividends later. In conducting workshops for teachers, I am often asked about handling specific discipline concerns. The reality in many of these cases is that the inappropriate behavior could have been avoided in the first place if the teacher had established some effective classroom management strategies. Classroom management (and discipline) is most effective when it is proactive rather than being reactive. Another benefit of taking a proactive approach is that it is less stressful and time-consuming than constantly reacting to problems instead of preventing them. The best solution for solving problems is to try to prevent them from occurring.

While I believe that the content of this book can make a positive difference in the classroom, I think it is important to recognize that the strategies and tips in this book cannot work miracles for every student. Unfortunately there are some students who bring concerns into the classroom that go beyond the scope of this book. Some of these students may require intensive counseling and/or alternate classroom or school placements. Hopefully the activities and thoughts in this book can help you to better ascertain which students need help beyond your expertise, or beyond the content of this book, and as such, you will be able to facilitate appropriate assistance for them.

While classroom management can help to establish a foundation for learning, it is critical to realize that the activities in this book are not intended to replace actual learning in your subject curriculum. Remember, the research shows that the greatest contributor to success is "on-task" learning (of your subject curriculum). While the activities in this book might (and should) have a greater influence during the first few weeks of a term or school year, it is very important to realize that the sooner you begin to teach (your subject curriculum), the better.

Years ago I wrote several books related to helping students improve their self-esteem. At the time it was felt that a high level of self-esteem contributed to academic success. I was often asked by teachers whether it was a higher level of self-esteem that contributed to academic success, or whether it was academic success that contributed to a higher level of self-esteem. The answer to this question seems to now be a little clearer as the current research tends to show that academic success makes a significant contribution to the development of self-esteem and positive attitude. Students who are successful in achieving curriculum objectives are generally the students who want to learn and who do not exhibit inappropriate behavior. As such, helping your students to be successful in your subject area may assist in classroom management and the prevention of discipline problems (see Chapter 10 for further thoughts in this area) and increase both self-esteem and positive attitude.

> "As achievement improves, students become more positive about school and, interestingly, teachers tend to become more positive about the work they are doing as teachers."
> Wayne Hutley and Linda Dier
> in *Getting By or Getting Better*, 2009

Effective teaching involves a purposeful step-by-step plan that progresses logically. Similarly, establishing solid classroom management learning also requires a step-by-step logical plan. While this book provides many principles (and related activities) to help you establish a consistent and meaningful system of classroom management, it is important for you to set some type of actual plan that includes timelines for achieving your goals related to classroom management. Chapters 9 + 10 can assist you further with this.

In a well-structured classroom, most behavior problems can be prevented when students know your expectations and there are clear consequences when students fail to meet your expectations. The classroom activities in this book can make a significant difference in your room, but they must be supported by assertiveness on your part to communicate what is expected and what will happen when expectations are not met. And when expectations are not met, logical consequences must follow. Without consistent consequences your students will quickly hijack your classroom, regardless of how many strategies and techniques related to classroom discipline you might arm yourself with.

There are a variety of personalities that can engage in effective teaching. As a counselor, it was fascinating to often meet with parents and students during the first week of school who were requesting a teacher change. The conversation sometimes went something like, "My daughter is in Mr. M's class. He is a very strict teacher who has a no nonsense policy in his class. My daughter is terrified of him and we think it would be much more appropriate for her to be transferred to another teacher who is more approachable, maybe someone like Mr. S." Interestingly, before the day ended I generally had another student and her parents who proceeded to tell me, "My daughter is in Mr. S's class. He is a very informal teacher and we don't think our daughter is going to learn well from him. We think it would be much more appropriate if my daughter was transferred to another teacher, maybe someone like Mr. M. who has better control of his class." In other words, some students learn better from different teachers. Similarly, some students may behave better for different teachers. As such, if you are having difficulties with a student, I think it is useful to talk to the student's other teachers. If there is a teacher who is not having concerns with the student, perhaps you can learn some specific techniques from this teacher to help you. On the other hand, if all the teachers are having problems with this student, I recommend that a curriculum leader, counselor, and/or administrator be involved in meeting with all the teachers to form a consistent plan to help this student (which could be based on some principles within this book). Regardless of your personality or teaching style I believe you can become an effective classroom manager.

While becoming an effective classroom manager can take careful planning and hard work, it important to note that an extensive review of many research sources in the area of student achievement confirmed the importance of classroom management (see the quote on the next page). It is my belief, and the research supports this belief, that awareness of some basic principles and the implementation of these principles can result in the making of effective classroom managers. By making the effort to become a more effective classroom manager, you can increase the level of student achievement in your class.

> "Classroom management rates first in terms of its impact on student achievement."
> Margaret Wang, Geneva Haertel, and Herbert Walberg, 1993
> (based on an extensive study of the research that had been done in the area of student achievement)

In using this book I suggest that you take a quick look through each of the chapters to familiarize yourself with the content. Chapters 9 + 10 in the book provide a framework to help you to establish an actual plan for implementing the principles and using the activities from this book. It is not necessary to use every activity throughout this book with your students. As has already been suggested, the content of this book is intended to help you establish an effective classroom management framework - it is not intended to replace your subject area curriculum. If you are implementing some principles from this book and you are beyond the first month of school, it is important to remember that you have already established your expectations and manner of doing things. Changing these may initially be confusing to your students so your results may not be as significant as they might be if you introduced these principles on day one of the school year. Throughout the book I provide some real-life case studies to support the principles being presented. The names within the case studies have been to changed to protect the anonymity of the students and the studies are sometimes the result of a compilation of work with several students to further protect the students involved.

> "After 40 years of intensive research on school learning in the United States as well as abroad, my major conclusion is what any person in the world can learn, almost all persons can learn."
> Dr. Benjamin Bloom

> "The main reason most people struggle professionally and personally is simply a lack of focus."
>
> Jack Canfield, Mark Victor Hansen, and Les Hewitt in *The Power of Focus,* 2000

PART A

WHAT SHOULD YOU DO DURING THE FIRST FEW WEEKS OF SCHOOL?

Perhaps you have heard a veteran teacher talk about what needs to be done during the first week or two of school. If not, here goes - the framework you establish related to classroom management during the first few weeks of school (perhaps even the first day of school) will generally typify the way your classroom is going to look throughout the term or year. Placing a high emphasis on an orderly classroom from the outset will help to ensure that you are teaching later instead of constantly struggling with student discipline. The first few weeks of school provide an opportunity for you lay the foundation for the kind of classroom where both you and your students want to be. During this time your efforts could focus on four areas: connecting with your students (Chapter 1), establishing meaningful rules (Chapter 2), setting routines and procedures that make a difference (Chapter 3), and creating a positive classroom environment where it is a joy to teach (Chapter 4). The manner in which your class begins on day one sets the tone for what will be happening on day one-hundred.

> "First comes thought, then organization of that thought into ideas and plans; then transformation of those plans into reality.
> The beginning, as you will observe, is in your imagination."
> Napoleon Hill

Let's then begin with this question, "What do you want your classroom to look like?" Close your eyes and visualize the appearance of your room. With your eyes still closed, watch as your students go about their daily tasks. Watch as you teach. In your mind, imagine how your perfect classroom would look and how your students interact with others including yourself. There are many articles and books related to success that stress the importance of forming a crystal clear vision of what it is that you want before you can set goals and actually achieve them. These same resources often talk about creating a "vision board", an actual visual representation of what your end result looks like.

Before you begin to implement any attempts to establish a system of classroom management, it is critical that you first identify what success will look like for you. It is possible that different teachers might have different visions in this regard although I expect there will be some commonalities between well-functioning classroom environments. Once again, I pose the question, "What do you want your classroom to look like?" Unless you form a mental picture of what you desire, it will be difficult to achieve any positive changes in your classroom management.

> "Formulate and stamp indelibly on your mind a mental picture of yourself as succeeding. Hold this picture tenaciously. Never permit it to fade. Your mind will seek to develop the picture...Do not build up obstacles in your imagination."
> Norman Vincent Peale

In the following four chapters you will begin to look at some concrete strategies that you can use during the first few weeks of school to lay a solid foundation for effective classroom management. First, and before you even begin to read further in this book, take some time to form a vibrant picture of what a well-managed classroom looks like. It is this mental picture that can help you to synthesize your learning from this book and also help you keep an unwavering focus during those moments when you are "tested" by some of your students. I would even recommend that you write down some thoughts on what your ideal classroom looks like (including the times when you are teaching or the students are working on assignments). Keep this outline handy and refer to it often.

It is normal for any teacher to feel some apprehension or stress before the first day of school. Being prepared can be the great stress reducer. There is a tendency for new teachers to place a great emphasis on the physical appearance of the classroom, often spending hours and sometimes even weeks before school begins to create that perfect looking classroom. While an attractive classroom can assist your students in feeling comfortable, it is more important to consider your classroom routines, rules and procedures and what you are actually going to teach on the first day and during the first week. Keep in mind that most students will arrive in your classroom on the first day ready to learn. In a sense this is the "honeymoon" period. As a result, you will generally have this immediate moment to begin your success in teaching, or if you are unprepared you will lose this opportunity.

> "By failing to prepare,
> you are preparing to fail."
> Benjamin Franklin

The next four chapters provide some basic principles related to establishing effective classroom management. While these principles are supported by research, I think it is more important to note that the activities presented have been personally field-tested in classrooms. It is recommended that you glance through each chapter and then choose 3 - 4 activities that you feel might work best with your students. It is not necessary to complete every activity that is listed in these chapters (or in this book) with your students. In addition, depending on your grade and the mix of students in your class, it may sometimes be necessary to take the intent of an activity and create a similar one that you feel might better meet the needs of your students. During the first two weeks of school, although your students may spend significant time in completing these activities, as has already been noted in this book it is important to begin the teaching of your curriculum as soon as possible. Although you won't be looking at curriculum in more detail until Chapter 10, I strongly recommend that during the first period with your students that some of this time is related to teaching a new lesson in your subject area. As you begin to teach, you will have the opportunity to help your students transfer their learning from the activities in the first four chapters to the reality of what you are going to expect from them throughout the year or term. In the end, your major goal is to help your students be more successful in your subject area; classroom management is simply the framework to allow this to happen.

"Trust is the glue of life.
It's the most essential ingredient in
effective communication."
Stephen R. Covey

CHAPTER 1

A SIMPLE BEGINNING
THAT CAN CREATE LASTING BENEFITS

Doesn't it feel good when someone takes a genuine interest in something you are doing? The unfortunate reality is that we live at a time when most people are so busy and so caught up in their own lives that it is unusual to have someone express a desire to learn more about us. In our schools, it is often this personal contact with students that makes a significant positive difference in their classroom attitude and behavior. I am often amazed at how many adults remember their best teacher as someone who took a personal interest in them. Connecting with your students (and this doesn't mean you have to be their best "buddy") can make a significant difference in helping you with your classroom management.

> *During the first week of one of my classes, two physically large fourteen year old boys were a constant disruption with their endless misbehavior. I tried various discipline techniques with them to no avail. Towards the end of the week, one day they both wore football jerseys to class. As they were leaving the class I asked them about their interest in football and discovered that they had a game that evening at a local park. Altering my evening schedule to attend their game created an unbelievable result as the following day, in class, the two boys suddenly became my strongest supporters. Their classroom behavior literally changed overnight. Showing a personal interest in them created acceptance and acknowledgement that they, in turn, returned back to me.*
> Grade 9 Teacher

This first chapter provides one of the easiest, and sometimes most successful, strategies to lay the foundation for your classroom management. The activities in this chapter can help you to get off to a strong start by connecting with your students which can be very beneficial when you then add other strategies and techniques in this book. Having a connection with each student helps to create an atmosphere where they will be more willing to accept what you are attempting to do in the classroom. There are, though, two important things to keep in mind as you establish connections with your students. First of all, taking a personal interest in your students does not mean you have to become their best friend and most certainly does not mean that your students need to know the intricate personal details of your own life. It is generally not appropriate to be sharing information related to your own personal problems with your students. Secondly, although you will spend some time during the first week or two establishing these connections, be careful that your students don't then constantly sidetrack your teaching in the following weeks and months wanting to talk about personal matters or interests. Remember, that success for your students comes with time on-task learning.

Activities #1 - 3 focus on learning the names of your students and helping them to feel welcome. Using a student's name is a powerful part of classroom management so the quicker you learn their names, the better. In addition, when you use a student's name (and when other students also use the names of their classmates) this helps everyone to feel more accepted and welcome. Activities #4 - 8 and #10 can help you to learn more about your students as individuals. Informally talking to a student about his/her interests, whether it is in the hallway, cafeteria or on field trips as examples, can create a positive connection between you and the student. This generally results in them being more receptive to your teaching. Activities #9, 11 and 12 can help students in a fun manner to feel more comfortable in the classroom which once again can help them to be receptive to learn. Activity #13 provides some further thoughts on how you can connect with your students throughout the year and Activity #14 explores the value of also connecting with your students' parents.

> "One looks back with appreciation to the brilliant teachers,
> but with gratitude to those who touched our human feelings.
> The curriculum is so much raw material,
> but warmth is the vital element for the growing plant
> and for the soul of a child."
> Carl Jung

ACTIVITY 1

WELCOME

1. Walk into Walmart and you are instantly greeted by a friendly staff member. If this approach works in one of the most successful businesses in the world then doesn't it make it sense to copy this in some way in your classroom. Here are some variations that I have seen work effectively.

    a) students line up at your door on the first day. Each student is personally greeted by you as they enter the room. As students enter one by one, tell them to give you their names. Repeat their names, look them in the eye and welcome each student with sincerity. It is important not to turn this into a frivolous activity and I wouldn't recommend that you use any form of joking or humor. Let the students know they are welcome, but through your non-verbal behavior convey that you are in charge. The purpose of this approach is to let students know that you are genuinely pleased to have each of them in your class, it is not intended to make students think you are "cool" or a "fun buddy".

    b) if it is impractical to have students line up outside your room, after they are seated at their desks, ask each student one-by-one for his/her name, welcoming him/her as you do this.

    c) as you read each student's name, ask the student to tell you something that he/she enjoys doing when he/she is not as school. This could turn into a mini-conversation between you and each student. This may also present at opportunity to reinforce that only one person at a time talks in your class.

    d) tell students whose name begins with the letter A to stand. Each student who is standing then repeats his/her name one at a time. Continue on to letter B and so on.

ACTIVITY 2

NAME MEMORY GAME

You can begin this game by stating your name. Next a student states his/her name and then yours. Next, another student (likely the one sitting behind the first student) states his/her name, then the name of the first student, and then your name. The next student repeats the process starting with his/her name and then continuing to name the others who have already stated their name. This process continues throughout the class until every student has been named. If you find that part way through a class that any student is struggling with all the names that came before him/her, then start fresh with this student and begin the activity over again. Once you have completed the task, begin once again starting with the student who was last before. This activity can be beneficial (especially for new students) even if most of your students already know each other. One of the real benefits of this activity is that you will quickly learn the names of all the students in your class.

ACTIVITY 3

OUR CLASS WORD SEARCH

There are a few variations of this activity. The first is that you prepare the word search beforehand using page 22 (and incorporating the names of all the students in your class). The disadvantage of this approach is the time involved in making it and the concern that some new students may be enrolled in your class at the last minute and their names might not be on the word search.

The preferred method would be to give each student a copy of page 22. Students design a word search incorporating the names of all the students in the class. To do this, you will need a list of your students posted in the class. Once students have completed their word searches they can either trade with a friend or you could collect them, make a few copies of each word search and use them over the next few days.

ACTIVITY 4

WHO AM I?

1. Each student writes a description of himself/herself including interests and hobbies.

2. The descriptions are collected and read, one at time, aloud. After each sentence in the description, the students attempt to guess who the student is. The clues continue, if necessary, until the complete description is read.

3. Repeat the process for another student.

OUR CLASS

ACTIVITY 5

HAVE YOU EVER?

1. Each student is given a copy of page 24. Students move around the class asking one student at a time if he/she has ever done one of the experiences listed on the page. If the answer is "yes", the student prints his/her name in the appropriate box (and only one box!).

2. After the sheets are completed, ask your students to share some of their stories that relate to the experiences on this sheet. A blank copy of the activity is also provided on page 25 in the event you (or your students) would like to design the activity.

> "A sign of an excellent teacher is someone that takes the time to listen to her students. I once had a teacher who used to spend her recess when she was on duty chatting with my best friends and I.
>
> Grade 5 Student

Have you ever . . .

performed on a stage?	been on a championship team?	won an award at school?	read a suspenseful book?
won a contest?	taken music lessons?	had an unusual pet?	moved to another country?
met a famous person?	ate an exotic food?	been a volunteer in your community?	watched an exciting movie?

Have you ever . . .

ACTIVITY 6

I AM UNIQUE

1. Discuss the meaning of the word "unique". In addition, talk about things that make people unique (stress positive characteristics as students provide suggestions). It would be useful to keep a list of personality traits, interests, hobbies, etc. that students identify as things that make people unique.

2. Each student is given a copy of page 27. You will require an ink pad or you could also use some washable paint. Each student uses the ink or paint to print his/her thumb print in the appropriate box.

3. Next, each student signs his/her autograph in the appropriate box.

4. Each student identifies three things that makes him/her unique (the list formed in #1 could be helpful to students in doing this). It would be useful for each student to share his/her results.

ACTIVITY 7

AN INTRODUCTION TO ME

1. Each student is given a copy of pages 28 + 29. Students complete the sentences on each of these pages.

2. Each student is paired with another student. Students share information about themselves with their partner.

3. Each student introduces his/her partner to the class based on the information shared in #2.

I AM UNIQUE

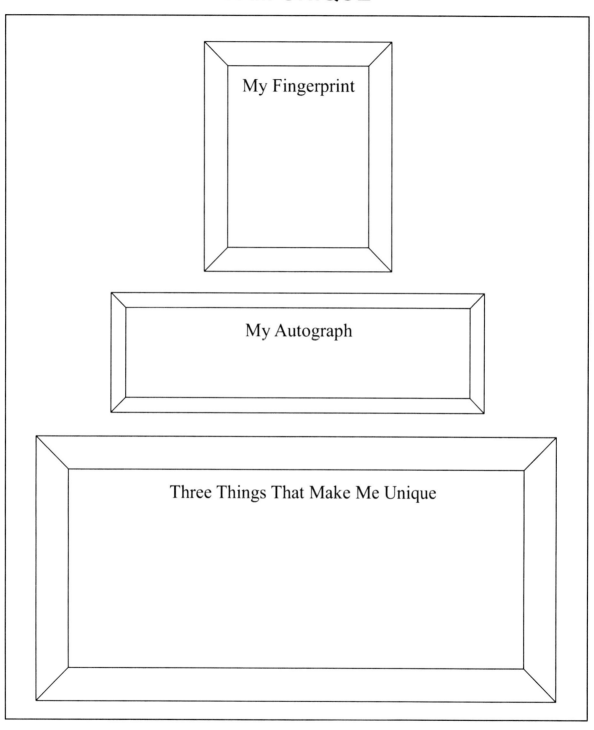

AN INTRODUCTION TO ME

My full name is ...

The name I like to be called best is ...

I enjoy reading books about ...

The thing I enjoy doing the most at school is ...

When I'm not at school I like to ...

My favorite subject at school is ...

If I could have any animal in the world for a pet, I would like to have a ...

The music I enjoy listening to the most is ...

If I could take a trip anywhere in the world, I would like to visit ...

AN INTRODUCTION TO ME

Some of the shows I enjoy watching on television are ...

If I was rich I would use some of my money for ...

Something I enjoy doing on a computer is ...

I think a best friend is someone who ...

A hobby or interest I enjoy is ...

I like it when ...

ACTIVITY 8

CHILDHOOD PICTURES

1. Each student brings in a childhood picture (or takes a picture from a magazine that best illustrates some aspect of childhood for him).

2. Pictures are arranged anonymously on a bulletin board, poster or wall and each picture is numbered.

3. Over the course of two or three days students write the number of each picture and then attempt to identify the student in each picture. Discuss the results and provide an opportunity for each student to tell his class a little more about the photograph.

ACTIVITY 9

NAME ART

Students enjoy seeing their names posted in the classroom. For this activity each student uses his name as part of a design or picture. Results are posted in the room.

ACTIVITY 10

SHOPPING BAG

1. Each student brings in a shopping bag that contains an article that represents something she enjoys doing when she is not at school. Samples might be dancing shoes, a baseball, video game, etc.

2. Each student creates 4 - 5 sentences that each give a clue about the object in the bag.

3. Any student begins the activity by providing a clue about what is in her bag. The other students attempt to guess the identity of the object. The student continues to provide clues until the object is successfully identified. Continue the process until everyone has had a turn. It would also be useful to encourage each student to tell a little more about her interest.

ACTIVITY 11

NAME TONGUE TWISTERS

1. Each student creates a tongue twister using her name. An example might be "Samantha Smith saved six small stamps from Switzerland, Spain, Sudan, Syria, Sweden and Somalia."

2. Share the results.

ACTIVITY 12

OUR CLASS AUTOGRAPHS
A PROUD CLASS

1. Each student is given a copy of page 33. Each student collects the autographs of all his classmates. Stress the importance of students writing serious autographs instead of adding "jokes" of some form to their names.

2. Students carry the autographs in one of their binders or notebooks as a reminder of their "proud class".

> "The only way to have a friend is to be one."
> Ralph Waldo Emerson

OUR PROUD CLASS

ACTIVITY 13

MAKING CONNECTIONS

As stated in the introduction of this chapter, the purpose of this chapter is to help you make connections with your students. As previously noted, knowing the names of each of your students can be a huge factor in helping students to feel accepted. In addition, addressing a student by name when it is necessary to provide some guidance for their classroom behavior is very important. The activities in this chapter can also help you to understand some personal information about each student. It is also possible that as students learn more about each other that this might create new friendships for them.

Showing an interest in your students can help you to bond with them which is often a very positive proactive way to gain their trust which can result in an acceptance of your rules and classroom procedures. Trust with your students can also help them to be more receptive to your teaching.

As a follow-up to the activities in this chapter, you can strengthen your connections with your students by following some or even all of the following suggestions:

- strive to use a student's name whenever you are talking to him/her
- as students complete activities in this chapter, keep a master list of some personal interests for each student
- attempt to talk to each student whenever possible about their interests (in the hallways, on lunch/recess supervision, field trips, etc.)
- keep a master list of your students where you place a check mark beside the name of each student after you have had an informal conversation with them. This helps to ensure that you build trust and create acceptance with every student in your class.
- during parent/teacher interviews don't hesitate to acknowledge out-of-school interests for each of your students. This not only demonstrates to parents that you are genuinely interested in their child, but the parents will often provide additional information that might be helpful.

ACTIVITY 14

EARLY PARENTAL CONTACT

Although initially time-consuming there is much to be said about contacting the parents/guardians of your students during the first week of school. This could provide an opportunity for a positive introductory conversation which helps to build some rapport with the adults in the lives of your students in the event you need to contact them at a future time. Your telephone call can also give a direct message to your students that you will involve their parents in what is happening in the classroom. Your call should simply state who you are and that you are pleased to have George or Julie in your class. You might also ask the parents if they have any questions about what you will be teaching this year. An empathetic approach (see Chapter 5) can help to leave the door open for a parent to express something that might be useful for you to know about their child. While this will certainly place an extra time demand on you during the first week of school, ask yourself if it is worth it if it later saves you time related to what is happening with students in your class?

For those who teach more than one class throughout the day, the time demands will usually be far too great to make individual telephone calls. In this case you might consider a letter or email to introduce yourself and use this as another opportunity to welcome the student to your class.

Regardless of your approach, keep your message short and positive. The contact may also give you some indication of the support you can expect from the parents in the event you need them to assist you in correcting any inappropriate classroom behavior for their child at some point. It would be useful to keep a record of any concerns or other specific information offered by the parents. This information could be helpful in later parent/teacher interviews.

"Unlike normative classroom values that are best created as a community, nonnegotiable rules are clear and should be chosen unilaterally by the teacher."
Matthew A. Kraft
in *Phi Delta Kappan*, 2010

CHAPTER 2

A FEW CLASSROOM RULES
THAT CAN MAKE A HUGE DIFFERENCE

For a moment imagine that you are leaving to go on a much needed vacation. You arrive at the airport, wearing some new clothes and full of excitement. After moving through the ticketing process, you are suddenly led into a large room with all the other passengers. Your pilot greets you and states that he would like you and the other passengers to set some rules of behavior for the flight. You groan at the delay that is now going to occur before you leave. Within minutes as the most vocal passengers begin to dominate the conversation, you begin to feel both frustration and anger at the pilot for initiating this discussion. After all, you think, isn't this the role of the airlines to establish in-flight rules? Finally, after more than an hour delay you get on the airplane with some vague rules about "respecting the rights of others."

About thirty minutes into your flight, your attempts to read a new novel are disrupted by the two people sitting beside you who are engaged in a loud animated conversation. You ask them to stop but they only glare at you and their conversation seems to increase in intensity. You call for a flight attendant to help you. After he arrives and listens to your concerns, he says to the others, "Remember, our number one rule is to respect the rights of others" to which the other two passengers quickly add that it is their right to be able to talk. An argument about the real intent of the rule transpires with more and more passengers now being disturbed by the opposing views of what this rule really means.

While you might think that the above example is preposterous, isn't this approach exactly what some teaches do? The students arrive on the first day of school, most of them excited to be returning back to school and many of them actually looking forward to learning. Then in the spirit of classroom democracy some teachers ask the students to help set some classroom rules. Yes, I know, this is generally done because if the students help to set the rules then this approach might help them to actually follow the rules because they, after all, have established them. While there might be some truth in this, is it possible that before the first hour of school has even ended that you have transferred your role as the classroom leader to some students in your class? Have you immediately conveyed to your students that you are not the person in charge? Have you immediately given permission for the most aggressive or vocal students to take over? And consider some other ramifications of letting your students choose the rules for your class. What would happen if the students chose rules that you don't agree to or you don't feel comfortable with? You might suddenly find yourself telling the students that you can't accept some of their rules, at which point you are, within the first hour of school, undermining your credibility to be trusted and/or communicating to your students that you don't respect or can't accept their suggestions. In addition, what about the silent majority of your students who really want to learn and quickly become frustrated and maybe even angry by the confusion as to who is really the classroom leader? What started with the best of intentions may end up doing more harm than good. And if one of your rules is something along the line of "respect the rights of others" then you may have permitted a rule that is going to be continually open to interpretation throughout the school year and may result in more confusion and ongoing disruption than you had hoped for. Remember that the manner in which your start your school year can set the tone for what happens next.

> "All effectively managed classrooms have rules although they can vary from classroom to classroom."
> Emmer, Evertson, and Worsham (2003)

Consider an approach where you assertively state 3 - 5 rules for your classroom There is no discussion. You immediately establish yourself as the classroom leader. Your rules establish some limits which is an important part of helping students to feel comfortable. In addition, your rules are the ones that you know as a professional teacher make the most sense and will make the greatest contribution to helping you to teach your curriculum. During the first day, if there is any confusion related to one of your rules, you can stop whatever is happening and ensure that your students understand exactly what the rule means and what would be the consequences of breaking the rule. Keep in mind, that as you will see in more detail in this chapter, that rules without clear enforceable consequences will not likely work. If every time the police pulled over a "speeder" on the highway and simply gave a warning, it wouldn't be long before many drivers were out-of-control. Rules require consequences and consequences need to be enforced.

> "A small number of rules will keep students from feeling overwhelmed."
> Cara Pitterman in *Scholastic*, 2011

In setting your rules it is best to avoid a list things that your students shouldn't do. A better approach is to word your rules in a positive manner so instead of "Don't speak unless you first raise your hand." it would be preferable to state "Raise your hand before I select you to speak." In addition, I think it makes sense to avoid generalized or vague comments. Although I have seen many classrooms where one of the rules was "Respect the rights of others", my experience tells me that this rule can be left open to individual interpretation and instead of helping to give you more on-task time to be teaching your curriculum, you may find yourself in constant arguments with some students whose views on respecting the rights of others is different than yours.

> "It is recommended that rules be positively worded."
> Thorson (2003)

Perhaps it might be useful at this time to actually define the word "rule". A dictionary definition includes the following:

- a guide or principle to govern action
- the usual way of doing something
(source: The Merriam-Webster Dictionary, 2011)

A thesaurus would provide some of the following words as synonyms for the word "rule":

- decree, guide, guideline, law, order, principle, regulation, ruling, standard
(source: Collins Thesaurus, 2011)

There are two key factors to consider in thinking about a rule. First, a rule describes the official and accepted way of doing something. Secondly, when a rule is broken some form of consequence will follow. The case study on the next page provides an example of breaking a rule and a teacher's approach to applying consequences.

What are your thoughts on the teacher's handling of the behavior problem related to the case study on page 41? Hopefully, you would agree that the teacher took far too long to get to the actual consequence for breaking the rule. The teacher could have simply given the student a warning to sit down and keep quiet. If this was not done, then a consequence could follow immediately. The more you talk and the longer you postpone any consequences as you beg, bribe, and argue with a student, the more time you are wasting for everyone else in class. Although a teacher may tell a student that he is wasting everyone's time through his misbehavior, another reality is that the teacher is also wasting time if she fails to quickly apply a logical consequence to the breaking of a class rule. It is strongly recommended that you consider a few consequences for the breaking of any class rules before you ever post them. There will always be some students who will "test" your rules and a failure on your part to enforce appropriate consequences will quickly devalue your rules leaving you with some students who constantly misbehave. Planning your consequences beforehand can help you to deliver them calmly and assertively (two important characteristics of an effective teacher - see Chapter 6). Your students will take your rules much more seriously when there are consequences that are enforced whenever a rule is broken.

As you consider your class rules, keep in mind that a vibrant class where students feel comfortable in making mistakes is more beneficial to learning than a classroom where students are fearful of making the slightest noise.

> "The rules we practice and are willing
> to support with consistent discipline
> are the rules kids respect
> and take seriously."
> Robert J. Mackenzie and Lisa Stanzione
> in *Setting Limits In The Classroom*, 2010

"Mike, please sit down and stop talking."
Mike continues to wander from friend to friend, still talking.
"Come on Mike. You know our rules state that you have to stay in your seat."
Mike continues to be out of his seat and is still talking to others.
"Mike, this is the last time I am going to tell you."
Mike continues to be out of his seat and is still talking to others.
"Come on Mike. You know that what you are doing is wrong."
Mike smiles at his teacher and continues to talk to others.
"Mike, how would our class function if everyone got out
of their seat and started talking to others?"
Mike shrugs and then starts to talk again.
"Mike, I'm getting angry. This has to stop."
Mike looks at his teacher as though he is assessing her level of anger.
"Mike, we've been through this before. You're not going to win so get in your seat."
Mike pays no attention to his teacher and keeps talking.
"Mike!!!"
For a moment, Mike stops talking and looks at his teacher as though
he is waiting to see what is going to happen next. After the brief pause,
Mike once again begins to talk to a friend.
"Mike, you need to stop talking right now and sit down."
"Why are you picking on me? Other people are talking and you're not saying
anything to them. Why are you always picking on me?"
"Mike, I'm not picking on you. You are breaking a class rule.
And this is not about other people in our class.
I will deal with them after I deal with you."
"But that's unfair. Why are you always after me?"
"Mike, I'm always after you because you are always misbehaving."
There is a general ripple of laughter in the classroom.
Mike looks proud of the response he is receiving from his peers.
""Mike, please sit down. This has gone on long enough. I'm losing my patience."
Mike moves on to another student and continues to talk.
"Mike, you are wasting everyone's time. You need to respect the rights of others."
"What about my rights?"
"Mike, I'm going to count to three and if you are not in your seat and quiet
by the time I get to three, you will stay in my classroom for the entire lunch today."

Grade 6 Teacher

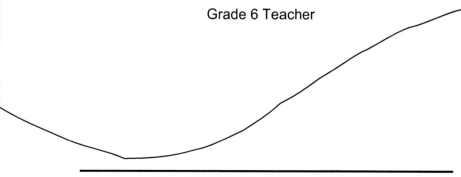

For many students, appropriate classroom rules set parameters for classroom behavior that creates some degree of comfort. Most students like to know what is expected and will honor limits as long as they are fair and enforced consistently. Another key to establishing a classroom that is conducive to learning is to ensure that your students understand your classroom rules and the rationale for them. In explaining any rule it is important that the rationale for the rule be clear. In some cases a rule might lead to increased learning for your students while other rules might be more of a safety concern. Whatever the case, ensure that your students are very familiar with your expectations and your reasons for them.

The activities in this chapter can help you to set appropriate rules for your class, help your students better understand the rationale for these rules, and help you set logical and fair consequences in the event that your rules are broken.

The first few activities (#15 - 19 + 22) look at workable classroom rules and the rationale for them. Although it is suggested that you provide 3 - 5 rules for your students, it is still worthwhile for your students to give you feedback on these rules. Next, two activities (#20 + 21) give you some thoughts on using silent signals (usually with your hands) to help remind students of your rules. Consider the hand signals similar to what an orchestra conductor might do to lead his musicians. The conductor has a system of hand signals that the musicians have learned and closely follow which generally prevents the need for the conductor to shout to gain control of the orchestra. Similarly a classroom teacher can use hand signals to lead her class in a quiet, more relaxed manner.

As already mentioned, consequences are an important part of establishing a foundation for classroom management. If there are no consequences when students break your rules, your rules will quickly become meaningless to your students. Activities # 23 - 27 can help you to provide meaningful consequences related to your rules. As noted in these activities it is important that you not only have consequences for students when they break your rules, but it is also effective to have some related consequences for students who routinely follow your rules.

Activity #28 looks at value of using games as a teaching strategy. Students enjoy games and these can be a fun way to increase curriculum learning. Your students can even play a major role in designing games based on any quiz games that are currently popular.

Finally, Activities #29 + 30 provide an opportunity to ensure that your students are aware of school-wide rules.

ACTIVITY 15

CLASS RULES

As stated in the introduction to this chapter I recommend that you choose 3 - 5 rules for your class that you feel comfortable with and that you know can make a difference in creating a comfortable teaching and learning environment. It is also suggested that these rules are already posted in your class when your students first arrive. By grade 5, your rules should not surprise any of your students so it is not necessary to provide a lengthy rationale for these rules (although other activities in this chapter can help your students better understand the reasons for these rules and the benefits they can gain by following the rules).

Here are three rules that I have personally used with success. In choosing your rules, if you are a new teacher it would be useful to talk to some experienced teachers in your school about the rules they have found to be successful in their classrooms. Remember these are your rules so choose those that you feel most comfortable with. As you set your rules, it is also important to consider the consequences that you will use if a rule is broken. You will note, in the list below, that I didn't mention anything about talking or getting out of your seat during times when students are working. I accepted students talking during these times, especially if they were sharing ideas or helping each other. This sometimes required students to move around the room. A key question to ask yourself (before telling your students to keep quiet) is the talking related to the lesson?

1. Raise your hand and wait until you are chosen to speak during a lesson or student presentation.

2. Be positive with everyone in our class.

3. Be ready to start our lesson on time.

What makes a good teacher?

A good teacher should be kind to his students, but should also be firm when necessary.

This should go without saying, but they should also teach well. By "teach well", I don't just mean that a teacher should simply teach the lesson. I think teaching well means that the teacher teaches the lesson, makes sure everyone understands it, and then reinforces the lesson later on, whether it's reinforced through homework, tests or projects, or even more schoolwork on the day the lesson was taught to help the topic stick in the student's mind.

Another trait of a good teacher is understanding. A good teacher understands that you already have a lot of work. I always appreciate it when a teacher takes the time to ask what else we have going on (projects, tests, etc.). This shows me that the teacher understands that we have a lot of other things to do and that they are trying their best to make our lives a bit easier.

Grade 7 Student

ACTIVITY 16

RULES IN OUR SOCIETY

1. Tell your students to identify some rules in our society. You could begin by identifying traffic laws such as speed limits. It is also important for students to consider rules that might apply to stores or even rules that relate to behavior among people in the community. It would be useful to list the rules as your students suggest them.

2. Using one of the rules as an example (perhaps the speed limit rule), students identify how they benefit from such a rule.

3. Each student is given a copy of page 46 to complete. Results are shared and discussed.

ACTIVITY 17

THE BENEFITS OF OUR CLASS RULES

1. It is important that Activity #15 is completed before doing this activity. Using one of your class rules as an example, students discuss the intent of the rule and how the rule can benefit them. It is important that students are aware that a major benefit of your rules is that they can be more successful in learning. Most students start the school year wanting to be successful. A major benefit of your rules should be that following the rules will help each student to be more successful in your subject area as there will be more time spent in learning instead of dealing with constant disruptions.

2. Students are given a copy of page 47 to complete. Results are shared and discussed.

A RULE IN OUR SOCIETY

1. An example of a rule in our society is . . .

2. I think this is a fair rule because . . .

3. Three ways that I can personally benefit from this rule are . . .

   i)

   ii)

   iii)

A RULE IN OUR CLASSROOM

1. An example of a rule in our classroom is . . .

2. I think this is a fair rule because . . .

3. Three ways that I can personally benefit from this rule are . . .

   i)

   ii)

   iii)

ACTIVITY 18

OUR CLASS RULES

Each student is given a copy of page 49. Students write the class rules on this sheet. It is recommended that each student places his copy of the class rules in a visible place in his binder or a notebook that is frequently used in your class. In listing the benefits, some of them may be identical to those identified in Activity #17.

You might even find it useful to have each student show this list to his parents and have his parents sign the bottom of this sheet.

ACTIVITY 19

IF I WAS A TEACHER

After you have introduced your rules and your students fully understand what they mean and how they can benefit from following them, it would be useful to give your students the opportunity to suggest rules they might introduce in a classroom if they were the teacher.

It would be useful to have your students write their rules and provide a rationale for them. It is suggested that you read what each student has done. This will help you to better understand each student's view on classroom rules and the results might even provide you with an additional rule or two that could be considered for you class.

It might also be useful to have students share some of their thoughts and provide an opportunity for the class to discuss the suggestions of their classmates.

OUR CLASS RULES

Some of the ways I will personally benefit from these rules are . . .

ACTIVITY 20

THE HAND OF SILENCE

As a teenager I worked at a summer camp. I clearly remember the first evening meal at the camp when more than 400 boisterous campers (who had less than an hour before arrived by a fleet of buses) and more than 200 staff members crammed into a massive wooden dining hall to create a volume of noise similar to a rock concert.

As the program director for the camp walked to a podium that was set to one side of the sprawling room, I wondered how he would ever gain control of the excited campers.

I was very surprised when he simply raised his hand without any words. Immediately the noise throughout the room changed to a buzz as veteran campers began to explain to the newcomers that the upward hand signaled to be quiet. Within a minute the once almost out-of-control mob was silent.

The program director then explained the importance of the hand signal and the need to follow it to maintain control in such a large room. As he began to welcome the campers and provide a few introductory rules for behavior in the dining hall, whenever the campers began to talk once again, he simply held up his hand and waited until his audience was ready. Throughout this summer, I learned a very important strategy for classroom management, one that I still constantly use as a teacher.

Throughout my teaching career, I have always quickly introduced the "hand of silence" to my classes. In fact, once I introduce the strategy, I then have my students practice it by giving them permission to talk to each other and then raising my hand to end the conversation.

The "hand of silence" provides a calm, easy-to-use, effective classroom management strategy that can help you to control your class without shouting.

ACTIVITY 21

SILENT SIGNALS

Once your students have learned to respond quickly to the "hand of silence" outlined in Activity #20, then you can build on this classroom management technique.

As an example, it can be annoying to have a few students talking as you are teaching. To stop whatever you are teaching to speak to a few students can hinder the pace of your lesson and be a distraction to other students. An easy hand signal to use during such an interruption is to simply continue teaching while your "hand of silence" is directed at the students who are talking. If you have established this concept well and students are aware that you enforce your rules with immediate consequences, then often the sight of your upraised hand will be enough to quiet the students without requiring a stoppage in your lesson.

This technique can be then developed further. At the front of your classroom you should have your "classroom rules" posted. If your first rule states to raise your hand before speaking, then if a student is blurting out answers during your lesson, you can simply hold up one finger to remind the student of your first rule. There is no need to stop your lesson. Your finger can simply be a silent signal to remind the student of the appropriate rule. Similarly, if your second rule is "to be positive with others", if a student needs a reminder of this, you can use two fingers to signal this message to a student without having to interrupt whatever else is happening in the classroom.

ACTIVITY 22

PRACTICING OUR RULES

An important aspect of establishing your classroom management techniques is to have your students practice them. After all, if you were teaching some concept from your subject curriculum, you would have your students practice various aspects of the concept until they had mastered it. It is strongly suggested during the first two weeks of school that you take time to review your classroom rules with your students and actually practice any hand signals that you have developed to remind your students of the rules.

Throughout the year or term, whenever your students seem to be slipping away from your rules, then take the time to once again review the rules and practice the accompanying hand signals.

ACTIVITY 23

CONSEQUENCES

1. To help students begin to think about the consequences of both breaking and following rules refer back to Activity #16 on page 45. Using a few of the rules that were discussed during this activity, write the headings "POSITIVE CONSEQUENCES" and "NEGATIVE CONSEQUENCES" in order that your students can view them.

2. Taking any societal rule (such as following a posted speed limit), first of all discuss the positive consequences a person might gain as a result of following this rule. The positive consequences could include things like "being safer", "feeling less stressed", etc. Keep a list of the identified rewards under the heading "POSITIVE CONSEQUENCES".

3. Next, discuss any negative consequences that could result from disobeying a societal rule (once again, such as the speed limit). Responses from students might include "might cause an accident", "might increase stress", "might get a fine", etc. Write the responses under the heading "NEGATIVE CONSEQUENCES".

4. Each student pairs with a partner. Each pair of students selects any societal rule (once again, these can come from the results of Activity #16 on page 45). Each pair then identifies and keeps a record of all the positive and negative consequences they can think of related to both following and breaking the rule they have chosen.

5. Students share their results. It is important that the students complete this activity with an understanding of the word "consequences" and that they are aware that there can be positive or negative consequences that may result from either obeying or breaking any rule.

> "Rules are just a waste of time if there are no consequences."
>
> Grade 6 Student

ACTIVITY 24

CONSEQUENCES FOR OUR CLASS RULES

Although you may have decided (and this is recommended in Activity #15 on page 43) to give your students a set of classroom rules (rather than them deciding on them as a class), it may still be useful to hear and consider their thoughts on the consequences for both obeying the rules and for breaking any of the rules. This information might provide some unique ideas that you have never thought of before. In addition, ask yourself if you spent as much time rewarding students for appropriate behavior as you do for giving attention to students for inappropriate behavior how would this change your class?

1. Each student is given a copy of page 56 to complete. You can tell your students that their thoughts will be seriously considered when you look at positive and negative consequences related to your classroom rules.

2. It is recommended that you read the responses from your students and then select a few to discuss further with your class, especially in the area of any reward systems that students mention that they have experienced before. If your students are entering your class already having experienced some system in their past that led to appropriate behavior and good work habits, then by all means explore these strategies further and give serious thought to whether there is value in using a system that your students are already familiar with. While it is likely that you won't make too many changes to the consequences you had in mind for students who break any of your rules (see Activity #26 on page 58), their thoughts related to positive consequences for obeying your rules would be useful to consider for implementation.

3. The information you gain from this activity could be particularly useful to you in working with any students who consistently break your rules. Such students may offer you some insights into the con-

sequences that they feel could work best to change their behavior.

ACTIVITY 25

TEN THINGS I'D LIKE TO HEAR FROM MY TEACHER

1. Tell your students to identify some words or phrases they would like you to say to them when they are working hard and achieving good results. This discussion can help your students understand that you want to acknowledge appropriate behavior and good work habits. In too many classes, students are primarily exposed to teachers who focus on what is wrong instead of what is right. This approach can quickly alienate and frustrate a large group of students who are genuinely interested in learning.

2. Each student is given a copy of page 57 to complete. Students can refer to the discussion in #1 above for help. I would recommend that you tell students that you will attempt to use their thoughts in praising both behavior and good work in your class.

3. Collect the completed sheets from each student and read one recommendation from each student. This can help to reinforce that you want to acknowledge and reward positive behavior in your class.

4. I would recommend that you keep the completed sheets and attempt to use the comments unique to each student during the next few months. You could put a check mark beside a comment once you use it. This would help you to ensure that you are distributing your comments fairly among all your students. It might even be useful to place the completed sheets in a brightly colored binder that your students recognize as you refer to it on a daily basis.

CONSEQUENCES FOR OUR CLASS RULES

1. Whenever students obey our class rules, three things I think my teacher could do are . . .

    i)

    ii)

    iii)

2. Whenever students disobey our class rules, three things I think my teacher could do are . . .

    i)

    ii)

    iii)

TEN THINGS I'D LIKE TO HEAR FROM MY TEACHER

1.

2.

3.

4.

5.

6.

7.

8.

9.

10.

ACTIVITY 26

MY CONSEQUENCES

Although already stated in this chapter, let me reiterate it one more time - "Rules without consequences will never work." Even the most caring, involved and conscientious parents realize that somewhere along the way there is a need for consequences to help guide the behavior of their children. For a teacher who has somewhere around twenty-five (or greater) students from all walks of life in his/her class, there will be even more occasions in which appropriate behavior should be rewarded and inappropriate behavior should be corrected.

While I have placed this activity adjacent to other thoughts on "consequences", the reality is that you need to have a clear picture on the first day of school regarding how you will react to both appropriate and inappropriate behavior. Back in Activity #15 on page 43, you outlined your rules for the class. The moment you tell your students your classroom rules (and for many teachers this will be one of the first things they do with their class), you need to be prepared for the obvious question - "What will happen if we break any of the rules?" Having a ready answer can help you to then respond calmly and consistently when students either obey or disobey your rules. If your consequences are non-existent, vague, illogical, or too severe, your rules will quickly lose their purpose which, after all, was to establish a classroom environment where you could teach effectively and students achieved greater success in their learning.

In considering your consequences, research supports the principle that praising effort can result in the longest lasting positive direct impact on achievement, therefore your central focus for individual students and for the class as a whole should relate to effort. In addition, your praise concerning effort should be as specific as possible related to the skills begin taught or the positive behavior that is being demonstrated by your students.

> "Praising students for effort inspires them to accept greater challenges."
> Carol S. Dweck, Ph.D., in *MINDSET: The New Psychology of Success*, 2006

How you will respond to students who disobey your rules often presents a significant challenge. I frequently hear teachers fervently ask, "What can I do when a student breaks one of my rules?" If you are using some form of token reward system in your class (see Activity # 27 on page 65), then your answer to this question will generally be found in the system of token rewards and punishments that you are using. For others, I have listed a seven step process on the next few pages that I have seen successfully used. As you complete page 63 + 64 (and I strongly recommend that you do this before the first day of school), keep in mind any school guidelines or policies related to disciplining students. For example, your school may have a very clear process (including the completion of some type of form) when a student is being sent to the office. Similarly, most schools have a very clear process for handling some situations such as bullying. Once again, if you are a new teacher talk to some veteran teachers and even one of your school administrators before you begin your first day to ensure that you are aware of any school policies or guidelines related to rules and discipline.

In establishing consequences in your class, it is critical to be consistent in applying them. To punish a student who is a known "behavior problem" but to ignore a student who is a known "non-behavior problem" for the same rule infraction gives mixed messages to your class, often creating resentment that increase the misbehavior of some students.

MY CONSEQUENCES
(for inappropriate behavior)

The following provides a framework for responding to possible rule infractions within your class. It is important that your response to behavior problems should be both calm and assertive (there are some "assertiveness tips" provided in Chapter 6). Remember that some students will go to great lengths to "save face" so anytime you can use silent signals (as suggested in Activities #20 + 21), these can be a great help in preventing the incident from being "fed" by others in the class. In addition, related to this, where possible talk to a student in private related to your concerns rather than in front of his/her classmates.

STEP 1 - Give A Warning
This can be either verbal or non-verbal. It should be based on one of your classroom rules if possible.

STEP 2 - Have A Face-to-face Meeting
I don't recommend giving students endless warnings. During the first few weeks of a school year especially, I suggest you give one warning and then take action. Let your students know that you intend to support your rules with consequences. A possible first consequence may be to tell a student that you would like to meet with him at the end of class. If the student attempts to argue this with you or even "mock" your request, be careful that you don't get "sucked" into an argument with the student. You have provided a consequence, and at this time it is important to prevent this incident from escalating which could force you to go through all the possible discipline steps you have at your disposal. Having said this, though, I certainly wouldn't ignore a continued flagrant increase of misbehavior from the student.

During your face-to-face meeting, assertively ensure that the student understands the purpose of your rule and how following this rule can assist in successful learning. Your meeting with the student is not a discussion. You are telling the student what is expected. At this time, you might outline the other steps you are prepared to take if the behavior does not improve.

STEP 3 - Make Up Any Time Wasted

As many of your rules will likely relate to "keeping on task", then students who break your rules will be wasting class time. As a result, a logical consequence of wasting time is to make up the time during recess, lunch, after school (when possible), or even during game times (see Activity #28 on page 65). Making up time generally works when it is appropriate to the amount of time wasted - in other words in the 5 - 10 minute range, otherwise you may be punishing yourself and even creating an inappropriate consequence that your students will rebel against creating a new set of problems.

STEP 4 - Change Seats

Sometimes an appropriate consequence that can lead to improved behavior is as simple as changing where a student sits in the class. In doing this, you might want to meet with the student after class if you feel that taking this action in front of his peers might fuel an escalation of the problem.

STEP 5 - Consult Other Teachers

It is recommended that you do this step as soon as you feel that you have an ongoing behavioral concern with a student. By talking to other teachers, you might learn a strategy or technique that they are using successfully with this student. On the other hand you might learn that this student is a behavioral problem in several or even all of his classes. If this is the case it would make sense to consult with someone in either administration or counseling before deciding on your next course of action.

In some schools, an ongoing study hall or detention room is sometimes used throughout the day for misbehaving students. If this opportunity exists in your school, then this might give you your next course of action with the student. Another possibility is to set up a meeting between the student and all his teachers. Chapter 9 will provide some further thoughts on school-wide programs to deal with inappropriate behavior.

STEP 6 - Involve The Student's Parents

During the first instance of contacting the parent, I recommend a telephone call. Ensure that you are prepared to explain your classroom rules that have been broken, the rationale for your rules, and a specific outline of how this student has broken your rule(s) and the previous forms of consequence you have followed. If this does not stop the behavioral problems, I would then go to the next step of asking the parents and student to attend a meeting with you to discuss the problem and problem solve some possible solutions.

STEP 7 - Involve Your Administration

Before involving the administration to assist you with behavioral problems in your class, I recommend that you meet with an administrator (and "administrator" here could be defined as a team/grade and/or curriculum leader before you talk to a principal or vice-principal) to discuss what you have already done in an attempt to resolve the problem and ask the administrator for additional strategy suggestions that you might consider before you ask for her actual involvement.

In addition to these seven steps, there are other suggestions provided in the remaining chapters of this book that might be useful to you as well. Sometimes, empathetic listening (Chapter 5) can make a significant difference in classroom management. For some people, being more assertive (Chapter 6) may be the ingredient you need for success. For others, understanding conflict resolution strategies (Chapter 7) or techniques in anger management (Chapter 8) and even the manner in which you teach (Chapters 10) might make a positive difference. If all else fails, there may be some specific tips and strategies in the chapter on discipline strategies (Chapter 9) that can help you.

MY CONSEQUENCES

STEPS I CAN FOLLOW WHEN STUDENTS DISOBEY MY CLASSROOM RULES

1.

2.

3.

4.

5.

6.

7.

MY CONSEQUENCES

REWARDS I CAN PROVIDE WHEN STUDENTS FOLLOW MY CLASSROOM RULES

1.

2.

3.

4.

5.

6.

7.

ACTIVITY 27

TOKENS

Some teachers very effectively use some system of token rewards (or the withdrawal of the reward) to assist with classroom management. For example, you might create paper money that is unique to your room. When you "catch" students following your rules, you give them a "money" reward. If a student is breaking one of your rules, you can "fine" them a specific amount of money to pay back to you (and it would be appropriate to give one warning before you apply any fine). At the end of the week (or every two weeks), your students can use their earned money to purchase small gifts from a class store that you set up (possibly candy, stickers or other small items from a "dollar store"). The money could also be used on a class-wide basis to earn time for classroom games (see Activity 28 on this page), a pizza party (once a term) or even an extended supervised recess (if your school permits this).

ACTIVITY 28

CLASS GAMES

Students love to compete in various games that focus on the content of what they are learning. These games can be played during the last ten minutes of class as a reward for appropriate behavior (and any students who broke your classroom rules during the class are disallowed from participating in the game). They could also be played for part of a period every Friday which gives your students something to work towards each week. The great thing about the games is that your students will see them as an enjoyable reward and yet the reality is they will be reviewing their learning in your subject area. Your students could even design such games based on current popular television quiz shows.

ACTIVITY 29

SCHOOL RULES

It is generally expected on the first day of school that you talk to your students about "school rules" in addition to your classroom rules. In some schools, there may be school-wide assemblies where an administrator might outline school rules. In either case, it is important that your students understand school-wide expectations as these rules often support or enhance the rules of your classroom.

> "An effective school is one in which, over time,
> students show improved achievement,
> more positive attitudes, better attendance,
> and more appropriate behavior."
> Wayne Hulley and Linda Dier in *Getting By or Getting Better*, 2009

When both teachers and administrators make a concerted effort to enforce school and classroom rules, students sense the consistent emphasis on learning within the school which generally results in an overall more effective school.

To ensure that your students are aware of any school rules, tell them to list what they consider are the most important rules in your school using page 67 as a handout. Discuss the results.

OUR SCHOOL RULES

ACTIVITY 30

THOUGHTS ABOUT OUR SCHOOL RULES

After students have been given a list of school rules (and the related rationale for each rule), it would be appropriate to provide an opportunity to discuss them. Discussing them shouldn't imply that your students can change them. The discussion can give you an opportunity to observe how individual students think about rules and may give you some clues as how to better motivate them to follow your classroom rules. In addition, the discussion can give you some insights into student perception related to your school rules which can be valuable information to share at a staff meeting if school rules are being discussed.

> "Habits are safer than rules;
> you don't have to watch them.
> And you don't have to keep them either;
> they keep you."
> F. Crane

Rules For My School

Rule #1
　　Students should be polite and courteous to their peers, teachers, other staff, and visitors to the school.

Rule #2
　　Students should help to maintain a clean school which includes their locker, desk, classroom, hallways and cafeteria.

Rule #3
　　Students should obey any requests from their teachers or others in a position of authority in the school who ask them to behave or cooperate in a more appropriate manner.

Rule #4
　　Students should respect the rights of others by refraining from bullying them in any manner or by destroying their personal property.

Rule #5
　　Students should behave in a manner in the classroom that allows a teacher to teach without being interrupted.

　　　　　　　　　　　　　　　Grade 8 Student

"A child wants some kind of undisrupted routine or rhythm. He seems to want a predictable, orderly world. For instance, injustice, unfairness or inconsistency seems to make a child feel anxious and unsafe."
Abraham Maslow

CHAPTER 3

CLASSROOM ROUTINES THAT WILL MAKE YOUR JOB EASIER

In the previous chapter, you explored classroom rules. In addition to classroom rules, it is important to establish some classroom routines. Classroom routines might include things such as:

- entering and exiting the classroom
- the process for leaving the room to go to the washroom or library
- emergency drills (fire, lock-down, etc.)
- what to do if a student is late for class
- process for handing in assignments
- procedure for sharpening a pencil or accessing any classroom materials
- procedure for using computers in class
- safety considerations
etc.

An important principle related to both classroom rules and procedures is that these are established to provide a framework for effective teaching. Their purpose is not is set up a sterile classroom where students are afraid to move, afraid to talk, and fearful of making any form of mistake. A vibrant learning environment (more on this in Chapter 4) is a place where students feel comfortable, a place where students are encouraged to make mistakes, and a place where students are excited about learning. Returning back to my suggestions for classroom rules in the previous chapter (see page 43), you will notice that I didn't say anything about students talking or getting out of their seats. A classroom where students are passionate about learning will encourage students to talk to each other (unless the learning task specifically requires them to be quiet) and encourages them to consult and work with other students. Similar to the previous chapter on rules, it is important for classroom procedures to be consistent for them to have the greatest impact on effective classroom management and student success.

Ineffective classroom routines can result in a great waste of time. To repeat the same instructions every day or to answer the same questions each day related to classroom routines and procedures can not only waste valuable learning time, but this can become a frustrating experience for both you and your students. In a well-structured classroom, many conflicts are often prevented because children know what is expected. When classroom rules and procedures are clear (and make sense), students feel more secure which encourages them to take the risks (and make the mistakes) that are essential to real learning. The best teachers manage their classrooms with procedures, not discipline. A class that is constantly misbehaving is often a sign of unclear rules and procedures and a lack of meaningful consequences to support them. In the end, it is actions and not words that will define your rules and procedures.

In the previous chapter, I suggested that you immediately begin your first class by stating your classroom rules, I would recommend that classroom procedures be established as the need arises. The exception to this might be the need to establish emergency drill procedures as a priority during your first class with students. Otherwise, it makes more sense to talk about classroom routines as the opportunity presents itself or a question related to a procedure is asked by a student. Overwhelming students with rules and procedures on the first day may encourage some students to immediately test your limits. The fewer rules and procedures that you start with, the easier it is to manage them. In considering classroom procedures, this might be an area that input from your students might be valuable. They might even have some ideas that you haven't thought of before. In addition, their participation could help to empower them to be more willing participants in following the procedures. The exception to this would be in the area of any school rules/procedures that directly affect what happens in your class. Examples of this might be emergency drills or even a school-wide policy/procedure related to students leaving the class to go to the library or washroom.

In setting classroom routines, you might ask yourself (or even your students) questions such as:

- what do I expect my students to do when they enter my class?
- what books/materials do I expect my students to bring to each class?
- are there some routines that can help students when they are absent?
- how can I help students keep more effective notes?
- how can I help students to be more organized?
- what can I do to help students learn better time management skills?

In addition to activities to help you establish appropriate classroom routines, there are also activities in this chapter to assist you in teaching your students how to be better organized and also related to time management. Although organizational skills and time management may not seem to be directly related to classroom routines, these areas all go hand in hand. While classroom procedures can lead to better organizational and time management skills, the direct teaching of organizational and time management skills can also enhance the learning and practice of classroom routines.

In looking at classroom routines (similar to rules), it is generally necessary to teach your students in the same way you would teach your subject matter (more information is provided on "effective teaching techniques" in Chapter 10). The start of the year is the ideal time to introduce your classroom procedures although, unlike rules, it would make sense to space the introduction of your procedures until they are relevant to something you are doing in class. Although by grade five, most students have a good idea of acceptable rules and classroom routines, unless these are specifically outlined your students may become complacent in following them and may even constantly challenge whatever is happening in the class because they want to see what your limits are. Set your rules and routines early in the school year, teach them to your students, practice them with your students, and apply consequences when they are not followed.

Daily routines can assist students in four major areas. The following provides a brief description of each benefit:

1) OFFER A FRAMEWORK FOR SECURITY

Students benefit from knowing their limits and from knowing what is expected of them. These expectations not only help create a safer environment (and research shows that student safety is an important factor in learning, whether their sense of safety is real or perceived) and also an environment where students feel comfortable making mistakes. If students don't feel comfortable in making mistakes, then they will resist taking risks which can result in the avoidance of learning anything new.

2) OFFER A FRAMEWORK FOR LEARNING

As previously mentioned in this book, student success (as it relates to learning) is directly related to time "on task". The more effectively your classroom routines focus on saving time, the more time you will have to teach and as a result, the more time your students will have to learn. In addition, smooth classroom procedures help to create an atmosphere that is conducive to teaching. Instead of constantly reminding students that they need to do this or that, you will be able to focus on your lessons and providing guided practice as your students attempt to master what you have taught.

3) HELP STUDENTS TO LEARN ORGANIZATIONAL SKILLS

Over the years in reading student report cards, a common comment I often viewed (especially for students who weren't doing well) said something about "poor organizational skills". Good classroom procedures can help teach your students how to be better organized and how to make more effective use of their time.

4) HELP TO LIMIT BEHAVIORAL PROBLEMS

Any type of confusion or uncertainty in a classroom can result in student misbehavior. Classroom routines can help provide a framework that gives students an exact and consistent way of doing things. This kind of approach helps to remove confusion and uncertainty and in the process it helps to reduce behavior problems. The best approach to stopping misbehavior is to prevent it before it begins, and meaningful, clear, classroom routines can play a significant role in the prevention of inappropriate behavior.

Activities #31 - 40 can provide some practical thoughts on actual classroom routines that you can use. Some of these are time-saving tips that can help you to keep a greater emphasis on helping your students to learn the content of your curriculum. These activities can also help to establish procedures in your class to prevent disruptions and misbehavior.

Given that a lack of focus sometimes occurs in classrooms when students have poor organizational and time management skills, there are also activities in this chapter to help your students learn better skills in these areas. Activities #41, and 46 - 50, look specifically at helping your students to be more organized while Activities #42 - 45 look more specifically at time management.

As in other chapters in this book, as your students learn some new concepts, take the time to assess your own habits and skills in these areas. In the end, remember that your example often provides a model for your students to copy. You might very well ask what level of time management and organization skills are you bringing to the class because both of these factors will have a direct impact on your students' learning.

ACTIVITY 31

CLASSROOM PROCEDURES

1. On page 71 is a sample list of some classroom procedures and routines. It is suggested that you post 2 - 3 of these as sample classroom routines and then ask your students to identify other procedures they have either experienced in other classes or procedures they think would be helpful to them. Keep a list of their additional suggestions.

2. It is possible that your school might have some rules that affect your classroom routines. For example, your might have some form of "hall pass" when a student is excused to go to the washroom or library. Similarly, your school might have an "entry pass" or procedure for students who are late. In such situations, you should outline the procedure that is to occur related to school-wide expectations for any of the routines/procedures that were identified in #1 above.

3. Next, in looking at the remainder of the routines on the list established in #1, it would be a useful activity for students in small groups (2 - 3 students in each group) to each be assigned one of the routines and then establish what they think is a fair and practical system for implementing the procedure in the classroom.

4. Each group presents their recommendations. Following each group's presentation, there could be further discussion related to the ease of use and potential results of the recommendations. It would be useful for you to keep notes and the suggestions being given. As a result of the student suggestions, you can state that you are willing to try their ideas for establishing the procedures, or you can tell your students that you will consider all the suggestions and in tomorrow's class you will provide an outline of your classroom procedures that is based on the student suggestions (but not limited to them).

ACTIVITY 32

BENEFITS OF CLASSROOM PROCEDURES

When adults understand the benefits to them for taking a certain course of action, this can help to motivate them to take the action. Students are no different. Sometimes rules and procedures are an annoyance for them simply because they don't understand how they can benefit from them.

1. It is suggested that you begin by having your class discuss the benefits students could gain from following emergency procedures such as "fire drills".

2 Next, using a list of classroom procedures assign one procedure to each group of 2 - 3 students. Each group's task is to identify all the benefits that can result if they follow the given procedure. Share and discuss the results.

ACTIVITY 33

TEACHER ASSISTANT

A significant time-saver for you and a great way to encourage more responsibility from your students is to identify a "Teacher Assistant" each day (some schools use the word "Ambassador" or "Classroom Monitor"). This person can have a set number of responsibilities that could include things such:

- taking the attendance
- collecting and handing out materials
- working at the "rental shop" (see Activity #35)
- sharpening pencils (see Activity #34)
etc.

ACTIVITY 34

PENCIL EXCHANGE

An activity that can be a distraction in a classroom is the sharpening of pencils with an irregular flow of students to your class pencil sharpener. A simple way to remedy this is to have a container of sharpened pencils in a convenient location in your classroom. When a student requires a sharpened pencil, the student simply trades his dull pencil for a new one. Towards the end of class, the Teacher Assistant for the day ensures that all pencils in the container are sharpened for your next class.

ACTIVITY 35

RENTAL SHOP

Although it would be wonderful if every student came to every class with the appropriate materials such as pens, pencils, etc., there will times when a student forgets one of these things which can lead to a disruption in your class just as you are about to start your lesson. One way to help prevent this disruption is to have a "rental shop" in your class. The rental shop contains items such as pens, pencils and rulers. You can decide whether your rental shop will also include books and/or paper.

Your class Teaching Assistant for the day looks after the rental shop during the first few minutes of class (see Activity #36 for suggestions related to the first 5 minutes of your class). To rent an object, students must provide something for payment such as a pen. The result of this is that you should be able to start your lesson with everyone having the appropriate materials. At the end of class, students who have "rented" materials return them and receive their "payment" back.

ACTIVITY 36

THE FIRST FIVE MINUTES

Although it would be great to start your actual teaching within a minute or two after your students enter your room, the reality is that tasks like taking attendance or some form of other administrative tasks will generally prevent you from starting right away. As a result, it is often during this unstructured time that behavior problems arise and the need to discipline these students takes additional time and can even disrupt some of the passion you might originally have had for your lesson.

It is recommended that each day you have some form of question, brain teaser, short activity, etc. posted in your room. As students enter your room, the expectation is that they work on this short activity as you and your Teacher Assistant complete any of the necessary things that need to be done before you begin your lesson. Educational supply stores are a great source for such activities or you can obtain "puzzle" books at a local bookstore.

ACTIVITY 37

ABSENT BUDDIES

It is a reality that some students will be absent from some of your classes due to illnesses, appointments, etc. When these students return back to class, it can be time-consuming to help these students (and disrupt both your lesson plans for the day and even your classroom routines).

A solution for this potential ongoing concern is for every student to select an "absent buddy" on the first day of school. You keep a list of the buddies that you can refer to when a student is away.

Whenever a student is absent, you simply tell her "buddy" to call or email her (individual students can decide which approach works best for them) to share the content of today's lesson and any related assignments. When the absent student returns back to school it should be her buddy's responsibility to review what was missed. The Success Book mentioned in Activity #38 can also be helpful in this regard.

ACTIVITY 38

SUCCESS BOOK

One of the most important aspects of effective teaching is to show students examples of "excellent" work. It is this modeling that can make a significant difference in inspiring student success. A Success Book can assist with encouraging student success and also providing a resource for students who are absent.

Whenever students are completing assignments (including notes on your lessons), choose one student whose work is excellent for that class. Next, photocopy this student's work for the class. The work is then placed in your class success book. It becomes an honor for students to be selected to have their work in this book (which can encourage excellence in your class) while providing a resource book that students can refer to if they have been away (and this also provides you with a terrific set of notes that you can use with future students to show them what excellent work looks like).

ACTIVITY 39

WORK DONE ACTIVITIES

Another classroom reality is that students generally complete their work at varying lengths of time. As a result, you will often have some students who become bored (which can lead to behavior problems) because they have finished their work before the majority of the class. In such a situation, you don't want to punish students who work quickly by giving them additional questions so it is important to have a classroom procedure established to meet this potential concern.

Some suggestions are as follows:

- have fun puzzles and/or activity sheets related to your subject area that are available to students who finish their work before others
- encourage students to help other students
(as students assist other students it reinforces their own learning in addition to giving you some often needed help in working with all your students)
- read
(you could have a library of subject related books in your room)
- assist you with some tasks
(such as stapling some papers or organizing files, etc.)
etc.

> Ken was a grade 8 student who constantly disrupted others and rarely completed his work. One day as I was helping another student, I turned to see Ken talking to another student. Before telling him to stop, I noticed they were both working on a question together. As I moved closer, I observed that Ken was actually helping the other boy. As he looked at me as though I was going to tell him to stop talking, I surprised him by praising his effort to help another student. It wasn't long before Ken started focusing on completing his work so that he could then help others.
>
> Grade 8 Teacher

ACTIVITY 40

ONE-A-DAY SUCCESS TIPS

Activity #36 recommended that you have a five minute activity that your students complete as soon as they enter your room. Another thing you could add to this is a quote or tip for the day which students could write into their notebooks and then attempt to apply the intent of the thought during the course of their day. Pages 82 - 88 provide some success tips that you could use with your students over the course of a year (and both you and your students could add others to this list as well).

ACTIVITY 41

ORGANIZATION SURVEY

On pages 89 + 90 is a survey related to being organized that your students can complete. Once they have finished, discuss each of the answers. It is recommended that you repeat this survey after you have completed many of the activities in this chapter in order to assess the progress your students have made related to being more organized.

> "People seldom see the slow and painful steps by which the most insignificant success is achieved."
> Anne Sullivan
> (Helen Keller's teacher)

SUCCESS TIPS

1. Write a list of reasons how doing better at school will help you.
2. You are in charge of your success. Don't let others get in your way.
3. Whenever you are successful, repeat whatever you did again and again.
4. Thank others when they give you feedback that will help you.
5. It is okay to adjust your goals.
6. Before you begin to study make sure you have all the materials you will need.
7. Keep your eyes on your goals. Keep a picture in your mind of being successful.
8. Think positive.
9. Expect obstacles. Everyone faces problems. The key to success is how you deal with them.
10. Learn from your mistakes and your failures.
11. Take action, one small step at a time in the direction of your goals.
12. Build on your strengths.
13. Find another student who can help you with work that you don't understand.
14. Every day write down something you did well that day.
15. When you do your homework, start with whatever is most important.
16. Check your due dates every day for assignments and tests.
17. When you have finished an assignment, cross it off your "to do" list.
18. Reward yourself for achieving any of your goals.
19. Always finding something nice to say about others can help you to be more successful.
20. Study in a place that works best for you.
21. Sometimes it is just better to get your work done on time than trying to make it perfect.
22. Don't spend too much time thinking about what you have to do, just start!
23. Constantly tidying or organizing your things could become a timewaster. Just begin!
24. Good grades can help you to feel better about yourself.
25. Ask questions in class.
26. How you spend your class time is one of the most important factors in being successful.
27. Be a positive participator in every one of your classes.

28. Choose your courses carefully. Ask for help from a trusted teacher or counselor.
29. If what you are doing is not leading to success, try a different approach.
30. Accept that everyone has bad days.
31. Accept that everyone makes mistakes.
32. Accept that everyone faces problems and obstacles.
33. Break your workload down into manageable chunks.
34. When you're confused, ask for help.
35. When things go wrong, don't blame others.
36. Be responsible for your life and for your success.
37. The best preparation for tomorrow is focusing on excellence today.
38. Study with others who also want to be successful.
39. Spend time with other students who are successful at school.
40. Join a school club or team.
41. Be flexible.
42. Remember your teachers are people. Thank them when they help you.
43. Laugh.
44. Be punctual.
45. Make sure you always have the correct books for class.
46. Attend your classes.
47. Be the hardest working student in each of your classes.
48. Write your goals.
49. Find some healthy ways to reduce stress in your life.
50. Get more sleep than you need.
51. Eat healthy foods.
52. Don't drink alcohol and don't take non-prescription drugs or smoke.
53. When you have a class presentation, practice.
54. Use visual materials during presentations.
55. Involve your audience during presentations.
56. On presentations or essays, find a catchy beginning and ending.
57. If you have a personal problem that is bothering you, get help.
58. Keep a daily journal recording only your successes.
59. Constantly tell yourself that you are a wonderful person.
60. Spend some time each day reading for pleasure.
Being a strong reader can contribute to success.
61. When you are reading school texts, summarize what you are reading.

62. Spend the greatest amount of your time on your most important assignments.
63. Whenever you find success, keep repeating what you did.
64. Always hand in your assignments on time.
65. Pay close attention when test questions are reviewed.
66. When you are given feedback on an assignment, ensure you understand what has been said.
67. Use diagrams and pictures to help memorize information.
68. As a teacher is teaching, think of questions you can ask.
69. Thank your teacher when a lesson is excellent.
70. Always be on time for school. Take responsibility for never being late.
71. Write down and study any sample test questions teachers give when they are reviewing.
72. Work with other students to identify and practice possible test questions.
73. Sometimes you have to change your attitude in order to change your life.
74. Use study cards 10 - 15 minutes each day to review your work.
75. Go for a walk.
76. Work out in the gym.
77. Make a list of reasons why you want to succeed.
78. Keep well organized files of all class work, old tests, assignments, etc.
79. Whenever a test is given back to you, always ensure that you have the correct answers.
80. When you study, practice questions from old tests.
81. When you have an essay to complete, first make a rough outline of your major points.
82. Have others (preferably successful people) proof your work before you hand it in.
83. Accept feedback. Whether it is positive or negative, you can still learn from it.
84. Write down whatever you have to do. Don't try to keep assignment details in your head.
85. Take short breaks every once in awhile when you are studying or doing homework.
86. Find what works best for you in any subject and keep repeating this approach.
87. If what you are doing isn't working then try another approach.
88. Believe you are going to have a great day.
89. Always be polite to your teachers.
90. See your principal or vice-principal to show him/her some of your excellent work.

91. Focus on your successes, not your failures.
92. Doing a little on a major project every day is a better approach than leaving everything until the last minute.
93. Before any exam, get a good sleep, make sure you have all your materials, and stay away from others who are really stressed-out.
94. When you write an exam, spend most of your time on the most important questions.
95. At the end of any exam or test, review your answers, and ensure that you have answered all the questions.
96. Improving your keyboard speed can be a great timesaver for you.
97. Success is your personal responsibility. No one else can do it for you.
98. Excuses generally lead to failure rather than success.
99. Being successful is a personal choice.
100. Eliminate bad habits. Repeat good habits.
101. Believe that success is possible for you.
102. Before others will believe in you, generally you have to first believe in yourself.
103. Don't spend time with negative people.
104. Don't spend too much time worrying about the past.
105. Watch what other students do to be successful and learn from them.
106. Always act as though you are already successful.
107. Nothing happens unless you first take action.
108. It is generally better to do it now than later.
109. Don't worry about things that are out of your control.
110. Improve a little at a time.
111. Keep a record of your successes.
112. It's not always going to be easy.
113. It is better to do it right the first time.
114. Never, never, never, give up on being successful.
115. You will become the average of the people you spend most of your time with. Spend your time with successful people.
116. There is a tendency to become whatever we think about the most. Think about being successful.
117. Hard work and success go hand in hand.
118. Keep your focus on what you want to achieve.
119. We can't change what happened yesterday,

120. Forgive. Hatred breeds misery.
121. Accept change.
122. Be the first person to compliment yourself.
123. Being a winner is the result of having winning habits.
124. Nothing changes until you do.
125. Be self-motivated. Don't wait for others to tell you what to do.
126. Be energetic and enthusiastic.
127. Let others help you.
128. Find what you love to do at school and build on these strengths.
129. Be a great listener.
130. Be honest.
131. What you say to others can take on a life of its own. Always be positive.
132. Be the person that everyone else respects.
133. Your best friends are the people who support you and believe in you.
134. A true friend brings out the best in you.
135. Success starts today.
136. The most difficult assignment begins with the smallest step.
137. Do something good for another person.
138. Better study habits often result in needing less time to study.
139. When you give your mind a goal, it will often work to help you achieve your goal.
140. The more attractive a goal is for you, the better your chances are of achieving it.
141. When you set a date for completing a goal, you are helping to create focus and purpose.
142. Give yourself reasons for reaching your goals.
143. Taking action keeps your goals alive.
144. Having a winning attitude means that you expect to be successful.
145. Spend time with people who believe in you.
146. Your character is built on your honesty.
147. Attempt to understand what motivates you.
148. Successful people are persistent.
149. Keep a picture in your mind of being the kind of person you want to be.
150. If you're improving, you are already being successful.
151. Compliment your teacher when he/she teaches a lesson you understand and enjoy.
152. Study in the same place as much as possible.

153. Drink water instead of soft-drinks.
154. When you are studying, put a "Do Not Disturb" sign on your door.
155. Read to understand, not to just memorize.
156. After you have studied some subject area, make an informal presentation to someone else regarding what you have just learned.
157. Whether you are studying or doing homework, take short breaks approximately every 30 minutes.
158. Spend most of your time doing the things that will contribute the most to being successful.
159. After any test ensure that you understand all the correct answers and then file the exam so you know where it is when you need to study again.
160. Thank others when they compliment you.
161. Write things down so you won't forget.
162. Get involved in your school.
163. Always do the right thing.
164. Don't make excuses. Accept responsibility for what is happening at school.
165. Don't be afraid of failure. It is better to try and fail than to do nothing.
166. Replace "what if" and "but" with "I can" and "I will".
167. The best investment you will ever make will be in yourself.
168. If you think you can, you can. If you don't think you can, you won't.
169. Be realistic when you set your goals. Get help from a teacher or counselor.
170. Take a few moments to check your homework before you hand it in.
171. Success rarely happens overnight.
172. The word success means different things to different people.
173. You must want to learn.
174. Work smarter, not harder.
175. Make a list of how being more successful at school will benefit you.
176. Consider all feedback to be valuable.
177. Thank everyone who gives you feedback even if it is negative.
178. Your attitude about school may be the single most important factor related to being successful.
179. When you are studying explain things to yourself.
180. Successful people take full responsibility for how they are doing.
181. The degree to which you will be successful is your choice.
182. When you set goals, it is okay to change them.

183. Managing your time more effectively can save you time.
184. If you are working hard but not getting very good results, you need to change the way you are working.
185. One of the best times to study is just before you go to sleep.
186. Everyone learns differently. Attempt to discover how you learn the best.
187. Find a way to make important things stand out in your notes.
188. Read the complete paragraph before you highlight anything in your text. It is better to highlight fewer words than more.
189. After you study some notes attempt to state in one sentence what the content was all about.
190. When you are away, contact a friend to find out what you missed.
191. Once you have written some rough notes for any major assignment or essay, show these to your teacher to ensure that you are on the right track.
192. When you are completing any assignment, read the assignment instructions every 15 - 20 minutes to ensure you are doing what you are supposed to be doing.
193. A perfect assignment that is never handed in is worth less than an imperfect assignment that is handed in on time.
194. Choose your courses carefully with the help of a teacher or counselor.
195. Don't blame others for your failures.
196. Whenever you have to make a presentation, practice. Focus especially on your beginning, ending, and meeting your time requirements.
197. Develop your keyboard skills and improve your typing speed.
198. Quiz yourself as you study.
199. As a teacher is teaching, attempt to guess what you think the teacher is going to say next.
200. If you are unhappy with an assignment mark, ask your teacher what you could have done to get a better mark.

"Become the change you want to be."
Ghandi

ORGANIZATION SURVEY

For each of the following sentences, select the statement that best describes you. Write the number beside the statement in the appropriate box.

always like me - 5

sometimes like me - 3

never like me - 1

1. I tend to be late for classes. ☐

2. I wait until the last minute before completing assignments. ☐

3. Often I lose things like books or assignments. ☐

4. Most nights I never get my homework done. ☐

5. I don't have the time to complete my homework. ☐

6. I tend to be unorganized. ☐

7. When I have a lot of homework, I feel a lot of stress. ☐

8. I rarely write down a list of my tests and assignments. ☐

9. Most days I feel overwhelmed with everything that I have to do. ☐

10. I tend to be a procrastinator. ☐

always like me - 5
sometimes like me - 3
never like me - 1

11. I tend to have trouble finding things. ☐

12. When I get home, I find that I left my homework at school. ☐

13. I rarely set a schedule for studying or doing my homework. ☐

14. I'm not very good at following instructions on assignments. ☐

15. I often forget to bring my work or books to class. ☐

16. If I have to be somewhere by a certain time, I'm usually late. ☐

17. I rarely ask teachers for help. ☐

18. It's easy for me to get distracted when I should be studying. ☐

19. I'm not very good at organizing my school work. ☐

20. My work habits at school are really not very good. ☐

Add your numbers together from the twenty boxes on both pages. After doing this, your total is ☐

ACTIVITY 42

RACE THE CLOCK

The goal for your students is to build a small bridge using only newspapers/glue/tape and scissors. No other materials may be used. When the bridge is finished the opening under the bridge must be large enough for you to put your hand through it. The group with the strongest bridge wins (as measured by placing books on the bridge). Students have 30 minutes to complete this task. When you say go, students must first decide how much time to spend on each of the following 4 tasks before they actually begin to build the bridge. One person in each group will record how much time is actually spent on each of these tasks:

1. Planning how to build the bridge.
2. Assigning a role for each person in your group.
3. Constructing the bridge.
4. Testing the strength of your bridge.

1. Students are divided into small groups and each group is given the above instructions along with the appropriate materials. Each group proceeds with the task for 30 minutes (can be variable).

2. After completing the task, discuss whether the time that was planned for each of the 4 tasks was the same as the time actually used. Discuss how this activity might apply to setting timelines for doing homework.

ACTIVITY 43

SETTING PRIORITIES

1. Each student is given a copy of the story on page 93. Students read the story and then answer the questions.

2. Discuss and share the results.

ACTIVITY 44

HOW I SPEND MY TIME

1. Each student completes page 94. Discuss the results and identify possible time-wasters. It would be useful to compile things such as the average time watching television for your class per week, or the average time on the computer or playing video games.

ACTIVITY 45

USING MY TIME MORE EFFECTIVELY

1. Each student is challenged to revise the chart they prepared in Activity #44 and find a way to gain 2 - 3 hours more time during a week for school related work (or the enjoyment of hobbies and/or recreational reading). Share the results.

SETTING PRIORITIES

Sandi was stressed about all the work she had to do. Today was Monday and already she had enough homework to last for a month. Tomorrow she had a science test and 15 mathematics questions to complete for homework. By Wednesday, she had to have a topic for a speech that she would be presenting in two weeks. As well, she had a major history project due by next Monday. She knew that she had soccer practices both tonight and on Wednesday. In addition, her favorite television show was on Tuesday nights and she didn't want to miss that. Her class had just been assigned a new book to read, and by Friday she had to read the first fifty pages. On Thursday night she remembered that she was going to go shopping for a friend's birthday which was on Saturday. In addition, she had homework in her computer class that had to be done by Wednesday and homework in her art class to be done by Thursday.

The more Sandi thought about everything she had to do, the more confused and upset she became. This was all so overwhelming that she felt like giving up.

1. Make a calendar showing everything Sandi had to complete over the next two weeks.

2. In your view, which things should Sandi begin to work on tonight?

3. Establish a plan with timelines that shows what Sandi would have to do every night to complete all her assignments on time.

4. When you feel overwhelmed by the amount of schoolwork that you have do, what are some ways you can reduce the stress that you feel?

> "If you want to make good use of your time, you've got to know what is most important, and then give it all you've got."
> Lee Iacocca

HOW I SPEND MY TIME AWAY FROM SCHOOL

INSTRUCTIONS: Complete the following chart on how you spend your time away from school. List all the things you normally do such as watching television, playing video games, chatting on the Internet, talking to your friends, doing homework, etc.

TIMES	MONDAY	TUESDAY	WED.	THURS.	FRIDAY
FROM AFTER SCHOOL UNTIL YOU EAT SUPPER					
FROM AFTER SUPPER UNTIL 7:00 pm					
FROM 7:00 to 8:00 pm					
FROM 8:00 to 9:00 pm					
FROM 9:00 to 10:00 pm					
FROM 10:00 until you go to bed					

ACTIVITY 46

DAILY TO DO LISTS

Using page 96 as a sample, each student keeps track of class assignments, tests, etc. over the course of a day. Once students have completed this you could tell them to set priorities and establish a schedule of when things have to be done. Students could modify the chart on page 94 to set their schedule of what has to be done. Share the results. Students could continue to use a "daily to do list" over the next week.

ACTIVITY 47

MONTHLY PLANNER

Using page 97 as a monthly calendar, students take the assignments, tests, etc. from their daily to do lists (see Activity #46) and transfer what has to be done to this monthly planner. Being able to look a month ahead and prioritize what has to be done can be helpful to prevent students from becoming overwhelmed with too much to do at one time.

DAILY TO DO LISTS

INSTRUCTIONS: During each of your classes, keep track of any homework or other reminders on this chart.

CLASS	HOMEWORK/REMINDERS

A MONTHLY PLANNER

INSTRUCTIONS: List any assignment due dates, tests, etc. over the next month on the calendar below.

NOTES:

ACTIVITY 48

STOP PROCRASTINATING

1. Discuss the meaning of the word procrastination. Invite your students to give examples of situations where they procrastinated.

2. In small groups, students identify some positive and negative benefits that could result from procrastinating.

3. Each group is given a copy of the "stop procrastinating" tips on page 99. Each group prioritizes the ten tips with #1 being the one they think might work the best, #2 being the next best tip and so on. Share the results and discuss any other thoughts your students might have to help others to stop procrastinating.

ACTIVITY 49

TIME MANAGEMENT TIPS

Each student is given a copy of page 100. In small groups, students identify the five tips that could make the biggest difference in helping them to better manage their time. Each group shares their results.

STOP PROCRASTINATING!

1. Prioritize your work, and start with your most difficult tasks first.

2. Do your most difficult work when you are most awake.

3. Reward yourself for completing something you really didn't want to do.

4. Break large tasks/projects into small, manageable steps, and set realistic deadlines for completing each step.

5. If you tend to delay starting things because you can't make up your mind, then set a deadline for making a decision, and then stick to your decision.

6. Develop a clear vision of what the task/project will look like when it is completed.

7. Sometimes, you will have to accept that a job 95% done might be better than not getting it done at all because you are constantly trying to do it perfectly.

8. Ensure that you understand what you are to do on any task/project. Misunderstanding can lead to procrastination.

9. Focus on one thing at a time.

10. Set aside an appropriate period of time to complete your work.

TIME MANAGEMENT TIPS

1. It takes less time to fix a problem before it happens.

2. Faster is not always better.

3. Working smarter is more important than working longer.

4. Judging others usually takes up more of your time than accepting them.

5. Do it right the first time.

6. A few minutes at the end of each day to organize yourself for tomorrow will generally take less time than if you leave this for tomorrow.

7. You will generally be more productive if you keep your schedule somewhere else than in your head.

8. Before you begin any task, ensure that you understand what you are to do.

9. Interruptions are only interruptions when you permit them to be that.

10. Prioritize all the tasks that you need to do, and then start with the highest priority first.

11. Learn to say "NO".

12. There are times when doing something well is better than doing something perfectly.

13. Make a "TO DO" list every day.

14. By reducing the amount of time you procrastinate, you will have more time to get things done.

15. Analyze how you use your time, and eliminate timewasters.

ACTIVITY 50

TIPS ON BEING MORE ORGANIZED

Each student is given a copy of page 102 - 104. In small groups, students identify the five tips they feel could make the biggest difference in helping them to be more organized. Each group shares their results.

The most difficult step is always the first.

TIPS ON BEING MORE ORGANIZED

1. Throw away what you don't need anymore, especially from your locker or backpack.

2. Organize your locker and backpack in a way that makes it easy to find things.

3. Avoid keeping loose papers. Either punch holes in them so you add them to a binder or put them in an appropriately labelled file folder.

4. Ensure that your name is on your backpack and binder, and any other things you generally carry around with you at school.

5. If you keep your notes in a three-ring binder, organize them by subject area and in the order that you have them each day.

6. If you are using a three-ring binder, use colored dividers to make it easier for you to immediately find your notes for each subject, your "to do" lists, your master assignment due-date calendar, and your timetable.

7. Always keep your pens/pencils in exactly the same place so you are never looking for them.

8. Always have a few extra pencils and pens in your locker or backpack.

9. If you use a three-ring binder, keep a pencil case inside.

10. You can punch three holes in a large envelope (or purchase a plastic sleeve) and then keep this inside your binder for small sheets of paper. You can also use a pocket in the binder. Remember to clean out this envelope once a week.

11. If you keep a separate binder for each subject, place your timetable in each binder. You might also want to have a subject specific "to do" list and assignment due date calendar in each of these binders.

12. Always back up your computer files on a regular basis. There are some companies that offer a few gigs of free storage space where you can automatically upload your school work which means you will never lose it, and you can access it from any computer. Do a "Google" search to find such companies, but never upload personal information.

13. On your home or laptop computer establish a separate file folder for each subject area.

14. There is much less chance of losing materials if you do your homework in the same room every night.

15. If you have a part-time job or you participate in community activities in the evening, use your time wisely at school to get as much homework done as possible.

16. If you find yourself constantly losing things, then this is a warning that you need to find a way to better organize yourself.

17. If you have several tests to study for, set up a schedule to organize your time.

18. When you are required to read a complete book, or a long passage in a book, set a daily schedule for yourself to ensure that you complete your reading by the required date.

19. Set aside a specific time at home each day to complete your homework (and it makes more sense for this time to be early in the evening before you get too tired).

20. Schedule reminders for assignment due dates into your cell phone, or computer, or your iPod, or MP3 player.

21. Being more organized with your school work can give you more time for yourself each day.

22. Being organized can help you to be more successful at school.

23. Being more organized can reduce your level of stress each day.

24. It is generally more important to hand assignments in on time, than keep trying to make them perfect and then as a result hand them in late.

25. A three-hole punch can be helpful to you as you attempt to organize your loose papers. Do you know where you can find one in your school?

26. Another way to back up assignments you have completed on a computer is to send them to yourself in emails as attachments, then store your emails.

27. If you use a USB memory stick (or any other kind of memory stick), remember to put it in the same place every time you are finished using it, or you may find yourself losing it.

28. If you use a local commercial business (for example, Staples or the Office Depot) to print assignments or projects, remember you can save time by emailing your files to them that need to be printed.

29. Heavy backpacks can injure your back. If you don't need to bring home all your books then leave them in your locker.

30. Use a timer when you study or do homework, especially if you tend to take too long on one assignment and then run out of time. Set a schedule for your homework and then use the timer to keep you on track.

31. Plan for the unexpected. Leaving your studying and homework to the last minute, especially on major assignments, can backfire on you if something unexpected happens the night before the assignment is due.

32. Spend some time doing something that is enjoyable to you each day. You might even want to schedule this into your evening homework schedule.

33. A great timewaster for some people is procrastinating until they get very stressed about what they have to do. Set a schedule for what you have to do with time deadlines as part of the schedule. If you don't complete a task by the required deadline that you set, stop yourself from watching television, talking on your phone, or chatting on the Internet. On the other hand, when you complete things on time, reward yourself by doing some things that you enjoy.

34. If you just can't decide what to do first, put your choices on separate pieces of paper, put the pieces of paper in a box, and then take out one piece of paper. Start with the assignment on this piece of paper.

35. When it comes to organizing yourself, pay attention to what works and then keep doing more of this.

36. Take 30 minutes to walk through any office supply store. As you walk through the store, keep looking for any materials that might help you to be more organized. A few dollars spent in helping you to be more successful can be a very wise investment.

37. Attend your classes every day.

38. Sit near the front of the room in all your classes.

39. Your notes should be a summary rather than an exact duplication of what you are being taught.

40. Use abbreviations and symbols in your notes to save time (you might even use abbreviations that you use in "texting").

41. Keep your notes neat so you can read them two months from now.

42. Put your name (first and last) on everything that you do.

43. Don't put off until tomorrow what you can do today.

44. Break large projects into smaller chunks.

45. Ask for help and thank people who help you.

46. Be on time.

47. Ask your counselor or teacher if your school has workshops related to study skills, organizing, or dealing with stress.

48. Use "spell check" on your assignments. In addition, have others proof your work.

49. Take pride in what you do.

50. Use any spare time at school to organize your notes, do homework, or read any required articles or text references.

"Rules and procedures vary in different classrooms, but all effectively managed classrooms have them. It is just not possible for a teacher to conduct instruction or for students to work productively if they have no guidelines for how to behave or when to move about the room, of if they frequently interrupt the teacher and one another. Furthermore, inefficient procedures and the absence of routines for common aspects of classroom life, such as taking and reporting attendance, participating in discussions, turning in materials, or checking work can waste large amounts of time and cause students' attention and interest to wane."

Emmer, Evertson and Worsham (2003)

"Happiness is an attitude.
We either make ourselves miserable,
or happy and strong.
The amount of work is the same."
Franesca Reigler

THE BENEFITS OF ESTABLISHING A POSITIVE CLASSROOM ENVIRONMENT

In conducting research in the workplace I have discovered that the number one personal trait employers look for when they hire is positive attitude, and interestingly the number one trait employees would like to have in their co-workers is also positive attitude. Positive attitude enables people to work together more harmoniously and when conflict or misunderstandings do occur, positive attitude encourages people to find solutions rather than continuing to fight over their differences. Helping our students to gain a more positive attitude can assist them in forming a characteristic that can contribute effectively to future success in school, work, and in personal relationships. A student with a positive attitude can develop a mindset that sees failure as a chance to grow. When students are in an environment where they are not afraid to make mistakes and where they are not fearful of taking risks, significant learning can occur. In addition, positive attitude can help your students better deal with change as they develop an optimistic outlook. And similar to what happens in the workplace, positive attitude can help your students to get along better with each other as well as you and other staff members in your school.

As educators, we are familiar with students who seem to have the ability to succeed but they lack the required attitude to fuel the motivation to be successful. In this chapter, you are going to look at some activities that can help both you and your students to better understand positive attitude and its role in contributing to effective learning in your classroom.

In attempting to define positive attitude, one word that best describes this is optimism. An optimistic person is one who can see the possibilities in difficult situations, someone who sees problems as opportunities, and also someone who sees the best in himself as well as others.

Related to positive attitude is our self-talk, the internal dialogue that we all carry with us. Our self-talk can be a direct contributor to either success or failure. Our self-talk is often the best indication of whether we have a positive or negative attitude. Communication experts tell us that we all have more than 50,000 thoughts go through our mind each day. These same experts also tell us that for most people 70% or more of these thoughts are often of a negative nature. It is typical for many students to hear more negative comments than positive comments during the course of a day, thus resulting in a self-talk dialogue that has a tendency to be more negative than positive. Although most teachers are well aware that praise is important, the question you might ask is "What kind of praise is most effective?" There will be further thoughts and activities related to this question in this chapter. There are times when we focus on one or two students who are doing something wrong instead of praising the majority of students who are doing something right. This is not to say you should ignore poor performance or behavior, but to establish a positive learning environment you need to use specific, supportive feedback with students that places an emphasis on effort as well as achievement.

While you might also ask "Is positive attitude the result of success in the curriculum, or is success in the curriculum the result of positive attitude?", the current research tends to support the former (further thoughts on this in Chapter 10). Considering that the first four chapters of this book focus on things you should be emphasizing during the first few weeks of school and considering that "Being positive to others" was one of the rules I recommended back in Chapter 2, I am therefore placing this chapter on establishing a positive classroom environment before curriculum considerations (in Chapter 10) even though success in the curriculum plays a significant role in the development of positive attitude for your students.

As students begin to think about positive attitude, it would be useful for them to identify positive role models (with you being a significant role model for them). In a world where the media often focuses on what is wrong, this can present a challenge for students to identify people who have set themselves apart from others by maintaining their optimism in spite of personal hardships or setbacks. Students may identify celebrities, athletes, people who have made a significant contribution to their community, or simply family members who set a positive standard. As there will be some students who have a shortage of role models, it will also be useful for students to identify books, movies, quotes, websites, etc. that deliver messages of hope and optimism.

In looking at positive attitude, it is important for your students to recognize that positive attitude translates into action. This action is generally demonstrated in a very strong work ethic, a persistent determination, a strong sense of responsibility and strong self-discipline. Without this action, positive attitude is simply a charade.

While positive attitude is often associated with a high level of self-esteem, it is important to note that this is not necessarily true. A team led by Roy Baumeister, Ph.D., who is a professor of psychology at Florida State University is uncovering some groundbreaking research in the area of self-esteem. For example, they found that violent criminals can have self-esteem, and it is their unwarrantedly high level of self-esteem that causes violence. In fact, their research shows that "pumping up" someone's self-esteem can actually backfire. It was shown that high levels of self-esteem did not necessarily increase academic success, career achievement, or lower the incidence of violent behavior.

> "There's no question that you get the best results with highly contingent praise and criticism. That means praising exactly what was done right, and criticizing exactly what was done wrong. Just praising kids regardless of how they do contains very little useful information, and if anything can even have a negative effect on learning."
> Dr. Roy Beaumeister
> in *The Journal of Social and Clinical Psychology*, 2008

An important aspect of teaching students is your use of praise. Some teachers constantly praise students for every little thing that they do. In such situations, it doesn't take long for the students to "turn off" to the praise. It is often so unwarranted that even the students know it is meaningless. In using praise, it is important to be specific. Telling a student that his work is good is not as effective as telling a student that his use of descriptive words in the story he has written is very impressive. Be specific, and let your students earn the praise. Recognition for actual achievement (and effort!) is far more important than an endless showering of perhaps well-intended, but meaningless, compliments. Similarly, students can benefit from specific criticism that focuses on helping them to better understand what they have done wrong instead of nebulous comments such as "You can do better", or "That is poor work". In her book "Mindset - The New Psychology of Success", the author Carol S. Dwek talks about the importance of praising effort. In fact, the "growth mindset" that she argues would lead to greater learning is generally the result of praise directed more towards effort than achievement. It is the praising of effort that helps people to develop a mindset that helps them to persevere and learn how to grow in spite of failure.

> "Praising students for effort
> inspires them to accept greater challenges."
> Carol S. Dweck, PhD.,
> in *Mindset: The New Psychology of Success,* 2006

In this chapter, you will have the opportunity to introduce some activities to help establish a more positive classroom environment. Keep in mind that one of the greatest characteristics of a positive classroom environment is establishing a place where students feel comfortable taking risks and making mistakes. A positive classroom is also a place where students learn and grow from their mistakes. Indicators of such a classroom will be an increased level of self-discipline, self-initiative, determination and an increased sense of personal responsibility.

First, students will explore some thoughts on defining positive attitude in Activities #51 - 53. Next, students will explore traits of positive people and how this can apply to them in Activities #53, 54 and 61. Activities # 55 - 60 can begin to help you better understand some forms of praise to use with students and that they can also use with each other, although it is important to add that any of these forms of praise will be much stronger when they contain references to specific things that are the root of the reason for the praise. Activities #62 - 64 begin to look at student self-talk. It is a student's self-talk that often best illustrates whether his thinking is optimistic or pessimistic. Finally, Activities # 127 + 128 provide some practical thoughts for the physical layout of your room that can all contribute in a positive manner to establishing a more effective learning environment.

ACTIVITY 51

POSITIVE ATTITUDE SURVEY

On page 112 is an informal positive attitude survey that you can use with your students. Students who score from 40 - 50 would tend to have a high positive attitude; scores from 25 - 40 would be average; and scores less than 25 would be below average (although what is average for you class or your school could be quite different than another class or school). If you have any students who have very low scores it might be beneficial to share this information with your school counselor or child care worker to ensure that someone is helping the student. A review of these questions could also be a part of Activity #52.

It is recommended that you repeat the survey with your students at the end of this chapter to see if there has been some growth.

ACTIVITY 52

WHAT IS POSITIVE ATTITUDE

After reviewing the answers to the questions in Activity #51, students discuss a definition for positive attitude. The definition could include words like:

- optimistic
- happy
- confident

In addition, their definition could include phrases such as:

- doesn't give up very easily
- learns from failures
- looks for opportunities instead of problems

POSITIVE ATTITUDE SURVEY

For each of the following sentences, select the statement that best describes you. Write the number beside the statement in the appropriate box.

always like me - 5
sometimes like me - 3
never like me - 1

1. I tend to believe that good things are going to happen to me. ☐

2. I believe that most other people treat me fairly. ☐

3. When I make a mistake, it inspires me to try harder next time. ☐

4. I would describe myself as a happy person. ☐

5. Whenever I face a problem, I work hard to solve it. ☐

6. When I have work to do, I don't give up until it's done. ☐

7. Even when others stop believing in me, I keep believing in myself. ☐

8. Other people tend to be attracted to me because I am a positive person. ☐

9. I feel good about myself. ☐

10. I believe that I am in control of my future success. ☐

Add your numbers together from the above ten boxes. After doing this, your total is ☐

ACTIVITY 53

TRAITS OF POSITIVE PEOPLE

1. Based on the results of Activity #52, discuss and list words that best describe people who are positive. The following list is the top ten traits of positive people that resulted from research outlined in Scott Ventrella's book "Power of Positive Attitude in Business":

> optimism, enthusiasm, belief, integrity, courage, confidence, determination, patience, calmness, and focus

2. From the student list developed in #1 above and from Scott Venrella's list, in small groups students identify their top ten list of words that best describe positive people. Share the results and then formulate a top ten list of the traits of positive people that your class can agree on.

3. Each student is given a copy of page 114. On the left hand side of this page, students write the top ten list of positive traits that your class developed in #2 above. On the right hand side of the page, students identify a person (could be a friend, relative, family member, neighbor, celebrity, famous person, someone in a book, etc.) that they think best represents one of the identified top ten traits and then writes this person's name beside the appropriate trait. The goal is for students to try to get a different name for each trait, but if this is proving to be too difficult you might decide to let them use a name more than once. This could also be done effectively as a small group activity.

4. Discuss the results with students providing a rationale for each person they chose.

TRAITS OF POSITIVE PEOPLE

TOP 10 TRAITS OF POSITIVE PEOPLE	SOMEONE WHO HAS THIS TRAIT
1.	
2.	
3.	
4.	
5.	
6.	
7.	
8.	
9.	
10.	

> "If you want your life to be more rewarding, you have to change the way you think."
> Oprah Winfrey

ACTIVITY 54

A POSITIVE QUOTE TO LIVE BY

1. Each student selects a positive quote that she thinks would be a source of inspiration or a guide for her to live by. Some sample quotes are provided on page 116, or your students could also research similar quotes.

2. Some of the things your students could do once they have selected a quote are:

- create a poster using the quote and an appropriate picture
- write the quote on a file card to carry with her
- create a small poster with the quote on it to be placed in a locker or somewhere at home
- write a poem or song about the quote

ACTIVITY 55

50 COMPLIMENTS

1. As a class, list some positive things that could be said to others when they are deserving of receiving a compliment.

2. In small groups, students identify 50 compliments.

3. Share the results from #2 and compile a list of the best 50 compliments.

4. Post the list somewhere in the class and challenge your students to use these compliments with others in the class.

POSITIVE ATTITUDE QUOTES

"Wherever you go, no matter what the weather, always bring your own sunshine."
Anthony J. D'Angelo

"I had the blues because I had no shoes until upon the street,
I met a man who had no feet."
Ancient Persian Saying

"Attitude is a little thing that makes a big difference."
Winston Churchill

"Every day may not be good, but there's something good in every day."
Author Unknown

"Happiness is an attitude. We either make ourselves miserable, or happy and strong.
The amount of work is the same."
Francesca Reigler

"If you don't like something change it; if you can't change it,
change the way you think about it."
Mary Engelbreit

"The only disability in life is a bad attitude."
Scott Hamilton

"It's not what happens to you that determines how far you will go in life;
it is how you handle what happens to you."
Zig Ziglar

"If you believe you can, you probably can.
If you believe you won't, you most assuredly won't."
Denis Waitley

"Happiness is not by chance, but by choice."
Jim Rohn

"Take charge of your attitude. Don't let someone else choose it for you."
Anonymous

ACTIVITY 56

50 ENCOURAGERS

1. As a class, list some of the words of encouragement that could be said to others when they are trying their best.

2. In small groups, students identify 50 phrases and words that could be used to encourage others.

3. Share the results from #2 and compile a list of the best 50 encouragers.

4. Post the list somewhere in the class and challenge your students to use these words of encouragement with others in the class.

> "Kind words can be short and easy to speak, but their echoes are truly endless."
> Mother Teresa

> "Perform a random act of kindness for someone: a smile, a compliment, or a favor just for fun.
> These will multiply and spread very rapidly."
> Steve Brunkhorst

ACTIVITY 57

OUR POSITIVE CLASS NEWS

1. In small groups, students design a 3 - 4 page class newspaper. The emphasis in this newspaper is to focus on anything positive that has happened in the class or to class members in the school or community. A sample template is provided on page 119 although students should be encouraged to design their own.

2. At the end of a specified period of time, each group presents their newspaper. This might even be an activity that could occur throughout the year with a group of students responsible for publishing a newspaper each month. The names of each person in the group could be posted and whenever students have positive news to share, they could provide this news to one of the group members. You might even decide to share the newspapers with parents and your school administrator(s).

ACTIVITY 58

A POSITIVE STORY

1. Each student shares a positive story. The stories could come from real life, a book, television show, movie, etc.

2. After the sharing of each story, discuss the factors that make the story positive. Students could refer to the traits of positive people that were developed in Activity #53.

OUR CLASS NEWS

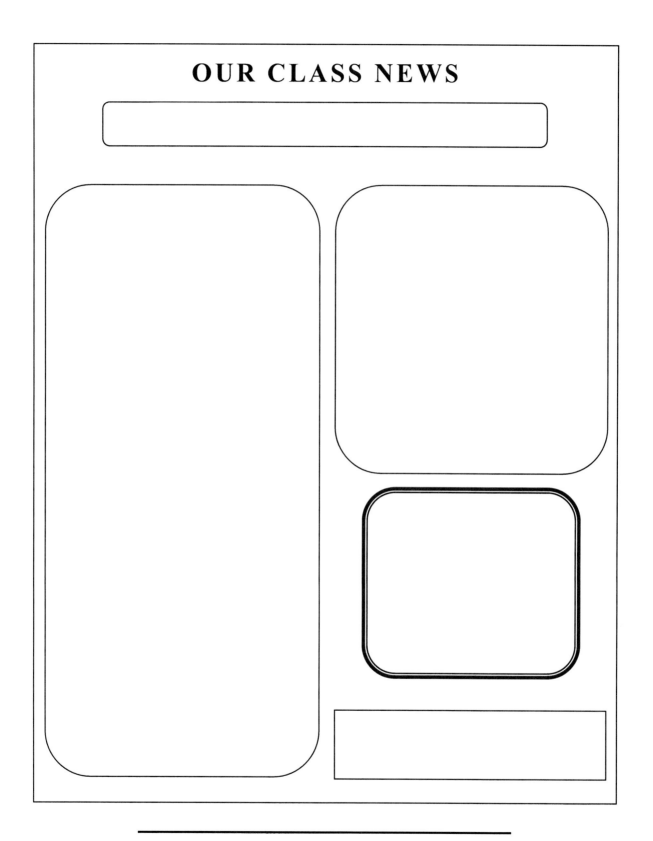

ACTIVITY 59

POSITIVE REFRAMING

1. Students are told to provide some examples of negative statements that they sometimes hear. Some examples might be:

- Life sucks.
- I'm no good at anything.
- I'm always messing up.
- I never do anything right.

2. For each negative statement that students identify, tell your students to rephrase the sentence so that it becomes positive. For example, the above negative statements might be changed to:

- Life is great.
- I'm really good at helping others.
- I'm getting better at being kind to others.
- I did all my homework perfectly.

3. In small groups, students identify 10 - 15 negative statements and then reframe them into positive statements. Results are shared.

> "Expect the best and get the best,
> expect the worst and get the worst."
> Dr. Norman Vincent Peale

ACTIVITY 60

REFRAMING A STORY

1. Each student finds a negative or unhappy story in a newspaper or magazine. Students rewrite their stories changing it into a happy or positive story.

2. Results are shared. It might also be useful to discuss whether the media should be placing a greater emphasis on positive inspirational stories instead of mostly focusing on the negative.

Grade 6 Student

ACTIVITY 61

POSITIVE TRAITS THAT BEST DESCRIBE ME

Each student is given a copy of page 123. Students complete the page and results are shared. In completing this activity it would be useful for students to have the list of positive traits developed in Activity #53.

ACTIVITY 62

SELF-LIMITING BELIEFS

1. Our beliefs (the way we view ourselves and the world around us) can have a strong impact on our level of success and happiness. Self-limiting beliefs that are learned from a variety of sources can prevent young people from being successful. Below are five common self-limiting beliefs that can have a negative effect on success and happiness:

> I'm a loser if I make mistakes.
>
> Other people are ruining my life.
>
> My life should be free of problems.
>
> I cannot control how I feel.
>
> Success is based on being lucky.

2. Each student is given a copy of page 124. Discuss the various success quotes in relationship to the self-limiting beliefs stated above.

POSITIVE TRAITS THAT BEST DESCRIBE ME

Some positive traits that best describe me are . . .

SUCCESS QUOTES

"It's okay to make mistakes.
Mistakes are our teachers - they help us to learn."
John Bradshaw

"You may be disappointed if you fail,
but you are doomed if you don't try."
Beverly Sills

"To achieve a major success,
you must assume 100% responsibility for your life."
Jack Canfield

"Nobody is free from having problems.
The successful person accepts his/her problems
and rises above them instead of dwelling on them."
Anonymous

"Every achievement, big or small, begins in your mind."
Mary Kay Ash

"You cannot always control what happens to you,
but you can control how you decide to respond to what happens to you."
Brian Tracy

"I am a great believer of luck,
and I find the harder I work the more I have of it."
Thomas Jefferson

"If you want the rainbow, sometimes you have to put up with the rain."
Dolly Parton

"I attribute my success to this:
I never made excuses."
Florence Nightingale

ACTIVITY 63

A PERSONAL SELF-LIMITING BELIEF

1. In reference to the five self-limiting beliefs in Activity #62 on page 122, students identify additional self-limiting beliefs.

2. Using the quotes on page 124, students match each of the self-limiting beliefs from #1 above and also from page 122 with the most appropriate quote.

3. Each student is given a copy of page 126 to complete. It is recommended that you collect this work and provide comments back to your students rather than sharing these in class.

ACTIVITY 64

REFRAMING SELF-TALK

1. Each student writes a self-limiting belief (could come from Activity # 63) on a file card.

2. Collect the file cards, shuffle them, and then give them to a student. The student reads the top card as it is and then repeats it again reframing it as a positive statement. This card is then placed on the bottom of the stack and the next student repeats the process.

A PERSONAL SELF-LIMITING BELIEF

1. A personal self-limiting belief I have is . . .

2. I think this self-limiting belief is the result of . . .

3. I think this self-limiting belief keeps me from being successful because . . .

4. Two quotes I could remember that could help me to overcome this self-limiting belief are . . .

    i)

    ii)

ACTIVITY 65

SEATING ARRANGEMENT

The seating arrangement in your class can have a dramatic effect on behavior and the establishment of a positive classroom environment. It is recommended that your seating arrangement provides a direct view from your students to you and to the area of the room where you would normally stand when you teach. This is especially important during the first few weeks of school, so it is not recommended that you start your school year with a seating arrangement where your students are in groups which might result in some of them having to always turn around when you need them to listen to you. Another recommendation is that your desk is located in a position where you have eye contact with all your students.

> "You will get better results
> if you arrange your room
> to permit orderly movement, few
> distractions, and efficient use of space."
> Emmer, Evertson, and Worsham (2003)

The key point here is visual contact with your students. When your students are constantly turning in order to see you, you lose the opportunity to use non-verbal cues (see Chapter 5) which can be so effective in communicating your expectations to students. To be able to look directly at a student and communicate to this student (often with your facial expressions) that his behavior is not appropriate is a lot less disrupting to the class than constantly having to talk (or even shout) to get a student's attention. Until you have established clear classroom expectations, set the desks in the arrangement that gives you eye contact with every student. This does not mean that your classroom has to be set up in straight rows with all the desks separated. Some of the most effective classroom have 3 - 4 desks touching each other (but facing the front of the room). This kind of arrangement also helps to provide more "moving around" space which is important for you as a teacher as you work with individual students.

Generally, you might decide to let your students choose their own seats for the first day with them being clearly told that you might change the seating arrangement before the week is over. Once you have had a chance to observe how your students work, take quick action to separate any students who are disruptive when they sit near each other. This action gives a clear message to your class that there are immediate consequences when your expectations are not met. Also keep in mind that the further any disruptive students sit away from you, the harder it can be to control their behavior. Proximity to where you normally stand in the room can assist in improving the behavior of some otherwise disruptive students.

Once you feel that classroom rules and routines have been established you can then ask students to suggest new seating arrangements which you might then implement every 3 - 4 weeks. The bottom line here is really a case of what arrangement best contributes to effective teaching and student learning. There can be many variations that work for you. If your current seating arrangement is not working, then make some changes. Strive to find the best seating arrangement that contributes the most to establishing a comfortable and positive classroom environment.

ACTIVITY 66

THE APPEARANCE OF YOUR ROOM

Some teachers go to great lengths to set up a room with attractive decorations, interesting pictures, etc. before school begins. Other teachers start with a "bare" classroom in order that their students become the major contributors to how the room looks. Although either approach can be effective, in the end it is important to post student work throughout your room as quickly as possible. Students love to see their own work. In addition, I recommend that there are a few things in your room that are important to you. These things might be something like a poster that represents a dream vacation for you or a picture that creates a peaceful feeling for you, or even a quotation that you find inspirational. There are times when we all need a mental break and something visual in your room that is special to you can help with this.

The following provide some further ideas to consider in setting up your room.

a) PICTURE FRAMES

A few cheap picture frames that you pick up a garage sale can be used for exceptional student work (even if it's not art). Students will feel incredibly proud when something they have done is placed in one of your picture frames for the next week. The frames with their work are displayed in a prominent place in your room. It is important over a period of time to recognize every student in your class through this approach.

b) BULLETIN BOARDS

A tremendous amount of work can go into arranging displays on classroom bulletin boards before school begins. Unless the displays directly relate somehow to making the students feel more welcome, perhaps it might make more sense to cut back on your efforts here and let your students participate on a regular basis in designing and arranging the bulletin boards in your class.

If you have two bulletin boards, as an example, it might be useful to reserve one to recognize student excellence and for the other one to focus on some aspect of your curriculum. The first bulletin board related to student excellence could be set up when students enter on the first day in terms of background and a title, but otherwise left blank. As quickly as possible during the first week, ensure that every student has some example of excellence posted on this bulletin board.

The second board, focusing on curriculum, could be used during the first two weeks of school to post any completed activities from Chapters 1 - 4 in this book. After this, it often works well to assign the task of setting up the bulletin board to a few students on a systematic schedule throughout the year. The bulletin board could be considered as an assignment for students that is evaluated similar to other assignments. This way, your bulletin boards can relate directly to the curriculum and you never need to spend any time in setting them up.

I would also recommend that you take pictures of your bulletin boards throughout the year so you can use these pictures with students in future years to show them examples of excellent work.

c) CLASS LIBRARY

It is recommended that you have a selection of reference books related to the current subject content that your students are studying. Similar to a main library, there should be some procedure for students to sign out the books (perhaps another job for your teacher assistant - see Activity #33). If possible, it would be great if there could be a few comfortable chairs (or a reading rug) in this area to give a "lounge area" feel.

d) COMPUTERS IN YOUR CLASS

In placing any computers in your class give some thought to the ease that they can be accessed so that students are not constantly disturbing others in order to reach them. Also consider their impact on nearby students. As some students use the computers, will this cause a distraction for nearby students? As well, consider lighting requirements. If your computers are near a west or south facing window, it might be difficult for your students to read the screens at various times during the day. Finally, it is important to establish procedures for using the computers which also requires a process for printing if you have printers hooked up to the computer. Your procedures should also include accepted internet usage guidelines.

If your students are using laptops it is essential that you have clear procedures for using and also storing the computers. Once again, a teacher assistant (maybe even a "technology assistant") could be a great help in this area.

e) SOMETHING FUN

It definitely makes sense to have a few things in your room that apper to be completely random and yet contribute in some way to fun. These could include board games, puzzles, funny posters, a joke box (a file box containing file cards with favorite jokes from students in your class), age appropriate magazines, etc.

f) SOMETHING ALIVE

Whether it is a few plants or even an aquarium, something that is alive in your room can be a real asset in establishing a calm, positive environment. Whatever you set up, give your students the responsibility of caring for the plants or fish. Spider plants, as an example, are an easy to care for plant that are also an excellent source of purifying the air in your room. Similarly, umbrella trees are easy to care for, grow well, and can have a very soothing effect when placed at the front of the room.

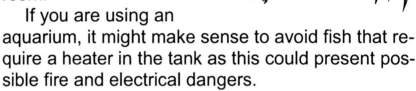

If you are using an aquarium, it might make sense to avoid fish that require a heater in the tank as this could present possible fire and electrical dangers.

g) SOMETHING FOR YOU

As has already been recommended in this chapter, it is important that there a few things in your room that are meaningful to you on a personal level. This could be a poster of some scenery that is significant to you, some reminder of your family, a quote that inspires you, etc. Remember, you classroom is your workplace as well as a place for your students. When you look after your needs as well as those of the kids in your class, everyone will be happier.

In looking after your needs, a great investment for some teachers may be obtaining a comfortable chair with appropriate back support as you may spend significant time sitting in this chair as you mark and prepare. In addition, a comfortable pair of shoes might also be a wise investment.

h) A GREAT $200 INVESTMENT

At a time of cutbacks in money for schools, it is common for teachers to be short of materials. If someone gave you $200, is there something you could buy for your classroom and students that would make your life easier? And if your answer to this question is "yes, there definitely is something you could buy that would contribute to you having a more positive classroom where both your students and you wanted to be", then my next question is "Would it then make sense for you to spend $200 of your own money to make this happen?"

If investing $200 in your classroom could help you to be more effective, then it follows that you would likely be happier and more satisfied with your teaching which then results in you being less stressed. Isn't $200 spent being proactive better than the time and money that you might spend if you encounter health problems because of stress?

It is recommended that if you have a teacher supply store near you (or even one online) that you visit this place frequently in an attempt to find timesaving ready-to-use materials for your room.

i) MONTHLY WALL CALENDAR

It can be very helpful to your students (and yourself) to have a visual reminder of upcoming assignments, tests, special days, assemblies, etc. posted in your room. At any business supply store you can purchase a large whiteboard calendar that you can reuse over and over again. A calendar that shows several months can be just as effective as a complete year calendar.

Calendars can be great timesavers, and if you have a student (or parent) who states that he/she didn't know when an assignment was due, you can quickly prove that there is no excuse for a student to miss a deadline as everything is publically displayed on the calendar in your classroom.

Some teachers also use websites to set up calendars for their students (see page 134).

j) A CLASS WEBSITE

Whether you set up a one page website, attach a page to your school website, or simply make use of email, this type of technology can provide a great way for you to communicate with parents and even students. First of all, it is important that you are aware of school and school board policies related to using emails and/or websites to communicate with your students and/or parents.

Contacting parents by telephone can be very time-consuming. Contacting all the parents by email can be effortless. An email once a month, as an example, could contain an outline of upcoming assignments and tests. Some teachers also make very effective use of sending a monthly summary of marks to individual parents and/or students.

Postings on a website can provide assignment due dates as well as the instructions for completing assignments. This can be very helpful to both students and parents.

k) VISIT OTHER CLASSROOMS

It has been said that success leaves clues. By visiting other classrooms, both in your school and in other schools, you can pick up new ideas that can contribute to success in your classroom. When you visit, talk to the other teachers to get a sense of their rationale for how they have arranged their rooms. It would be useful to directly ask them what they think are the most important things that contribute to creating a positive classroom environment.

Other teachers can be a great source of help. Take the time to cultivate relationships with them that result in a willingness for them to share and help you grow as a teacher.

l) SUGGESTIONS FROM YOUR STUDENTS

Empower your students to be more actively committed to having a positive classroom by asking for their input. It would even be useful for your students to form small groups with each group discussing and then presenting their recommendations to their peers related to establishing a more positive classroom.

If you take this approach, it is important that you actually implement some of the suggestions.

m) IN-BOX

The start of any class can be disrupted as students bring notes from home, field trip forms, etc. It would be far less disruptive to have a procedure in place for dealing with each of these (and your teacher assistant could help you with this).

Suggestions include having a box in a convenient place that is your in-box. Whenever students bring in forms or notes from home, these pieces of paper are automatically placed in your in-box by your students. At some point during the class, your teacher assistant can file or organize the content of your in-box according to your instructions.

Similarly, you might have a homework or assignment box so that students place these materials in a box as they enter the room with your teacher assistant later using a class list to check off the names of students who have handed in their work.

Along the same lines, you could also have an out-box where forms to go home, as an example, are placed. Once again your teacher assistant can hand out the materials.

As a teacher, your major focus should be on teaching. Wasting time doing tasks that many of your students would enjoy doing for you (and would also build a sense of responsibility for your students) does not make a lot of sense.

n) A TIME-OUT PLACE

There will be situations when it may be necessary to have a student sit away from other students as a result of misbehavior or even to re-write a test. As such it would be useful to set an area with a desk that can be used for such purposes. You can refer to this place as the "time-out" place or even the "quiet" place.

Some teachers even effectively partner with other teachers in this regard so that your student may be sent to another classroom. If you are taking this approach, it is important that your student has work with him when he leaves your room.

"Time-outs" should be timed and in most situations a short period of time (10 - 15 minutes) is more effective than longer periods of time.

> "People rarely succeed unless they are having fun in what they are doing."
> Dale Carnegie

> "I took violin lessons from age 6 - 16,
> but had no luck with my teachers,
> for whom music did not transcend
> mechanical practicing. I really began
> to learn only after I had fallen in love
> with Mozart's sonatas. The attempt
> to reproduce their singular grace
> compelled me to improve my technique.
> I believe, on the whole, that love
> is a better teacher than sense of duty."
> — Albert Einstein

"To be effective with others, we must see, hear, and interpret (perceive) them accurately."
George M. Gazda and others in
*Human Relations Development:
A Manual for Educators*, 2005

PART B

HOW TO DEAL EFFECTIVELY WITH INAPPROPRIATE BEHAVIOR

An educator might have great creative skills, a solid knowledge of both curriculum and teaching techniques, yet without the communication skills to effectively communicate this expertise to students and also to use these appropriate communication skills to better understand the needs of individual students, this apparent expert teacher may be doomed to fail. Teaching is communicating. A solid grasp of effective communication techniques can enhance the success of any teacher and also builds the foundation for meaningful conflict resolution. In looking at communication skills, this section of the book will include both listening and speaking. This is often described as interpersonal communications or human relations skills.

Two characteristics that often underline interpersonal skills are empathy and genuineness. Empathy is often defined as "putting yourself in someone else's shoes" while genuineness may be described as sincerity. Hein (2004) in a review of recent research in the area of extraordinary teachers found that one of the major factors was "ability to connect exceptionally well with students". The first chapter of this book commenced with activities related to connecting with your students and now we return back to this theme from a different viewpoint.

> "Teachers trained in interpersonal skills produced students who had fewer discipline problems, attended school more frequently and earned significantly higher gains on cognitive tests."
> Aspy, Aspy, Russel, and Wedel, 2000

As a teacher, you are constantly a model for your students. Being a warm, empathetic and genuine teacher can help your students to learn these positive interpersonal skills which in turn can reduce behavioral problems in your class. In the workplace if you were to ask employees what they value in fellow workers, you would hear some of the following:

- someone who is optimistic
- someone who will listen to me
- someone with a sense of humor
- someone who doesn't judge me
- someone with patience

Similarly you will find that students also respond best to teachers who exemplify these desirable characteristics. The process of learning requires an environment that accepts mistakes, a willingness to accept criticism and a comfortable level of interacting with others. A teacher, as the class leader in interpersonal communications, has a strong influence on all these factors.

Effective interpersonal skills are not only crucial in your work with students but also have a direct impact with parents, administrators, co-workers, and other non-teaching staff such as custodians. You might wonder why I included custodians. A clean classroom contributes to your students' learning. I have been in some schools where teachers set up desks in such a way that it was very difficult for custodians to keep the room clean, or in other situations where the teacher allowed the room to become so messy that custodians did not do their best job in cleaning up after the teacher's indifference. Like anyone else in the school, treat your custodian with respect and your job will be easier.

A variety of sources (Carkhuff, Egan, Kottler, Glasser, Alberti) have recognized three major skill areas related to being an effective communicator. These three skills areas may be summarized as follows:

1. Empathetic Listening
2. Constructive Assertiveness
3. Conflict Resolution/Problem Solving

The next three chapters will look further at each of these areas of interpersonal skills. As in previous chapters, activities will be provided to teach your students these skills as well. As your students learn to be more effective communicators, you will have the opportunity to refine your skills along with them.

To be effective with others, you need to correctly understand what they are saying to you, and similarly they must correctly perceive what you are trying to say to them. Effective communications is a two-way street that includes both the speaker and listener. Sometimes the essential message in any attempt to communicate may be lost because of poor speaking and/or listening skills. The message may also be lost as a result of biases, expectations and defense mechanisms that all affect perception. If you find yourself repeatedly having difficulties communicating with another person, it might be useful for you to consider some of these factors as they affect the perception that is occurring. There is a saying that we tend to hear what we want to hear, and in our communications with others they may also hear what they want to hear even if this results in perceiving a different message than we are trying to deliver. Empathetic listening, as explained further in Chapter 5, can help you and your students to better communicate with less misunderstanding.

> "Many behavioural problems ultimately boil down to a breakdown in teacher-student relationships."
> Rosa Sheets and Geneva Gay (1996)

Chapter 6 looks at constructive assertiveness. "Assertive behavior is the ability to stand up for one's legitimate rights in ways that make it less likely that others will ignore or circumvent them" (Emmer, Evertson, and Worsham, 2003). Another way that assertiveness might be defined is looking out for your own wants, needs and rights while at the same time being aware of the wants, needs and rights of others. Your students should expect and receive respect for their wants, needs and rights. The word constructive has been added to assertiveness here as a reminder that it is constructive praise or criticism that can make a difference in your students' learning.

Assertive people tend to be more admired by others. Assertive people stand up for what they believe and this is certainly an important trait to instill in your students. Non-assertive people tend towards either being passive (in their relationships with others) or aggressive. Neither of these characteristics lead to effective communications and in the classroom neither of these approaches leads to effective classroom management, and as a result meaningful learning. Non-assertive teachers tend to find themselves repeating the same things over and over again with their students. When a confident teacher assertively gives a set of instructions, there is a greater likelihood that these instructions will be followed by the students. When either constructive criticism or praise is used by a teacher in an assertive manner, the results will have a greater impact.

Chapter 7 looks at conflict resolution. While the content of Chapters 1 - 6 can help to prevent or reduce conflicts in the classroom, even the most effective teachers will still encounter some conflicts in their classroom. Classroom conflicts can provide an opportunity to teach your students some skills that can make a huge difference throughout their lives. Conflicts with others in the workplace are often identified as the number one source of stress in the workplace. Helping your students to learn skills in successfully resolving conflicts can not only reduce stress (and conflicts) in your classroom, but it can prepare your students for a more successful future. This chapter presents a model for conflict resolution that you can teach to your students. The skills used in implementing this model build on the skills learned in Chapters 5 + 6.

Conflicts in the classroom can result in a great deal of time and energy being taken away from teaching your curriculum. Having a specific procedure for dealing with conflicts, such as the model given in Chapter 7, can help to expedite solutions in a more positive manner. Another aspect of conflict resolution relates to problem solving or decision making. Chapter 7 will also provide a model for problem solving that you can teach to your students. When your students are more familiar with a process for solving their own problems this can alleviate the need for you to be constantly handling concerns between students.

> "The problem is not that there are problems.
> The problem is expecting otherwise
> and thinking that having a problem
> is a problem."
> Theodore Rubin

Another aspect of conflict resolution relates to anger management. While it might be a small number of students in your class who need help with anger management, these students can cause significant disturbances, and even pose safety concerns, when they express their anger in inappropriate ways. Helping your students learn skills in expressing their anger in more appropriate ways can once again be a factor in success not only now, but in their future as well. Chapter 8 provides some thoughts and activities related to anger management.

> "Children who had been consistently angry in childhood were more likely to be unsatisfied with life at age 30."
> Columbia University College, 2000

As has already been stated several times throughout this book, the manner in which you present yourself as a classroom leader can have a significant impact on how your students interact with each other. One of the most effective anger strategies your students will learn is how you deal with conflict. Becoming more familiar with conflict resolution tips and techniques as well as anger management strategies can help you to better model appropriate behavior for your students. Recently as I was presenting a workshop to parents on conflict resolution, a mother approached me at the end of my workshop to tell me about her ten year old daughter who routinely expressed her anger by screaming, slamming her bedroom door, and then pounding on it. When I asked the mother how she responded to these inappropriate outbursts, she replied that she yelled back at her daughter and sometimes found herself pounding on the other side of her daughter's bedroom door as she screamed at her daughter to stop. This is a pretty obvious case of a child learning inappropriate behavior by modeling a significant adult in her life.

Chapter 9 provides some specific discipline strategies that have been successfully used within classrooms and schools. Some of these techniques require the commitment of all staff members while other discipline strategies can be used by individual teachers. In the end when all staff members work together to support each other in making the school a cleaner and safer environment, and when discipline outside the classroom is viewed as being equal to behavior expectations within the classroom, everyone benefits and greater learning occurs.

"If I were to summarize in one sentence the single most important principle I have learned in the field of interpersonal relations, it would be this: Seek first to understand, then to be understood. This principle is the key to effective interpersonal communication."

Stephen Covey

CHAPTER 5

THE BENEFITS OF DEVELOPING EMPATHETIC LISTENING SKILLS

For more than twenty years, I have been involved in teaching interpersonal communication courses to teachers. Most teachers, by their own admission, state that they are much better "talkers" than "listeners". Effective communications, and similarly effective teaching, depends on developing strong listening skills. When students feel that you have heard and understood them, they feel validated and accepted. This can often lead to a stronger bond and sense of understanding between you and your students which can in turn lead to improved behavior and greater participation in learning. As previously stated in this book, when a person attempts to get into the shoes of another person, this is known as empathy. Empathy results in an understanding of both the content of what a person is saying and also the underlying feelings reflecting the emotions the person is experiencing.

> "Students initiate more out-of-class communication with teachers who show a high level of empathy in the classroom, which enhances the classroom climate."
> Phillips, 2003

CLASSROOM MANAGEMENT

Every day we hear other people talking. Words surround us. From the media, to our families, colleagues and students, come endless attempts to communicate. Although we constantly hear the voices, we don't always hear the message. Communication difficulties are often the first area identified in marriage breakdowns, in parent-child conflicts and, in general whenever people have concerns with others. While you have likely heard that practice makes perfect, for many people years of improper practice has led to habits of poor listening. Both parents and teachers can often be heard telling kids to listen better, yet the reality is that some parents and teachers have set a poor example of how to listen effectively and the students are simply copying what they see.

From the moment of our first arrival in this world, we have been hearing others speak and just as quickly we learned how to be selective in our listening to ensure that our needs (and wants) were met first. For example, many of the first words we focused on were related to satisfying our basic needs such as food, comfort and protection. Our world was very "me" centered. As a consequence, our listening skills were influenced greatly by selfish gratification. By the time we started our formal schooling, many of our basic communication skills were already established. Although formal education often improved our skills in both speaking and writing, there was generally little in the curriculum to improve listening skills. Although most of us were likely told, at some time or another, to "listen better", we were rarely instructed as to how to do this.

Listening is an art. It is comprised of specific skills which necessitate instruction and practice before they can be mastered. Interestingly, I have found over my many years of being an educator that some of the students who were the best listeners were often the children of professionals involved in the "counseling field" or were themselves clients who had been exposed to professional counselors. These children learned from the role models in their lives who had significant skills in listening. These students also readily confirmed for me that effective listening skills can be learned and that a primary source of learning occurs when students have role models who are proficient in the use of these skills.

> "A wise old owl sat on an oak:
> The more he saw, the less he spoke:
> The less he spoke, the more he heard:
> Why aren't we like that wise old bird?"
> Albert Einstein

Empathetic listening keeps the lines of communication open between you and your students, and is essential in identifying problems that may contribute to conflicts. As empathy contributes strongly to acceptance, improving your skills in this area can help you to have a class of willing learners. When students feel accepted, they will want to be in your classroom. A central skill to the mastery of empathetic listening is paraphrasing what your students say to you. Paraphrasing can focus on the actual content of what is being said, or it can focus on both the surface or underlying feelings. Paraphrasing can sometimes be brief with only a few words being spoken while other times it might better be described as providing a summary of what is being said.

Empathetic listening is sometimes described as being "reflective" in nature. In fact, in many books related to interpersonal communication skills you will often find thoughts related to empathy in a chapter titled "Reflective Listening". Reflection is a nice analogy for empathy as the word reflect implies looking in a mirror. Empathy is really an attempt to hold a mirror in front of a student as he is talking and reflecting back to him the content and emotions of what has been said. In doing this, it is critical that your reflection be one of genuineness, otherwise you may simply be "parroting" or providing a parody of what the student is saying which can quickly lead to a lack of rapport and trust between you and the student.

> "The great gift of human beings
> is that we have the power of empathy."
> Meryl Streep

Once you have developed further skills in empathetic listening (and the activities in this chapter can help both you and your students to do this), it becomes important to recognize that empathy in itself does not necessarily move you and your students towards some form of resolution. If you are attempting to problem solve or resolve a conflict, chapters 6 - 9 can better provide some strategies related to problem solving and conflict resolution (and the strategies in these chapters depend on you first developing effective communication skills). Having said this, establishing empathy with your students can be a wonderful preventer of classroom conflicts and misbehavior. When students feel understood and accepted, they are much less likely to "cry out" for attention in inappropriate ways.

verbal assurances you give to the student that you care about him. In such situations, the student may appear to willingly go along with what is being said only to never again seek help from the teacher. The resulting lack of empathy and respect can sever any connection you had with the student which can then lead to a lack of willingness for the student to participate in learning in your classroom.

While the eyes are often considered to be the most important aspect of giving our full attention to a student who is talking to us, it is also useful to remember that some students either lack the confidence or cultural background to maintain eye contact, and in such situations our unwavering eye contact may be perceived as being more threatening than accepting. There may be times when we have to adjust our non-verbal behavior to that of a student to provide that best "reflection" of what a student is saying and to provide the most comfortable environment for the student to openly talk. In addition, remember that your non-verbal behavior may reveal your true feelings about what a student is telling you, so you have to be aware of your own biases and focus on getting yourself into the shoes of the student rather than forcing the student into your shoes.

> "First of all," he said, "if you can learn a simple trick, Scout, you'll get along a lot better with all kinds of folks. You never really understand a person until you consider things from his point of view - "
> "Sir ?"
> " - until you climb into his skin and walk around in it."
> Harper Lee in *To Kill A Mockingbird*

Research shows that the majority of our communication is non-verbal. The ability to interpret non-verbal cues and to be more aware of our own non-verbal behavior is a powerful tool in communicating effectively. The manner in which you look, move and react to a student all provide clues for the student as to whether you genuinely care about him. In teaching counseling skills, I often state that students will be very forgiving if you ask the wrong question, or even misinterpret something they have said, if they perceive that you genuinely care about them. As well, there will be times that the words a student is presenting to us are different than the non-verbal behavior the student is exhibiting. In such situations, understanding the non-verbal cues becomes an important part of interpreting the message.

Respect is also a component of effective listening and it is closely tied in with empathy. When you accurately perceive and reflect what a student is saying to you, the understanding and acceptance that results generally leads to increased respect towards you from the student (and vice versa). This respect can be very important in motivating students to better listen to you both when you are teaching and when you are involved in both problem solving and conflict resolution. You may have sometimes heard a teacher (and/or parent) say that his students don't respect him. Respect is something that we earn in our relationship with students, and skills in empathetic listening can go a long way in helping to establish this respect.

> "When a teacher expresses warmth, it perpetuates itself and spreads."
> Neidigh, 1991

Another component of empathetic listening is warmth. Gestures, posture, tone of voice, etc. may also communicate warmth. Effective listening then also involves awareness of non-verbal communications, both on your part and on the part of your students. While the "teacher stare" may be an effective non-verbal discipline technique, it is important to drop the stare and adapt eyes that convey warmth when you are seeking to understand something a student is trying to tell you. There are times when we can almost instantly say whether we like a person, or not. Such first impressions are generally based on non-verbal cues we observe in the other person. Similarly, students perceive your non-verbal behavior and as such may perceive what you are saying in a completely different light than what you are intending. This discrepancy between words and perception illustrates the need for teachers at some point to have an unbiased and qualified educator assess their teaching. In addition, self-evaluation through the use of video may also provide an enlightening look at whether your verbal message matches your non-verbal behavior.

It has been said that we are always communicating. Whether we are speaking or whether we are listening, we are still communicating, and what we are communicating (through our non-verbal behavior) when we are listening may speak much louder then our eventual words. For example, when a student is talking to you, if you are focused on something else (such as trying to read a book or mark an assignment), the student will quickly determine that you are not interested in spite of any

> "What you do speaks so loud
> that I cannot hear what you are saying."
> Ralph Waldo Emerson

Activities in this chapter can help both you and your students to become more effective listeners. As in other chapters, the activities are intended to help your kids learn some new skills, but this is definitely one chapter where you should carefully consider your own skills in listening and as much as possible use the activities for your own person growth as well. The best strategy to teach your students empathetic listening skills is for you to model them.

The chapter activities begin with a look at non-verbal listening. Activities #67 - 75 can help to teach your students more about non-verbal listening skills. As you work through these activities, keep in mind that students from other cultures may perceive non-verbal listening cues differently. As well, this is an area where it might be very helpful to have one of your students or a colleague take a video of you as you teach so you can better analyse your strengths and weaknesses.

> "The most important thing in communication
> is hearing what isn't said."
> Peter F. Drucker

Activities #76 introduces three listening skills: paraphrasing, clarification and open-ended questions. These are the major skills that can help you to establish empathy with your students. They are also the skills that contribute to your students feeling more comfortable in talking openly. Activities #77 - 80 look closer at paraphrasing. Activities #81 + 82 explore clarification, while Activities #83 + 84 provide information on using open-ended questions. Finally, Activities 85 + 86 provide a review of interpersonal communication skills taught in this chapter.

Being an effective communicator, and in this chapter the focus is on your listening skills, can help you to become an outstanding teacher.

ACTIVITY 67

WHAT IS NON-VERBAL LISTENING

1. Give your students some examples of what non-verbal communications refers to. Through a class discussion, develop a list of ways to communicate non-verbally (for example: eye contact, gestures, posture, etc.). It would be useful for students to be as specific as possible (for example: How many different ways can messages be conveyed through non-verbal cues?).

2. In pairs, one student tells the other student about an interest, hobby, favorite television show, etc. The student who is listening cannot speak and attempts to show interest in what is being said through non-verbal listening. It is suggested that this activity be timed between 1 - 2 minutes and then the students reverse roles.

3. Students share their experiences from this activity and discuss the role of non-verbal listening skills in communications.

> ". . . and be silent that you may hear."
> Shakespeare in *Julius Caesar*

ACTIVITY 68

MINIMAL ENCOURAGERS

1. Discuss examples of minimal encouragers such as "mm, hm", "ah," etc.

2. Repeat Activity #67 using a theme such as a favorite sport, book, or even using articles from a newspaper with students this time using minimal encouragers as well as non-verbal cues.

3. After each student has had an opportunity to be both a speaker and a listener, discuss the use of minimal encouragers in listening to others.

ACTIVITY 69

NON-VERBAL MESSAGE OPPOSITES

1. Discuss how the message that a person gives non-verbally may be different than what a person is actually saying. For example, someone might say that everything is okay, but meanwhile they may be "wringing" their hands and trembling in some manner.

2. In small groups, students prepare a short skit that illustrates a conversation where one person in the group is saying something that is opposite to what his/her non-verbal behavior is illustrating.

3. Discuss each of the skits in order that your students better understand how we sometimes convey a different message non-verbally than what we are actually saying.

ACTIVITY 70

BLIND WRITING

1. Give your students a short poem. In pairs, one student closes his eyes while the other student recites the poem line by line with the "blind" student writing the poem. The student who is reciting the poem can give the student verbal directions related to improving and correcting the writing.

2. After a specific period of time, students reverse roles.

3. Discuss the role that vision plays in communicating and in completing tasks.

ACTIVITY 71

SILENT STORIES

1. Students will require a picture from a magazine. Explain that they will be drawing the pictures so it is important to select one that is not too complex. Students form pairs. In each pair, one student attempts to describe her picture (without actually showing the picture to the other student) using only non-verbal cues and sign language of her own making while the other student then draws what she perceives the picture to be.

2. After a specific period of time, students reverse roles.

3. Discuss how body language can be used to communicate specific ideas.

> "I have walked with people whose eyes are full of light but who see nothing in sea or sky, nothing in city streets nothing in books. It were far better to sail forever in the night of blindness with sense and feeling, and mind, than to be content with the mere act of seeing. The only lightless dark is the night of darkness in ignorance and insensibility."
> Helen Keller

ACTIVITY 72

SILENT DISCUSSIONS

1. Teach your students some basics of "signing" (they could even do this as a research project). If there is a teacher in your school who is trained in this area, this teacher could give your students some further instruction.

2. In small groups, students attempt to engage in a discussion (topic chosen beforehand by the teacher) using signing.

3. Each group repeats some aspect of their discussion with the other students discussing their interpretation.

4. This may also be an excellent opportunity to discuss some possible non-verbal signals that could be used in the classroom (see Activity #21).

ACTIVITY 73

A QUIET LISTENING ASSIGNMENT

1. Students watch a video that shows people interacting in some way with each other.

2. Students answer the following questions:

   a) Identify specific examples of people communicating non-verbally.

   b) Give some examples of people communicating a non-verbal message that is different than their verbal message.

3. Discuss the results.

ACTIVITY 74

CULTURAL NON-VERBAL DIFFERENCES

1. If you have students in your class from other cultures, it would be useful to have them share how some of the non-verbal forms of communication that you have been looking at so far in this chapter may be interpreted differently in their culture.

2. Another option for completing this assignment would be for students to research differences in cultural interpretations of non-verbal behavior and present their findings. Discuss the implications of the results from both #1 and 2.

ACTIVITY 75

MY TEACHER'S NON-VERBAL COMMUNICATION SKILLS

1. Each student is given a copy of page 160 or 161. After your students complete this activity, collect their results. The purpose of this assignment is to give you direct feedback from your students on your use of non-verbal communication skills. You can decide whether you want to discuss the results with your class or simply use them for your own awareness and growth.

ACTIVITY 76

THREE IMPORTANT LISTENING SKILLS

Three listening skills that can contribute to developing empathetic listening are "paraphrasing, clarification, and open ended questions". The following provides a definition of each of these skills.

PARAPHRASING: This is one of the best techniques to ensure that you understand what another person is saying to you. Paraphrasing is basically repeating back to a person the essence of what she has said. For example, a student might say "I really enjoy my math. class, but I have a lot of trouble with my homework. It seems like as soon as I get home I forget how to do the questions. This is so frustrating for me." In response, using a paraphrase, the teacher might say, "You feel frustrated because you think you understand your math., but as soon as you get home you seem to forget what we did in class." In this particular instance, the teacher has paraphrased both the content and the accompanying feeling. There may be times in which you only paraphrase the content and there may be other times when it is more important to reflect the emotions. In either case, you are helping the student to feel understood because you have reflected the intent of his words and/or emotions back to him. Also keep in mind, that your non-verbal cues are also important as you paraphrase. If you paraphrase something a student has said to you, but don't even look at the student, your message may be interpreted that you don't care. Similarly, if you paraphrase that the student is feeling sad but you do so with a smile on your face, your non-verbal message may be perceived as being different than your verbal message. In paraphrasing, it is important to be genuine and demonstrate this genuineness through your non-verbal communication skills as well as your verbal message.

After you paraphrase something a student has said to you, the student will often then reply with words such as "right" or "that's not entirely correct", or perhaps smile or frown. The student's feedback after you paraphrase then tells you whether you have correctly interpreted what she said, or not. If your paraphrase is not accurate then you can move on to a second important listening skill which is "clarification".

Paraphrasing, although it may seem simple, is a wonderful way to demonstrate understanding (empathy) which helps a student to feel accepted and more likely to engage in a further discussion with you which could eventually lead to some form of problem solving.

CLARIFICATION: Sometimes when a student is telling you something, it may be useful to clarify what she is saying to ensure that you really understand what she is trying to tell you. There are even times when you paraphrase the intent of what a student is saying, only to have her reply back to you that you are not really understanding her. In such situations, it is necessary to clarify her message to you. Without clarification, you may make incorrect assumptions and jump to solutions without having identified the problem. It is quite alright to say to a student that you are not quite sure what she is saying to you. This shows the student that you are really trying to understand, and most students will respond in a positive manner to your request. In addition, it is often useful to ask the student for specific examples to illustrate what she is saying. For example, a student might tell you that she is being bullied. An important aspect of clarifying this message is to ask for specific examples of what she means by bullying, when it has occurred and who is doing it. This is an example of clarifying something that a student has said to you to increase your understanding.

There may also be times during a conversation when you summarize what a student has been telling you. Summarizing is similar to paraphrasing except that it is often longer and may also include references to any responses you received related to questions of clarification. After summarizing, it is then appropriate to ask the student if this is what she is trying to say to you. If she says no, ask her to tell you which parts of your summary are correct and which parts require further understanding.

OPEN-ENDED QUESTIONS: An open-ended question is really a statement that turns into a question. Open-ended sentences can be very effective in encouraging students to talk more openly. They are also an excellent form of communication to use to encourage discussion with your students. Open-ended sentences often begin with phrases such as "Tell me more about . . .", or "Give me some examples concerning . . .", or "Describe . . .", or "Explain . . ." In each case these phrases encourage the student to talk more openly.

The opposite of an open-ended question would be a closed question. Some examples of closed questions might be "Is your homework done?", or "How old are you?", or "Did you bring your field trip form?" Closed questions generally elicit a short, often one word, answer. While closed questions serve a purpose, closed questions can stifle a discussion if used too frequently. In a one-to-one conversation with a student closed questions can block the student from talking freely.

In a sense, minimal encourages such as "mm, hm" could also be considered open-ended questions as could a smile or the nod of your head.

SUMMARY: A person with effective listening skills often uses a paraphrase to ensure that what is being said is understood and then follows this up with an open-ended question to encourage the person to continue to talk openly. At various times during the conversation, the listener will also use some form of clarification and summarizing to ensure that the message is being understood.

Before continuing with the next few activities that relate to paraphrasing, clarification, and open-ended questions, it would be useful to share these terms with your students so they have a basic understanding of them.

MY TEACHER'S NON-VERBAL COMMUNICATION SKILLS

1. I have noticed that when I am talking to my teacher, something that he does non-verbally to make me feel like he is really listening to me is . . .

2. I have noticed that when students misbehave, some non-verbal communication skills that my teacher uses to discourage students from misbehaving are . . .

3. I think a really good non-verbal communication skill that my teacher uses is . . .

4. I think my teacher's non-verbal communication skills would be even more effective if he . . .

MY TEACHER'S NON-VERBAL COMMUNICATION SKILLS

1. I have noticed that when I am talking to my teacher, something that she does non-verbally to make me feel like she is really listening to me is . . .

2. I have noticed that when students misbehave, some non-verbal communication skills that my teacher uses to discourage students from misbehaving are . . .

3. I think a really good non-verbal communication skill that my teacher uses is . . .

4. I think my teacher's non-verbal communication skills would be even more effective if she . . .

ACTIVITY 77

PARAPHRASING IN THE ROUND

1. Any student starts this activity by stating 3 - 5 sentences that describe a personal interest or hobby.

2. A second student paraphrases what the first student said. Next, a third student paraphrases what the second student said. Continue for four or five students with the focus on maintaining the essential meaning of the original comments from the first student.

3. Repeat the process with another student talking about a hobby or interest.

ACTIVITY 78

PARAPHRASING PRACTICE

Each student is given a copy of page 163. Students complete the assignment. Share the results.

> "To listen well, is as powerful means
> of influence as to talk well,
> and is as essential to all true conversation."
> Chinese Proverb

ACTIVITY 79

THE IMPORTANCE OF PARAPHRASING

Paraphrasing can help your students to better understand what is being said to them, whether they are listening to a teacher or another student. After you have introduced the concept of paraphrasing and students understand what it is, the following provide some practical ways for your students to learn how to paraphrase effectively.

1. A paragraph is read from a book (preferably from a current unit of study in your class). Students take turns orally paraphrasing what you have said. After a few students have provided a paraphrase, read another paragraph and repeat the process. Generally a paraphrase should have less words than you initially spoke and it is okay in paraphrasing to repeat a few key words from the original paragraph.

2. During a 2 - 3 minute period of any lesson being taught, the students paraphrase (in writing) what you have been teaching. This activity can be repeated often to teach your students how to paraphrase. Similarly, as students provide answers to your questions, you can paraphrase what they say to model skills in paraphrasing.

3. As students watch a video in the classroom, pause the video after a person has spoken and have your students paraphrase what was said.

4. As an assignment, your students could paraphrase the daily announcements in your school or even a segment from a news broadcast.

5. Students, grouped in pairs, share a memory of a birthday or an event that was a happy time for them. One student shares the memory while the other student paraphrases what is being said. After a specific period of time, reverse roles.

INSTRUCTIONS: On a separate piece of paper, write a paraphrase for each of the following paragraphs:

1. He was very difficult to work with - always complaining and never working very hard. Sometimes I just wanted to tell him to quit so the rest of us could get on with our group project.

2. She helped me so much. When I didn't understand what I was supposed to do, she explained things carefully to me. She even took the time to help me with my math. homework. Without her help I would have been lost.

3. He was strict, but also fair. I learned to listen carefully to what he said had to be done because he didn't like to repeat instructions. When I did my homework though, he praised me and made me feel great about what I had accomplished.

4. She was great in sports. It seemed like no matter what sport she was involved in, she was the best player on the team and she was also a great leader as she always encouraged others to do better.

5. Sometimes I don't understand what I have to do for homework. It is really frustrating to get home and open my books and then forget what I am supposed to do, or sometimes I forget how I am expected to do it.

6. I like teachers who are caring. I also like teachers who help me to learn. When a teacher takes the time to carefully explain whatever we are currently doing, this is a great help to me.

7. My best friend would do anything for me. It's nice to know that somebody like my best friend really believes in me. I enjoy being with my best friend and it's nice to just be accepted for who I really am.

8. There are times when, no matter how hard I work, I just can't get everything done on time. Sometimes I feel overwhelmed with everything that I have to do. At times like this, I find it helpful to take a break and go for a walk, or listen to a few of my favorite songs before I start to work again.

ACTIVITY 80

PARAPHRASING FEELINGS

1. Your students develop a list of feelings such as anger, frustration, job, sorrow, etc.

2. Students are once again given a copy of page 163. This time, tell your students to use just one sentence that would describe or paraphrase the emotion that the person might be feeling in each situation. Share the results.

3. Tell your students to identify, and then discuss, situations where it might be more appropriate to paraphrase the feelings that a person is expressing before paraphrasing the actual content.

> "Saying nothing . . .
> sometimes says the most."
> Emily Dickinson

ACTIVITY 81

A TIME I WAS MISUNDERSTOOD

Each student is given a copy of page 165. Students complete the page and results are shared. Keep a list of the answers that students provide for the last question related to things that a student could do whenever they misunderstand something that is said to them.

A TIME I WAS MISUNDERSTOOD

Here is the description of a time when I was misunderstood by someone else . . .

In this situation, some of the emotions I felt were . . .

I think that most people when they are misunderstood feel . . .

Whenever I misunderstand what someone else says to me, I could . . .

ACTIVITY 82

CLARIFICATION PRACTICE

Each student is given a copy of page 168. While the intent of this activity is to help students become more comfortable asking questions when they are confused or don't understand something that is being taught in class, the reality is that this activity can enhance student success as your students learn to ask for help and clarification.

This activity can be used over the course of a day or week. Every time a student asks a question to clarify her understanding of something that has been said in class, she places a check mark in the appropriate column and writes the question that she asked. At the end of a specific period of time, you will be able to see which students are comfortable asking for clarification on a regular basis.

ACTIVITY 83

ENCOURAGING LIVELY DISCUSSIONS

An effective way to encourage lively discussions is through the use of open-ended questions (and also paraphrasing). Open-ended questions encourage a response that is longer than just a word or two. Examples of open-ended questions are:

>Tell me about . . .
>Describe . . .
>In what ways . . .
>Explain . . .

Each of these responses with encouraging body language can

result in your students responding in a more open manner. During a lesson where you would like to inspire a vibrant discussion try using some of these open-ended questions. As students respond, it would also be useful to paraphrase what they say which helps them to feel understood which also encourages further discussion.

    One of the real keys to a vibrant discussion is to talk less than your students. This may be hard for you to do because you may be accustomed to doing most of the talking. Through the effective use of silence, open-ended questions, paraphrasing and clarification, you can initiate and maintain fabulous discussions, and another real benefit for your students is that you will constantly be modeling these effective interpersonal skills.

"Most men talk too much.
Much of my success has been due
to keeping my mouth shut."
J. Ogden Armour

CLARIFYING WHAT IS BEING SAID

INSTRUCTIONS: Every time you ask a question of clarification in class, put a check mark in Column 1, the time and date in Column 2, and the actual question in Column 3.

1.	2.	3.

ACTIVITY 84

OPEN-ENDED QUESTIONS

Give your students some examples of open-ended questions (could come from Activity 83). It would also be useful to give some examples of closed questions. Discuss the benefits and application of each type of question as well as the drawbacks. The following provide some thoughts on helping your students to better understand the use of open-ended questions.

1 In small groups, students identify and list ten examples of open-ended questions. The results are shared and a master list is kept.

2. Using the chart on page 170, students record open-ended questions that were used in class. This activity would work well during a discussion on some aspect of what you are currently teaching. Share the results.

3. You could also use the chart on page 170 for a homework assignment where students note open-ended sentences that were used in a conversation on a television show or movie.

> "We have two ears and one mouth
> so that we can listen
> twice as much as we speak."
> Epictetus

EXAMPLES OF OPEN-ENDED QUESTIONS

INSTRUCTIONS: Every time someone uses an open-ended question, put a check mark in Column 1, the time and date in Column 2, and the actual wording of the question in Column 3.

1.	2.	3.

ACTIVITY 85

LISTENING SKILLS SUMMARY

Each student is given a copy of page 172. After the page is completed, share and discuss the results.

> "If there is any one secret of success,
> it lies in the ability to get the other person's
> point of view and see things
> from his angle as well as your own."
> Henry Ford

ACTIVITY 86

LISTENING SKILLS REVIEW

Each student is given a copy of page 173. This page can be completed based on your students observing conversations within your class, within the school, or even from watching a television program. After the page is completed, discuss the results. It would also be useful to consider having your students use this page to evaluate you.

> "When you start to develop your powers
> of empathy and imagination,
> the whole world opens up to you."
> Susan Sarandon

EMPATHETIC LISTENING SKILLS SUMMARY

INSTRUCTIONS: Explain each of the following terms and then give an example from a conversation to illustrate what the term means as well as the benefit of using this listening skill.

a) Non-verbal Listening

    i) Definition -

    ii) Example -

    iii) Benefit -

b) Paraphrasing

    i) Definition -

    ii) Example -

    iii) Benefit -

c) Clarification

    i) Definition -

    ii) Example -

    iii) Benefit -

d) Open-ended Questions

    i) Definition -

    ii) Example -

    iii) Benefit -

LISTENING SKILLS REVIEW

INSTRUCTIONS: During the course of a day, place a check mark in the column immediately beside each of the listening skills listed on the chart below. In addition, write some specific examples of what was said to actually illustrate each of the listening skills.

LISTENING SKILLS	CHECK MARKS	SPECIFIC EXAMPLES TO ILLUSTRATE EACH LISTENING SKILL
NON-VERBAL LISTENING		
PARAPHRASING		
CLARIFICATION		
OPEN-ENDED QUESTIONS		

> "The way we communicate
> with others and with ourselves
> ultimately determines
> the quality of our lives."
> Anthony Robbins

CHAPTER 6

CONSTRUCTIVE ASSERTIVENESS

When someone criticizes you, how do you respond? If a student "talks back" to you when you are attempting to discipline her, what do you do? When you give your class instructions for completing an assignment, do you have to repeat yourself several times? Are there any students in your class who are easily influenced by their peers? Each of these examples relates to the way you communicate with others or the way your students communicate with each other. A person who is assertive would tend to handle each of these situations in a positive manner because assertive people look out for their own wants, needs and rights as well as considering the same for others.

This chapter focuses on how others understand you in contrast to the last chapter that focused on how you understood others. The manner in which others interpret your communication to them is interpreted by your communication style (which also includes your non-verbal behavior as discussed in the last chapter). Effective teachers will sometimes need to be firm in addition to being kind. To teach effectively, it is important that students follow your directions without the need to continually repeat yourself. This chapter can help you to become more assertive. In addition, we live at a time when there is great talk in our schools about bullying. The reality is that assertive people are less likely to be bullied, so introducing some form of assertive training in your class can be a useful supplement to your efforts to reduce bullying among students.

> "Students and teachers who are assertive are not just more capable, they are also more appealing and lovable."
> George M. Gazda, et al, in *Human Relations Development,* 2005

Not only can assertive training help your students to better resist bullying, but such training can also help your bullies to learn more appropriate behavior in their relationship with others.

> "Rejected children often show aggressive behaviors towards their peers. It is recommended that teachers help such students by teaching them social and assertive skills."
> Kim (2003)

Assertiveness training can help your students to build more positive relationships with others, including both adults and their peers. Improvements in empathetic listening (from the last chapter) as well as improvements in being constructively assertive can be a significant contribution to increasing positive interactions in your classroom, and as a result contribute greatly to learning. When students learn to be more assertive, they are less likely to be disruptive as they learn appropriate ways to express themselves.

The term "constructive" assertiveness is used in this chapter because it implies that your assertiveness can help your students to grow in a positive manner. As assertiveness can sometimes be misinterpreted as being aggressive (which is generally considered to be of a more negative nature), the adjective constructive is provided here as a reminder to use your assertiveness to help your students to learn rather than creating a sense of fear that may impede learning in your classroom.

Communication styles tend to fall into one of three categories: passive, assertive, or aggressive. Any of these styles could be demonstrated by our non-verbal behavior (such as our eye contact, body position or the tone of our voice), as well as our determination and level of confidence in presenting our thoughts. The following provides a general definition of each of these styles.

PASSIVE
A person with a passive communication style tends to refrain from stating her beliefs or feelings. Such a person tends to quietly react to any form of confrontation and often feels very uncomfortable in the presence of people who have an

aggressive style of communication. People with a passive style of communication are often indecisive and in group situations tend to resist making any kind of decision or stating their views. A passive communicator may also have a fear of hurting the feelings of another person and as such may constantly try to please others by being sensitive to their wants, needs and rights. Although a person with a passive communication style may be perceived by some to be extremely kind, polite, caring and thoughtful, the reality is that this person has difficulty saying "no" which can lead to the person being overworked and being "taken advantage of" by others. Such a person tends to run away from problems which in the case of teaching often leads to ignoring student misbehavior until it gets out of hand instead of confronting it when it first starts. This style of communication is also often expressed non-verbally with poor eye contact, nervousness, and a soft, sometimes whiny tone of voice. A passive person may feel that she is not in control of her own happiness and destiny and as such will often let others make her decisions for her, vacillate in making a decision, or even blame others for her failures.

ASSERTIVE

An assertive person is aware of her own wants, needs and rights and is willing to stand up for these at the same time as respecting the wants, needs and rights of others. Assertive communicators tend to be straightforward and honest in their relationships with others. Their communication with others could be considered to be more socially acceptable than either passive or aggressive communicators. An assertive person tends to accept and respect others while expecting the same in return. An assertive person tends to confront problems in a calm, in-control, and constructive manner and looks for fair resolutions in conflict situations. Like a passive communicator, an assertive person can also be caring and polite, but an assertive person, unlike the passive person, can be firm and persistent in achieving her goals. An assertive person tends to be confident and decisive in making decisions. An assertive person generally feels in control of her own happiness and destiny and acts accordingly taking responsibility for what is happening in her life. This style of communication is often accompanied by direct eye contact, a confident body posture, and an even, although sometimes expressive, tone of voice. An assertive teacher has clear rules and procedures in her classroom with fair expectations for student behavior and a consistent approach to constructively dealing with inappropriate student behavior.

AGGRESSIVE

While some people may have trouble distinguishing between assertive and aggressive communications styles, one of the key differences is that an aggressive person does not consider the wants, rights and needs of others. In other words, in the context of this book, a person with an aggressive style fails to understand another person's point of view (or develop empathy as discussed in the last chapter). In addition, a person with an aggressive style of communication may attempt to force her values and her beliefs on others in an abusive, deceitful, manipulative and controlling manner. In a conflict situation the aggressive person attempts to win at all costs. There is often no room for compromise or discussion when an aggressive person faces problems or conflicts. An aggressive person tends to attack the person instead of the problem, often bullying the person into accepting her point of view or rules. An aggressive person is often viewed as being pushy and even at times out of control. Her approach, when she doesn't get her way, is to often create an environment of fear. While an aggressive person may appear to be successful, it is often her own insecurities that fuel her inappropriate behavior. Victories, at the expense of others, are necessary to cater to a weak self-esteem. Non-verbally, a person with an aggressive style of communications can have a stare that is filled with venom, body posture that may suggest physical attack, and a tone of voice that is often extremely loud. In the classroom, most students fear teachers with an aggressive style of communications. As a result, students rarely take risks knowing that failure is unacceptable. Learning suffers as students are uncomfortable asking questions or expressing their creativity or independence.

While most people would tend to have their communication style best described as being either passive, assertive, or aggressive, some people have a combination of styles and some teachers, in particular, may have developed a style in the classroom that is different than their normal communication style out of school. This may sometimes occur because some teachers believe that the only way to get students to behave is to employ an aggressive communication style. Hopefully, the content of this book will successfully dispel such an unfounded and often harmful notion.

> "Most students who do not want to come to school
> or who dislike school do so primarily
> because they dislike their teacher."
> Cornelius-White (2007)

> "Students should feel safe and learn to understand others.
> Teachers should demonstrate that they care
> for each student and empathize with them."
> Cornelius-White (2007)

Having an assertive communications style can help you to be more confident and positive in your relationship with others. Being assertive can also help you to be more influential with others.

Consider the benefits for your students in learning how to be more assertive. People skills can have a huge impact on both current and future success. People skills are identified by employers as being one of the major factors they consider in hiring. Recently I spoke with the president of a company who was hiring for a new branch of his business that was opening. I asked him what he looked for as he read through the hundreds of applications he had received for about eighty job positions. His response was immediate as he replied that first and foremost he wanted employees who got along with each other. Although I will reflect on this more in the next chapter, the reality is that assertive people, being more confident and positive, are in demand in the workplace and also tend to have healthier personal relationships. Helping your students to be more assertive gives them a very important lifelong skill that can contribute to success in so many areas.

Being assertive can help your students to respect each other and themselves. I have heard some teachers say that they wish that their students had more respect. Providing assertiveness training along with empathetic listening skills is one area of improvement that can directly contribute to developing this respect.

> "The basic difference between being assertive and aggressive is how our words and behavior affect the rights and well being of others."
> Sharon Anthony Bower

There are also health benefits related to being assertive. Being more assertive can also help you to reduce stress as you don't bury your feelings (as a passive person often does) and you don't find yourself prone to anger (as an aggressive person often is). An assertive person tends to resolve conflict in a win-win manner which can lessen the anxiety for all involved. Passive people tend to carry unresolved conflict around with them, often leading to various forms of illness. Passive people, who often see themselves as victims, may find themselves bubbling with anger that can remain buried within until it surfaces in some form of illness. Aggressive people tend to steamroll over others in conflict situations which can lead to strained relationships with others that can result in feelings of insolation and even increased anger for the aggressive person. Blaming others (which both passive and aggressive people tend to do) often results in greater stress for the person who is doing the blaming.

In the end, although there is much to be said about being yourself, if your communication style is best defined as being either passive or aggressive, this could definitely be getting in the way of creating a comfortable and well-managed classroom environment for your students. While this chapter is relatively short, it can provide some thoughts and tips on helping you to move more into an assertive style of communications. The activities can also help your students to learn to be more assertive which can also help them create more positive relationships with others. As you work through this chapter, if you find yourself concerned with your style of communication, it might be useful to find a mentor or even a counselor who could help you to learn a more assertive style of communication. The manner in which you communicate not only affects your effectiveness as a teacher, but it also has a direct impact on the quality of your relationships with colleagues and in your personal life as well.

> "We are injured and hurt emotionally,
> not so much by other people
> or what they say and don't say,
> but by our own attitude and our own response."
> Maxwell Maltz

Remember that the way you respond to others is often first practiced in your mind, so consciously visualize being more assertive until this manifests in your actual behavior. One of the most powerful words to master is "no". Unfortunately, many classroom discipline problems result from the lack of a teacher's assertiveness in saying "no", and similarly there are many personal relationships that suffer because one person in the relationship said "yes" when they really wanted to say "no". And yes, for some people the more difficult word to say might be "yes" because this might mean letting go of something they don't want to give up or it might mean making a commitment.

Unfortunately, being assertive does not come easily for some people. Some people have grown up with role models who were either passive or aggressive (or a combination of each of these communication styles which can be even a more confusing role model). To help your students become the change you would like to see, it is possible that you will first have to become this change. The most effective lessons related to the learning of appropriate interpersonal skills, as has been pointed out before in this book, will occur when you consistently demonstrate the appropriate use of these skills.

If you want to learn to be more assertive, consider some of the following tips:

- maintain eye contact with others when you talk although you also need to be aware that some students, either due to cultural differences or low self-esteem may have difficulty maintaining eye contact. In such situations it is generally beneficial for you to reduce your eye contact.

- speak with a calm, but confident, voice. Be careful that your voice doesn't fade away at the end of your sentences.

- avoid qualifying or disclaiming your thoughts by adding words such as "but" (I would like to do it, but . . .).

- when you are interrupted in the middle of a conversation, politely, yet firmly, finish what you have to say.

- don't turn your statements into questions (such as to your class "Will you please be quiet?").

- be firm when you say "no". There is no need to apologize for saying no although you can provide an explanation.

- be careful that you aren't non-verbally agreeing with everything that is being said to you especially if you disagree with what is being said (for example, constantly nodding).

- don't say yes when you really mean no.

- Focus on the problem, not the person, by using "I" statements such as "I feel . . . when you . . ."

- Acknowledge the other person's wants, needs or rights, but also ensure that the other person is aware of your wants, needs and rights.

- use the empathetic listening skills from Chapter 5
to ensure that you understand the other person.

- if you have difficult saying "no", begin by practicing
with strangers in non-threatening situations
(such as someone selling a product, you don't want, over the telephone).

- identify someone you consider to be constructively assertive
and model his/her behavior.

- If you know you are going into
a situation where you want to be more assertive,
practice your possible responses beforehand.

- set small achievable goals for yourself
and reward yourself when you are successful in being more assertive.

In this chapter, Activities #87 + 88 can help your students to identify their communications style. The key here is not labeling your students but helping them to better understand the factors that contribute to being more assertive and how this can contribute to being more successful in their relationship with others. As one aspect of communicating effectively relates to "fitting in" or getting along better with others, Activities #89 + 90 provides some further thoughts in this area. Finally, Activities # 91 - 96 can help to provide some tips on how to be more assertive.

ACTIVITY 87

COMMUNICATION STYLES SURVEY

Each student is given a copy of pages 184 - 186. It is recommended that students write their answers on page 186 and that you collect the answer sheets for your own information. Activity #88 provides a recommended approach to follow up the use of this survey.

From your student's standpoint, the purpose of this activity is to help them be more aware of the three communication styles: passive, assertive, and aggressive. As the goal of this chapter is to help your students improve their skills in being more assertive, there is no need to provide the results of this survey back to your students. It is recommended that you consider the results for your information giving you some further supporting evidence of what you already likely know about each of their communication styles. As you complete Activity #88, your students will be more aware of their results but in a manner that is hopefully more informative than labeling.

Activity #95 can also be useful in looking at the learning that can occur related to helping your students to develop assertive skills.

ANSWER KEY FOR PAGES 184 + 185

PASSIVE
  1 - c, 2 - a, 3 - c, 4 - b, 5 - c, 6 - a, 7 - a, 8 - b, 9 - a, 10 - c, 11 - a, 12 - b, 13 - a, 14 - c, 15 - c

ASSERTIVE
  1 - b, 2 - b, 3 - b, 4 - a, 5 - a, 6 - b, 7 - c, 8 - a, 9 - b, 10 - b, 11 - b, 12 - c, 13 - c, 14 - a, 15 - b

AGGRESSIVE
  1 - a, 2 - c, 3 - a, 4 - c, 5 - b, 6 - c, 7 - b, 8 - c, 9 - c, 10 - a, 11 - c, 12 - a, 13 - b, 14 - b, 15 - a

COMMUNICATION STYLES QUIZ

INSTRUCTIONS: Read each of the following statements and choose the answer that best describes how you would generally respond in each situation.

1. One of your friends has blamed you for a problem that wasn't your fault. You would likely
   a) get angry at your friend
   b) explain to them that you didn't cause the problem
   c) accept the blame so that you don't create further conflict

2. In most situations whenever teachers criticize you, you tend to
   a) keep quiet and stay out of their way
   b) talk to them further about what they have said
   c) argue with them and strongly state your point of view

3. If some of your friends told you what they think you should be wearing each day to school, you would likely
   a) get angry at them and tell them to leave you alone
   b) tell them that you are capable of deciding what you want to wear
   c) please them by wearing the clothes they suggested

4. You have just found out that someone you know has been gossiping about you behind your back. You would tend to
   a) talk to this person about what you have been hearing
   b) do nothing
   c) strongly tell this person what you think of him/her

5. Whenever you are speaking in a group situation, others would likely say
   a) they respect what you say
   b) you tend to dominate the conversation
   c) you need to speak louder

6. Another person is expressing his/her anger at you. You would tend to
   a) look away from him/her and try to ignore what he/she is saying
   b) maintain good eye contact, listen to what he/she has to say, and express what you are feeling when it is appropriate
   c) raise your voice and argue with him/her

7. If someone else received recognition from a teacher for work that you did
   a) you would likely keep your mouth shut
   b) get angry at the person who got the recognition
   c) tell the teacher the truth about who did the work

8. In an argument, you tend to
   a) present your viewpoint calmly and logically
   b) feel very stressed
   c) lose control of what you are saying

9. If someone asked you to help him/her with his/her work, you would
   a) help him/her even if it was inconvenient for you
   b) help him/her if and when it was appropriate to your schedule
   c) tell him/her to go bother someone else

10. If you were told by a teacher that you needed to do better work, you would
    a) be a difficult person to get along with the rest of the day
    b) attempt to discuss exactly what your teacher was referring to
    c) accept what was said even if your teacher was wrong, and try harder

11. A friend tells you that you have hurt his/her feelings. You would
    a) immediately apologize
    b) attempt to resolve the situation by talking about it
    c) tell your friend that he/she needs to toughen up a little

12. You have been given what you consider is an unfair mark on an assignment. You would
    a) strongly argue with the teacher
    b) not talk to the teacher even though you are angry about the mark
    c) politely discuss your thoughts with the teacher

13. You give a friend $20 to buy lunch for you. The lunch costs less than $10 but the person does not give you any change when he/she returns. You would
    a) not likely ask for it
    b) accuse your friend of trying to take your money
    c) ask the other person for the change

14. If a friend asked you to do something that you really don't feel comfortable doing,
    a) you would say no to his/her request
    b) you would tell this person you didn't want to be his/her friend anymore
    c) you would likely say "yes" even though you know you should say "no"

15. Another student accuses you of something you didn't even do. You would
    a) argue with this other student
    b) calmly explain the facts of what really happened
    c) say nothing

Your Name . . . .

COMMUNICATIONS SKILLS

ANSWER SHEET

INSTRUCTIONS: Write the letter that corresponds to your answer for each question.

1 -   9 -

2 -   10 -

3 -   11 -

4 -   12 -

5 -   13 -

6 -   14 -

7 -   15 -

8 -

ACTIVITY 88

THREE STYLES OF COMMUNICATION

1. Using the information on pages 176 - 178, provide a definition for each of passive, assertive and aggressive styles of communication.

2. Using pages 184 + 185 as a guide (and after your students have completed the survey), divide your class into small groups, with each group attempting to categorize each of the statements on these pages as being either passive, assertive or aggressive.

3. Share the results from #2.

4. Discuss student perceptions on which of these styles of communication would contribute the most to being successful. It may be useful to use quotes or other information from this chapter or even the next chapter to support the thought that being assertive is a preferred communication style that leads to success.

> "Perhaps you will forget tomorrow
> the kinds words you say today,
> but the recipient may cherish them
> over a lifetime."
> Dale Carnegie

> **ACTIVITY 89**

THE IMPACT OF YOUR COMMUNICATION STYLE ON OTHERS

Once your students have a better understanding of the three communication styles, tell your students to complete page 189 in small groups. Share the results.

"Say what you mean, and mean what you say, but don't say it mean!"
Lisa Johnson

"Words are, of course,
the most powerful drug used by mankind."
Rudyard Kipling

THE IMPACT OF YOUR COMMUNICATION STYLE ON OTHERS

	PASSIVE	ASSERTIVE	AGGRESSIVE
How do other people generally respond to this style of communication?			
What do other people generally think of people who use this style of communication?			
What are the potential consequences of a conversation where both people use this style of communication?			

ACTIVITY 90

TIPS ON FITTING IN

1. It would be useful to begin this activity by sharing some story related to success at school that focuses on the importance of getting along with others. People who get along with others tend to be assertive communicators rather than passive or aggressive so this activity can provide some practical thoughts on helping your students to become more assertive.

2. In small groups, your students are instructed to develop a list of "do's" and "don'ts" that could help people to be more effective in fitting in. Share the results. Keep a master list of the suggestions.

3. Each group is given a copy of page 191 to compare to the suggestions they have given. Each group uses their suggestions, the suggestions of others, and the recommendations from page 191 to identify a list of the "top 10 factors" to contribute to fitting or getting along with others. Share the results from #4.

4. You might even have a class debate on the pros and cons of "fitting in".

> "Never be bullied into silence.
> Never allow yourself to made a victim.
> Accept no-one's definition of your life; define yourself."
> Harvey Fierstein

TIPS ON FITTING IN

1. Always find something good to say about others if you have to say anything at all.

2. Do what you say you are going to do. Honesty brings respect.

3. Show concern for the feelings of others.

4. Listen to others as they share their interests and ideas.

5. Be a positive person. Leave your aches, pains and problems at home.

6. Be an optimistic person. Look for the best in any situation instead of the worst.

7. Keep an open mind. Learn to accept the differences of other people.

8. When you are presenting your point of view, remain calm and deal with the facts.

9. Be quick to forgive.

10. Take pride in your work.

ACTIVITY 91

TIPS ON BEING MORE ASSERTIVE

In small groups, students look at the tips on being more assertive from page 193. Students should identify the tips they think could work and then add additional tips that are suggested in their groups. Results are shared. It might be beneficial to post a "top 10" list in your room.

ACTIVITY 92

SAYING "NO" ROLE-PLAYING

1. An effective way to help your students learn to be more assertive is to have them role play various situations they may encounter where peer pressure makes it difficult to say no. Discuss some possible situations that your students feel relate to peer pressure.

2. In small groups, students prepare a skit related the situations identified in #1. Each group presents their skit followed by a discussion on the value of learning to say no.

> "Half the troubles of this life can be traced to saying yes too quickly and not saying no soon enough."
> Josh Billings

TIPS ON BEING MORE ASSERTIVE

1. Learn to make decisions based on your needs and feelings.

2. Learn to say "no" and don't feel guilty about it.
When you say no, you are rejecting the request,
not the person.

3. Don't apologize if you have done nothing wrong.
Do not neglect your own needs
in order to make other people happy.

4. Where possible, plan your responses in anticipation
of difficult situations that you might find yourself in.

5. Make your feelings and needs known to others.
Don't expect them to read your mind. Express yourself
honestly and clearly, maintaining good eye contact.

6. Avoid starting sentences with the word "you"
because this is often interpreted as being aggressive
instead of being assertive.
Begin your sentences with the word "I" such as,
"I get angry when you arrive late because it wastes my time."

7. Minimize your contact with people who don't bring out the best in you.

8. Avoid exaggerations, either in your mind or in what you say.
Attempt to keep your thoughts and words based on fact.
Avoid using words like "always" or "never".

9. Look for solutions to problems where other people (or even yourself)
don't have to be losers. Attempt to find "winning together solutions".

10. Remember that the underlying theme in being more assertive
is to demonstrate respect for yourself and for others.

ACTIVITY 93

I FEEL... WHEN YOU... BECAUSE...

In potential conflict situations, beginning a response with the word "you" is often perceived as being aggressive. For example, "You make me angry," or "You are the reason I am having problems". A more appropriate and assertive manner to reply to others in such situations is to use a sentence such as "I feel angry when you don't listen to me because I have to repeat what I already said." Including the "because" in a response to another person is more effective that simply expressing your anger. This approach is also important when it is necessary to discipline your students. This helps to focus on the problem instead of he person. This kind of response has three parts as follows:

>I feel . . .
>when you . . .
>because . . .

1. As a class, identify potential conflict situations that often occur at school. Responses could include student/student conflicts as well as teacher/student conflicts. Keep a master list of the situations that your students identify.

2. Using file cards, write "I feel . . . when you (insert here one of the situations your students identified in #1) because . . . For example, a card might read "I feel . . . when you push me because . . .," or another card might read "I feel . . . when you gossip about me because . . ." Each of your students could also write a card.

3. Give the resulting stack of cards to one of your students. The student reads the card aloud and fills in the blanks (after "I feel . . ." and "because . . ."). This card is then placed on the bottom of the stack and the next student repeats the process with the next card. At any time, you can stop to discuss the appropriateness of a response.

ACTIVITY 94

ASSERTIVE BODY LANGUAGE

1. Discuss how body language (particularly posture, tone of voice and eye contact) all affect what is being communicated. Have various students demonstrate the typical body language that would portray each of the three communication styles (passive, assertive, and aggressive).

2. Using the cards developed in Activity #93, in groups of three, one student reads the card to another student (using an assertive style of communication) while the third student then provides feedback regarding the student's body language as he/she stated the message of the card to the other student. Repeat with students changing roles until everyone has had a turn being the assertive communicator.

3. Choose a few students who did particularly well to demonstrate their assertiveness to the class by reading one of the cards to another student.

> "Assertive eye contact is important in maintaining discipline in the classroom and in other leadership roles."
> Webbink (1986)

ACTIVITY 95

ASSERTIVENESS DETECTIVES

During the course of a day (doesn't have to be in your classroom), students watch for other students who are expressing themselves in an assertive manner. At the end of a day or week, students share their discoveries. It might even be useful to recognize your assertive students in some way - perhaps the "Assertive Student of The Day" or even "Week".

ACTIVITY 96

ASSERTIVE REVIEW

It is recommended that students repeat the Communication Styles Survey on pages 184 + 185. This time, students should be instructed to purposely choose the statements that are the best examples of being assertive (whether this would be their natural choice, or not). Discuss the actual answers and congratulate those students who score high because this is an indication that they have learned more about being assertive (even if they still need further practice in transferring the theory into practice).

QUOTES RELATED TO COMMUNICATING EFFECTIVELY

"The greatest problem in communication is the illusion that it has taken place."
George Bernard Shaw

"To effectively communicate, we must all realize that we are different
in the way we perceive the world, and use this understanding
as a guide to our communications with others."
Anthony Robbins

"Kind words can be short and easy to speak,
but their echoes are truly endless."
Mother Teresa

"Deep listening is miraculous for both the listener and speaker.
When someone receives us with open-hearted, non-judging,
intensely interested listening, our spirits expand."
Sue Patton Thoele

"The most important thing in communication
is to hear what isn't being said."
Peter F. Drucker

"One of the most valuable things we can do to heal one another
is to listen to each other's stories."
Rebecca Falls

"The first duty of love is to listen."
Paul Tillich

"Listening is a magnetic and strange thing, a creative force.
The friends who listen to us are the ones we move toward.
When we are listened to, it creates us, makes us unfold and expand.``
Chinese Proverb

"A good listener is a silent flatterer."
Proverb

"Man's inability to communicate is the result of his failure to listen."
Carl Rogers

"Remain calm, serene, always in command of yourself. You will then find out how easy it is to get along."
Paramahansa Yogananda

CHAPTER 7

HOW TO SUCCESSFULLY RESOLVE CONFLICTS

While the previous chapters in this book can help to prevent conflicts and even create a foundation for positively resolving them, the reality is that even in the most encouraging classrooms with the most effective teachers conflicts can still occur. To believe and think otherwise is to ignore human behavior and the fact that some students will enter our classrooms with inappropriate habits that have formed over many years. The purpose of this chapter is to provide a framework to integrate some of the skills both you and your students have learned in other chapters in order to resolve conflicts in what I term a "winning together" manner. Winning together implies that both you and your students will benefit from effective conflict resolution techniques and the resulting outcomes.

While conflicts in the classroom are often viewed as being a stressful intrusion, something that is both unpleasant and a distraction from learning, there is another way to look at conflicts. Helping your students to learn conflict resolution skills may be one of the greatest gifts you give them in contributing to both their current and future success. It has been said that life is a series of conflicts. Certainly, as we examine the lives of successful people, one of the clues that we will find is that their success is often directly related to their ability to problem solve and handle conflicts. Conflict in the workplace is often identified as a number one cause of stress, whether the conflict is between co-workers, workers and management, or even workers and customers. Similarly, conflict in a school or classroom can also be a great cause of stress, and left unresolved can poison a learning environment.

While a dictionary definition of conflict tends to focus on the opposition to ideas or a clash that leads to irreconcilability, for purposes of this book (and particularly this chapter), I will look at conflict as a disagreement between a teacher and a student(s) or a disagreement between two or more students that cannot be resolved immediately by the other tips and strategies that have been presented so far in this book. In some instances these conflicts may require a combination of several strategies and tips as previously outlined in this book. In other cases, the conflicts will require a more specific approach as provided in this chapter, and in some situations the conflict may need to be addressed by other more appropriate professional assistance beyond the scope of this book. In some schools there may be some teachers and/or other support staff members (such as administrators, social workers, child and youth counselors, etc.) who have formal training in the field of conflict resolution, restorative justice, peace keeping, mediation and/or negotiating. These staff members can provide invaluable support, mentorship and leadership in helping any teacher to be more knowledgeable and skillful in the area of conflict resolution.

In teaching conflict resolution to students, many schools take this a step further and train peer mediators. While it is not the intent of this chapter to provide a peer mediator program, some of the activities here could certainly be used in such a program. In addition, as you work through these activities with your students, you will likely become more aware of students in your class who could become successful peer mediators and whom you could recommend to participate in a program if it exists in your school. For information on such programs you might find it useful to look at The International Network for Conflict Resolution Education at http://www.creducation.org or the National Center for Dispute Resolution in Special Education at http://www.directionservice.org

Physical violence is an unfortunate reality in some of our schools and classrooms. While the previous chapters in this book can help to establish a learning environment that prevents some forms of violence, this current chapter (and Chapters 8 + 9) look closer at how to respond when conflicts (which could include violence) do occur. One of the goals of any program in conflict resolution is to help students gain some skills for resolving conflicts in a peaceful manner.

> "Conflict resolution programs achieve improved student attitudes towards conflict, increased understanding of nonviolent problem solving, and enhanced communication skills. They also yield positive changes in classroom climate, moderate or significant decreases in physical violence in the classroom, less name calling and few verbal insults, improved self-esteem among children receiving training, and greater acceptance of differences."
> Richard J. Bodine and Donna K. Crawford
> in *The Handbook of Conflict Resolution Education,* 1998

Conflict resolution focuses on identifying needs, wants and interests and helps to find solutions based on these in a manner that best satisfies everyone involved. Understanding a problem solving process is essential to conflict resolution. Sometimes conflict resolution may also be referred to, or be a part of programs in negotiating, restorative justice, mediation, social justice, collaborative problem solving, and even peace education. Whatever name it is given, it is the underlying problem solving process and the interpersonal communication skills (as outlined in Chapters 5 + 6) that are the keys to its success.

> "We can intervene successfully to prevent conflicts from escalating into violent acts by providing young people with the knowledge and skills needed to settle disputes peacefully. Conflict resolution education can help bring about significant reductions in suspensions, disciplinary referrals, academic disruptions, playground fights, and family and sibling disputes."
> U.S. Attorney General Janet Reno and Secretary of Education Richard W. Riley in *Conflict Resolution Education : A Guide to Implementing Programs in Schools, Youth-Serving Organizations, and Community and Juvenile Justice Settings*, 1996

As previously mentioned in this chapter, conflict is a part of life. Sometimes conflict can create an opportunity for growth - both personally and socially. As students learn techniques in conflict resolution, there can be a strengthening of relations. An important aspect of looking at conflict is that dealing with conflict presents a choice. One choice is to focus on perceiving conflict as something negative and/or responding to the conflict in an inappropriate manner. Another choice is to perceive conflict as an opportunity to resolve issues in a manner that creates harmony and growth. The first choice tends to be the way most people respond out of habit. The second choice can be the result of further training and awareness in the areas of conflict resolution. The manner in which you resolve conflict in your classroom can serve as a role model to your students in terms of whether conflict is perceived in a negative or positive context.

While there are a wide range of possibilities to consider in conflict resolution training, there are three primary underlying considerations in this book. First is the need to understand and master effective interpersonal communication skills. It should also be noted that a major emphasis in these skills relates to listening. Effective empathetic listening skills create understanding and it is this understanding that is generally critical for resolving conflicts in a positive manner. Unless problems and concerns are properly understood it is difficult to find appropriate and lasting solutions. Secondly, there is a need for a basic framework for responding to a conflict. This can include factors such as dealing with the conflict in private rather than attempting to resolve a conflict in a public setting where peer pressure may negatively affect the willingness of students to engage in constructive problem solving. Finally, there is a need for students to understand a problem solving approach that is appropriate to their age level and experiences. Although a sample model is presented in this chapter, there are many other possibilities. This chapter can provide an overview for teaching some components of conflict resolution but it is certainly not all-encompassing, and readers who would like to introduce formal conflict resolution programs or consider alternatives to the content of this chapter should consider the websites related to conflict resolution that are provided on page 200 or the related resources in the bibliography at the end of this book.

This chapter begins with a survey (Activity #97) that can be used to help your students begin to understand that there are appropriate and inappropriate ways to express and deal with conflicts. Activities #98 + 99 look at typical conflicts that occur at school. This information can be useful to both you and your students in understanding the scope of conflicts that students typically face. Activities #100 - 102 provide an introductory look at both preventing and resolving conflicts. As stress can be a factor in causing conflicts and also in resolving them, Activities #103 - 106 look at identifying stressors and also tips for resolving them. Activities #107 - 114 provide a basic framework for resolving conflicts that is named Conflict CPR. As previously mentioned in this introduction, central to conflict resolution is some form of a problem solving process. Activities #115 + 116 provide a model that can be used to help students understand a framework for solving problems. Finally, Activity #117 provides a chapter review.

ACTIVITY 97

CONFLICT RESOLUTION SURVEY

1. Each student is given a copy of pages 204 + 205 to complete. It is recommended that you collect the completed surveys and record each student's mark so that they can be compared to this chapter's post-test. When you return the survey back to your students it is important to review the correct answers as this will provide an introduction to their learning in conflict resolution. The answer key for the best answers is as follows:

1 - c	6 - c	11 - c	16 - c
2 - b	7 - b	12 - b	17 - a
3 - a	8 - c	13 - b	18 - c
4 - c	9 - b	14 - a	19 - b
5 - b	10 - c	15 - b	20 - a

ACTIVITY 98

TYPICAL CONFLICTS AT SCHOOL

Students share examples of some of the conflicts they may encounter at school. Keep a list of the conflicts as these examples can be used in later activities. As students share their conflict examples, this would be an opportunity for you to show your interest in their concerns by using your empathetic listening skills (primarily paraphrasing, clarification and open-ended sentences as learned in Chapter 5). This activity can also help you to gain some insights into the types of conflicts that some of your students experience and also a look at what they perceive to be a conflict. It is not necessary to look for solutions to their conflicts at this time although this may occur in some cases.

CONFLICT RESOLUTION SURVEY

INSTRUCTIONS: Circle the phrase that best describes you in each of the following:

1. Whenever you find yourself in a conflict with another person,
   a) you tend to get very angry at the person
   b) you tend to walk away talking to yourself
   c) you tend to talk to the other person calmly about the problem

2. You are the kind of person who
   a) seems to always be getting into arguments with others
   b) tends to get along with most people
   c) tends to mistrust other people

3. You would best be described as someone who
   a) is a strong listener
   b) likes to argue your point of view
   c) avoids any kind of conflict with others

4. Whenever you find yourself in a conflict with another person,
   a) you tend to blame the other person
   b) you tend to blame yourself
   c) you try to resolve the conflict instead of blaming anyone

5. One of the best ways to resolve conflicts with others is by
   a) being forceful
   b) having the ability to understand their point of view
   c) knowing your rights.

6. When you get really angry,
   a) you tend to explode at whoever made you angry
   b) you tend to take it out on a friend
   c) you try to find a way to calm down before you do anything

7. Other people tend to be attracted to you because
   a) you have problems
   b) you have a cheerful attitude
   c) they feel sorry for you

8. Praising others is
   a) a good way to lose their respect
   b) a good way to look weak
   c) a good way to build positive relationships

9. In general, you tend to
   a) get angry very easy
   b) be calm most of the time
   c) be stressed out a lot of the time

10. A good way to build a positive relationship with another person is to
    a) leave them alone
    b) tell them about yourself
    c) show an interest in them

11. The greatest cause of stress in most companies is
    a) having to work too hard
    b) lack of job security
    c) conflicts between co-workers

12. A healthy way to deal with anger is to
    a) scream or yell at the person who is causing your problem
    b) go for a walk
    c) keep it inside

13. If you are really upset at another person you tend to
    a) very strongly tell him or her exactly what you are feeling
    b) calm down before you talk to him or her
    c) avoid him or her

14. Feeling angry is
    a) a normal thing
    b) a problem
    c) a sign of low intelligence

15. When other people ask you to do things
    a) you always say yes
    b) you only say yes if you have time to do what they are asking
    c) you always say no

16. The best way to fit in with a new group of people is to
    a) talk about things you like to do
    b) avoid eye contact
    c) be a good listener

17. When other people have hurt you, you are the kind of person who
    a) will forgive them if they are truly sorry
    b) will stay away from them
    c) will find a way to get even

18. You tend to be the kind of person who
    a) talks about your problems with anyone who will listen
    b) keeps your problems to yourself
    c) talks about your problems with a close friend

19. When you talk to other people you tend to be
    a) nervous
    b) confident
    c) sarcastic

20. You tend to be the kind of person who
    a) shows concern for others
    b) really doesn't care about others
    c) who likes others only if they first like you

ACTIVITY 99

CONFLICT GRAPH

1. As a follow-up to Activity #98, it would be useful to post the examples of the conflicts that were identified and then categorize them under headings suggested by your students. Headings might include "homework", "not listening", "not completing assignments", "bullying", etc. It is important in looking at conflicts that students don't share conflicts from home, nor conflicts (especially with the names of other teachers) that might have occurred in other classes.

2. In small groups, each group could be given one of the headings from #1 and then list as many specific examples they can think of that are related to this heading. Results are shared.

3. As an assignment, each student asks 15 - 25 other students which conflict heading best describes the area of conflict where he/she experiences the most conflicts. From these results, students make a graph to illustrate their findings. This activity would be more interesting if students also asked their friends who are not in their class. The graph below shows an example that was completed by a grade 8 student.

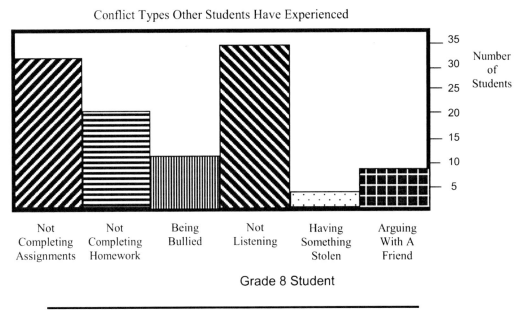

CLASSROOM MANAGEMENT

ACTIVITY 100

PREVENTING CONFLICTS

1. Based on some of the most frequently mentioned conflicts that were identified by your students in Activities #98 + 99, prepare a list of 10 -15 typical conflicts. Your students could also prepare such a list in small groups.

2. One by one, progress through the conflicts that were identified in #1 and discuss possible strategies and tips that might have prevented each of the conflicts from occurring in the first place. The emphasis in the activity (and for that matter in this book) is that the majority of conflicts that your students might experience could have often been prevented and that it generally takes less time and stress to prevent a conflict from occurring than it does to deal with it once it has happened.

ACTIVITY 101

A FIRST LOOK AT RESOLVING CONFLICTS

1. In small groups, students identify 2 - 3 typical conflicts that were identified in Activities #98 - 100. For each conflict, each group discusses possible ways to resolve the conflict.

2. Results are shared.

3. Based on #1 and #2, each group prepares a list of their "top 10" suggestions for resolving conflicts. After the results are shared, it would be useful to identify the best "top 10" suggestions from your students.

ACTIVITY 102

TIPS FOR RESOLVING CONFLICTS

In small groups, students are given copies of page 209. Each group compares the list of suggestions developed in Activity #101 with this new list and prepares a new "top 10" list of suggestions. After each group shares their results, it would be useful for your class to develop a top 10 list of all the suggestions. It is recommended that this list be posted somewhere in your classroom.

> "Whenever you are confronted with an opponent, conquer him with love."
> Mahatma Gandhi

ACTIVITY 103

STRESS AT SCHOOL

1. Discuss how stress can contribute to causing conflicts and can also contribute to mishandling them.

2. Students discuss causes of stress at school. Keep a list of the stressors that students identify.

3. Each student identifies the number one cause of school stress for him. As a class, rank the stressors from #1 showing the greatest stressor, as identified by the class, to the least stressor.

TIPS FOR RESOLVING CONFLICTS

1. Try to resolve conflicts before they happen.

2. Be slow to anger, especially over little things.

3. If you find that you are wrong, admit it. On the other hand, if you are not wrong, once you have taken the time to understand the other person's point of view, then be assertive in voicing your needs and rights.

4. Don't be too quick to blame others before you consider your own role in the conflict.

5. The first step in successfully resolving a conflict is attempting to understand the other person's point of view, rather than attempting to convince him/her of yours.

6. Be willing to forgive.

7. Most of the time, you shouldn't try to resolve a conflict when you are angry.

8. Attempt to have the conflict handled in private instead of in front of other students.

9. Clearly identify the problem before you attempt to find some solutions.

10. Attempt to find some solutions that are best for everyone involved.

ACTIVITY 104

SCHOOL STRESS GRAPH

1. Using the five top causes of stress that were identified in Activity #103, students are told to survey other students (including friends in other classes) to explore the major causes of school stress. It is recommended that each student surveys at least fifteen other students.

2. Each student prepares a graph (similar to page 206) to show the leading causes of stress at school.

3. Each student presents his/her graph. Once all the graphs have been presented, prepare a master graph incorporating the results from all the students.

> "The more tranquil a man becomes,
> the greater is his success, his influence,
> his power for good."
> James Allen

ACTIVITY 105

TIPS FOR REDUCING STRESS

1. In small groups, students brainstorm suggestions for reducing stress. Results are shared.

2. Each group is given a copy of page 212. Comparing these suggestions to the lists developed in #1, each group prepares a list of the their top 10 suggestions. After the results are shared, your class identifies their top 10 tips for reducing stress.

"The cyclone derives its powers from a calm of center. So does a person."
Norman Vincent Peale

"Nothing gives a person so much advantage over another as to remain always cool and unruffled under all circumstances."
Thomas Jefferson

TIPS FOR REDUCING STRESS

1. Ask a teacher or counselor for help.

2. Go for a walk or exercise in a gym.

3. Learn some relaxation techniques such as deep breathing.

4. Talk to a friend about what is bothering you.

5. Get more sleep.

6. Eat healthier foods.

7. If possible, avoid the situations that are causing stress for you.

8. As you look at your schoolwork, focus on just one thing at a time.

9. For difficult assignments, break the assignment into smaller parts.

10. Focus on what is most important and don't sweat the small stuff.

11. Avoid extreme reactions.

12. Do something for someone else.

13. Avoid alcohol, drugs and tobacco.

14. Spend some time just relaxing each day.

15. Laugh.

16. It is usually far less stressful to forgive than to seek revenge.

17. Don't criticize others.

18. Be with people who bring out the best in you.

19. Take breaks throughout the day.

20. Sometimes you need to say "no" to requests that you don't have time to do.

ACTIVITY 106

DEALING WITH STRESS

Each student is given a copy of page 214 to complete. Share the results.

> "Calmness is the cradle of power."
> J. G. Holland

ACTIVITY 107

CONFLICT CPR

1. Discuss what "CPR" is. It is likely that some of your students will have had "CPR" training as the result of babysitting courses or swimming lessons.

2. Tell your students that Conflict CPR is a three step process to assist in handling conflicts with others. In small groups, students attempt to identify three steps they think would be important in handling a conflict. Share the results.

3. Tell your students that in Conflict CPR, the acronym CPR stands for "calm, private and reflect". The next few activities will elaborate on this.

DEALING WITH STRESS

Three things that are stressful for me at school are . . .

1)

2)

3)

Ten tips that can help me to better deal with stress at school are . . .

1)

2)

3)

4)

5)

6)

7)

8)

9)

10)

ACTIVITY 108

CONFLICT CPR BENEFITS

1. Begin by further explaining the acronym CPR as it relates to conflict resolution. The "C" represents staying calm in the face of a conflict. The "P" represents resolving the conflict in private. The "R" represents reflective listening which includes understanding the underlying emotions and the content of what a person is saying so that the emphasis is on understanding the other person's point of view before expressing your own.

2. In small groups, students identify what they think would be the benefits of remaining calm, of dealing with the conflict in private, and of reflective listening to understand the other person. You might find it useful to give each group one of the three CPR terms to look at. Share the results.

ACTIVITY 109

REMAINING CALM

1. Based on Activities #104 - 108, students identify tips for remaining calm.

2. For an assignment, students are told to identify a situation that occurred during the course of a day when they might normally get stressed, but using one of the tips suggested in #1, they managed to remain calm.

3. Share and discuss the results from #2.

ACTIVITY 110

THE IMPORTANCE OF DEALING WITH A CONFLICT IN PRIVATE

1. Tell your students to identify the benefits of a conflict being handled in private as opposed to being handled in front of others. The discussion might include some of the following:

- how other students watching a conflict can "feed" it
- how resolving a conflict in private can lead to better solutions
- how resolving a conflict in public might be embarrassing to those involved
- how people might try to "save face" in publicly handled conflicts
- how public conflicts can start with just two people involved and may soon escalate to involving others

2. It would also be useful to discuss how to "move" the conflict into a private setting by discussing some of the following as examples:

- choosing the right time and place to resolve the conflict (in other words, most conflicts don't have to be handled immediately)
- involving a teacher/counselor to help move the conflict into a more private setting and perhaps to help mediate the conflict
- finding a healthy way to deal with your emotions before trying to resolve the conflict

3. It would also be useful to discuss the role that a friend (or third party person) might play in helping to resolve the conflict. Activity #111 can provide some further thoughts in this area. This might include some of the following thoughts:

- how a third person might help the people involved in the conflict better understand each other's point of view
- how a third person might be better able to suggest some solutions

ACTIVITY 111

MEDIATION TIPS

1. Discuss the concept of mediation and tell your students to identify some of the benefits that mediation could bring to a conflict.

2. In small groups, students identify tips they think would be helpful for a mediator to consider in helping to resolve a conflict. Share the results.

3. Each group is given a copy of page 218 to discuss in comparison to the tips they developed. Using their tips from #2 and the tips from page 218, each group prepares a top 10 list of mediation tips. Share the results and prepare a master list of the top 10 tips from your class.

ACTIVITY 112

THE IMPORTANCE OF REFLECTIVE LISTENING IN A CONFLICT

1. The word reflecting suggests a mirror. In a conflict situation, it is important to really understand what others are saying. One of the best ways to do this is through paraphrasing which is often also called "reflective listening". Sometimes the reflective listening focuses on the content of what is being said, while other times it focuses on the emotion.

2. In pairs, and using some of the conflicts identified in Activity #98, students prepare a skit that involves one person complaining to another student about something that has occurred while the second student

TIPS FOR MEDIATING A CONFLICT

1. Give each student in the conflict an opportunity to "calm down" before attempting to resolve the conflict.

2. Find a private place that is convenient for the students involved in the conflict to meet.

3. Set a time that is convenient for the students involved in the conflict to meet.

4. Have one student talk at a time. Ensure that the listening student understands the other student's point of view before presenting his/her point of view.

5. After each student has presented his/her point of view in the conflict, summarize what they have both said to ensure that both you and the other students clearly understand what is being said. Make sure that everyone fully understands the problem before you begin to look for solutions.

6. Keep the focus on the problem rather than letting students "attack" each other's character.

7. Ask each student to share his/her thoughts on possible solutions.

8. Attempt to find a solution that somehow meets some of the needs of everyone involved in the conflict.

9. Identify what will have to happen next for any solutions to work.

10. If the students are unable to come up with a solution, then a teacher/counselor can begin to suggest some possible solutions. In some situations, it may be necessary to simply end stating that you will meet again in a day or two. The time in between meetings gives each person an opportunity to consider some solutions for when you get together again.

attempts to paraphrase either the content of what is being said or the emotions behind it.

3. Choose some students to present their skits and discuss how paraphrasing (reflecting) can help people to feel understood and how being understood can both help to prevent conflicts and help to better resolve them when they do occur. Students could also be given copies of page 220 for further discussion.

ACTIVITY 113

CONFLICT SOLUTIONS

1. Discuss the concept of "win-win" solutions or "winning together" where a solution to any problem has some benefits for everyone involved.

2. Each student is given two file cards. On each card, students describe a typical conflict that sometimes occurs at school.

3. The cards are collected. Before continuing with the activity, it is recommended that you review each of the cards to check their appropriateness (don't permit the names of others, situations involving other teachers, or specific home conflicts). Groups are formed with 4 - 6 students in each group. One group is chosen to be the "judge".

4. Read one of the conflict cards. Each group has 3 - 5 minutes to come up with possible "winning together" solutions to the conflict. After each group presents their best 2 - 3 solutions, the "judge" group provides a score out of 10 and some feedback for their score rationale. Repeat the process so that every group has a turn being the "judge".

BENEFITS OF PARAPHRASING IN HANDLING A CONFLICT

1. Paraphrasing can help calm an emotional person because it is hard for him/her to argue against his/her own words.

2. Paraphrasing gives you an acceptable way to interrupt in a heated argument because you are not fighting against the other person's point of view, but simply trying to understand it.

3. When you calmly paraphrase, you can establish a softer level of conversation.

4. Paraphrasing helps you to understand the other person's point of view which can help you find more satisfying solutions to the problem.

5. Paraphrasing can help the other person be more aware of what he/she is saying. Sometimes, this will result in a person being more realistic about his/her actual concerns instead of exaggerating what has happened.

6. Paraphrasing can help to save face. Unfortunately, some conflicts occur in front of other people. Paraphrasing doesn't take sides or make demands. By saving face, people can work towards more positive solutions.

7. Paraphrasing helps to prevent you from stating your views and opinions. During the emotional first part of a conflict, your viewpoint, regardless of how logical it might be, may simply fuel the conflict instead of helping to find a solution. Once the emotions have been diffused, you can more effectively present your views and needs.

8. Paraphrasing helps to create empathy. Simply stated, empathy is the ability to put yourself in another person's shoes. This helps to create better solutions to the problem.

9. Paraphrasing helps to create respect. As you attempt to understand other people in a conflict situation, they will develop respect for you because you are taking the time to listen to them instead of demanding your way.

10. As you use paraphrasing in attempting to understand others, they, in turn, will be more likely to be willing to try to understand you.

ACTIVITY 114

CONFLICT RESOLUTION ASSIGNMENT

1. For this assignment, each student observes a conflict between two people. This conflict could be a real-life conflict that occurs at school or in the neighborhood, or it could be from a movie or television show. Each student answers the following questions:

   i) Describe what happened in the conflict.

   ii) In what ways was the conflict either resolved by using some aspect of Conflict CPR, or was made worse by not using some aspect of Conflict CPR?

   iii) How might the conflict have been handled differently?

2. Share and discuss the assignments.

ACTIVITY 115

A MODEL FOR PROBLEM SOLVING

The previous activities in this chapter can help to provide some of the communication skills and an overall strategy for resolving conflicts. What is missing is a specific problem solving approach so that once the problem has been understood you can then work towards a winning together solution. Although a basic model will be presented on the next page, it would be useful in most classrooms to adapt whatever problem solving approach your students have already learned as part of one of their subject areas (often learned in science or social science). The purpose of this activity is to ensure that your students understand some steps involved in solving a problem. Activity #116 will help your students to actually practice a problem solving model in resolving conflicts.

Problem solving is a process that can be learned. Add empathetic skills and Conflict CPR to this and you have a practical and powerful system for resolving many of the conflicts that might occur in your classroom. Problem solving models often have anywhere from five to ten steps in the process (Maruska 2004; Robbins 2004). Similar to the previous discussion in this book related to classroom rules, I would recommend that the fewer steps in the process the better. If you can keep the problem solving process to between five and seven steps, there is a better chance that your students will remember the model. The following model provides six steps that are generally found in problem solving models. Each step will be discussed further in the following pages.

A PROBLEM SOLVING MODEL FOR CONFLICT RESOLUTION

STEP #1 - Identify the problem.

STEP #2 - Attempt to understand how this problem affects each person involved in the conflict.

STEP #3 - Ask each person involved in the conflict to share a workable solution.

STEP #4 - From the possible solutions offered in #3, find some common ground to establish the best "winning together" solution.

STEP #5 - Establish a step-by-step course with appropriate timelines for implementing the solution identified in #4.

STEP #6 - After a specific period of time, evaluate the success of the solution that was implemented. If necessary, modify the solution and repeat any of the previous steps in the problem solving approach.

contribution to moving towards an acceptable solution for everyone involved in the conflict.

> "Any fool can criticize, condemn, and complain, but it takes character and self control to be understanding."
> Dale Carnegie

STEP #3 - Ask each person involved in the conflict to share a workable solution.

Simply asking each person involved in a conflict for their thoughts on possible solutions can not only provide insights into the needs and wants of those involved in the conflict, but may also provide some workable solutions. One of the key words here is workable (which would also suggest that any solutions need to consider the viewpoints of others involved in the conflict). While it is generally beneficial for everyone involved in the conflict to hear these suggestions (without commenting on them), in some conflicts you might find it useful to have each person write down a solution that you can present to the parties involved in a calm, non-threatening manner. Another option is to take the written suggestions without sharing them and find some common ground in them that can be used as the basis for a solution.

Sometimes, brainstorming with an emphasis on being creative can result in solutions that might not have otherwise appeared. With students, the brainstorming sessions can offer a fun way to look at the conflict and often help to diffuse the tension and emotions involved.

STEP #1 - Identify the problem.

Perhaps the most important aspect of any problem solving model is to identify the problem. Sometimes a great deal of time and effort is spent in trying to resolve a conflict without fully understanding the scope of the problem. As problems are frequently partly and sometimes wholly due to misunderstandings, it is very important to clarify the problem before attempting to find solutions. In fact, in some conflicts once you identify the problem for all involved, you might even find that the conflict quickly resolves itself because it was due in large part to misunderstanding. In identifying the problem, it is important to ensure that it is considered from all sides involved in the conflict. In situations where the problem is complex, identify various parts of the problem and begin the problem solving process by first tackling some aspect of the problem that you feel comfortable can be quickly and satisfactorily resolved. This can help everyone involved in the process to gain confidence before moving on to some of the more serious aspects of the problem. As the problem is identified, it is important for everyone involved to share specific examples related to the "how, when, where, what" of the problem.

> "It isn't that they can't see the solution.
> It is that they can't see the problem."
> G. K. Chesterton

STEP #2 - Attempt to understand how this problem affects each person involved in the conflict.

Tied very closely to Step #1 is the need to understand how the problem affects each person involved in the conflict. As stated in Step #1, often it is a misunderstanding (a different perception) that may have contributed to the problem in the first place. Give each person involved in the problem an opportunity to state how the problem affects him/her. The key here is to use reflective listening skills to ensure understanding. This can make a very positive

> "Believe it can be done.
> When you believe something can be done,
> really believe,
> your mind will find the ways to do it.
> Believing a solution paves the way
> to the solution."
> D. J. Schwartz

STEP #4 - From the possible solutions offered in #3, find some common ground to establish the best "winning together" solution.

Remember that a winning together solution involves trying to find some benefits in the solution for each party involved in the conflict. Even in situations where a student is clearly at fault in breaking a classroom or school rule, the solution can sometimes provide benefits to all involved (including both the perpetrator and any possible victims). A solution that prevents a student from further disregarding the rules benefits everyone in the class (including the teacher) by providing a more positive learning environment. The perpetrator in any conflict can benefit by understanding that he is making a contribution to this environment through his changed behavior. He can also benefit by avoiding any future punishments by following the agreed upon solution which will hopefully prevent him from being a source of further conflicts. The suggestions that students make in steps #3 + 4 of this process will often provide clues that can form the basis of winning together solutions.

In considering solutions it is important to consider the consequences of each solution on all the students involved in the conflict. The reality of consequences as they apply to decision making is a very important concept to teach to your students.

> "While we are free to choose our actions,
> we are not free to choose
> the consequences of our actions."
> Stephen R. Covey

STEP #5 - Establish a step-by-step course with appropriate timelines for implementing the solution identified in #4.

Sometimes solutions can be overwhelming to students. Like any other learning task it is important to break the solutions down into manageable steps with specific timelines. Successful solutions involve action, and this action is best achieved when the steps involved are achievable. As a student gains confidence in achieving each step, there is a greater likelihood that the solution will be successfully attained. Having measureable steps with specific timelines can assist in students being meaningfully engaged in implementing solutions.

In some conflict situations, you will find it helpful to set each step of the solution into some form of written contract between the students involved. The contract should include a clear wording of the solution as well as outlining any steps and the dates for their completion. It would also be useful to list the benefits the students will gain by successfully implementing the solution.

> "A goal without a date is just a dream."
> M. H. Erickson

STEP #6 - After a specific period of time, evaluate the success of the solution that was implemented. If necessary, modify the solution and repeat any of the previous steps in the problem solving approach.

There may times in resolving a conflict that you have an excellent solution but the students involved are having trouble achieving it because the plan of action was not practical. Of course, there may also be times when the solution itself was not workable. If the solution to a conflict is not working, then consider repeating some of the steps in your problem solving model to see if you can either come up with a more workable solution or a better plan of action for implementing it. Sometimes the goals are best achieved with a flexible process and sometimes it is our goals that need to be revised. Page 228 provides some further thoughts on setting and achieving goals.

> "Insanity is doing the same thing over and over again, and expecting different results."
> Albert Einstein

Conflicts, although they can be stressful and disruptive in the classroom, can provide a teaching opportunity as well. As has already been mentioned in this book, successful people are proficient at handling conflicts and in problem solving. Helping your students to gain skills in conflict resolution and in problem solving can contribute in a very positive way to both their current and future success. Taking the time to use some classroom conflicts as an opportunity to put your students' problem solving skills into action may be a wise investment of your time. As students gain proficiency in conflict resolution and problem solving this can help to reduce the number of these occurrences in your classroom and when conflicts do occur you will find that they can be resolved in a positive less time-consuming manner.

TIPS ON SETTING AND ACHIEVING GOALS

1. The most important thing about setting your goals is having one.

2. Write your goals and look at them often.

3. Take action. A goal without action is still just a dream.

4. Use a journal to keep track of your results as you work towards achieving your goals.

5. List all the ways you will benefit from achieving your goals.

6. Write a step-by-step plan for reaching your goals.

7. Set specific deadlines for achieving your goals and also for completing each step along the way.

8. Talk to someone you respect and trust about your goals and your plans to achieve them.

9. Prioritize your goals so that you know which one is most important to you.

10. Spend most of your time working on your most important goal.

ACTIVITY 116

RESOLVING CONFLICTS
USING A PROBLEM SOLVING APPROACH

1. Review whatever problem solving approach you developed in Activity #115. It would make sense to post the steps somewhere in your room.

2. Select 4 - 5 typical school conflicts that were identified in Activity #98. After forming small groups, each group is given one of the conflicts from #1 to apply the problem solving steps to resolve. Each group should discuss the implications of each of the problem solving steps related to the conflict they are looking at. Share the results.

3. It would also be useful for students to role play various conflict situations and demonstrate their learning from both Conflict CPR and a problem solving model to resolve the conflicts.

ACTIVITY 117

CHAPTER REVIEW

It is recommended that your students complete the survey on pages 204 + 205 once again. It is also recommended that as you discuss the answers to each question that your students be encouraged to refer to their learning in this chapter to support their thoughts.

> "Anyone who angers you conquers you."
> Confucious

CHAPTER 8

HOW TO TEACH YOUR STUDENTS ANGER MANAGEMENT

Another source of conflict can result from problems with anger management. These problems can be the result of teachers who have difficulty controlling how they express their anger or these problems can be with students. It is estimated in the U.S.A. as an example, that one in five people have problems with anger management. While anger itself can be a natural emotion, it is how this anger is expressed that can cause problems and trigger inappropriate behavior. When both teachers and students learn how to better manage their anger and express it in appropriate ways, anger can become a positive contributor to success instead of a negative force causing conflicts.

A dictionary definition of anger might be a strong feeling of displeasure with synonyms being words such as rage, wrath, fury, and indignant (The Merriam-Webster Dictionary, 2011). Anger can result from any of the following:

i) loss
ii) threats
iii) frustration
iv) lack of acceptance
v) helplessness
vi) learned response

i) LOSS

In looking at the various phases that a person goes through in grieving a loss (such as death of a parent, friend or even a pet, or loss that can result from separation/divorce, or having an absent parent, or even a 'break-up' with a close friend), anger is considered as one of those stages. In some situations, you may be well aware of some form of loss that a student is experiencing that can help lead you to be more empathetic with the student (and more understanding of any anger that is exhibited). On the other hand, you may have no idea that a student has experienced some form of loss. When you experience demonstrated anger that is out-of-character, it would make sense to talk to the student (and possibly her parents) about any recent changes in the student's life that may be contributing to her anger. Simply said, loss is the disappearance of something that was cherished.

The good news about this expression of anger is that as a stage, it is generally temporary although the timelines for its duration will be different for every student. Helping students who are experiencing loss to express their anger in an acceptable manner (such as talking to a counselor) can often be very helpful in assisting these students to handle this time in their lives when they are hurting and need some way to express their feelings, wants and needs.

> "Allowing children to show their guilt,
> show their grief, show their anger,
> takes the sting out of the situation."
> Martha Beck

ii) THREATS

Unfortunately, bullying (as an example of a threat) is an issue in our schools. Although teachers may not always see or hear the threats that may be occurring, there are definitely some students who come into our classrooms who have been threatened in some way, whether it happens in the hallway, playground, school bus, in the washroom, or even at home. In spite of the best plans, teachers can't be everywhere. Bullying will sometimes occur without our knowledge. In addition, bullying may occur in subtle non-verbal ways and for some students, bullying may be more of a perception problem than an actual reality. Whatever the case, a student who is bullied or feels threatened in any way will often be in inner turmoil and could unexpectedly explode at someone else. Sometimes it is the bully who has in some way been bullied. Although anti-bullying programs are not, per se, part of this book, they can certainly play an important role in both conflict and anger management. Having said this though, the reality is that much of the content of this book can assist in preventing and constructively resolving bulling issues as students learn more effective communication skills and better ways to deal with conflict.

> "Since a lot of bullying is caused by anger,
> help your child to learn anger management techniques."
> Harvey Karp

iii) FRUSTRATION

As will be explored further in Chapter 10, success or failure related to any subject curriculum can have a huge impact on a student's behavior at school. In 2000, the percentage of fourth-grade students performing at or above the *Basic* level of reading achievement was 63 percent. Performance at or above the *Proficient* level -- the level identified by the National Assessment Governing Board as the level that all students should reach -- was achieved by 32 percent of fourth-graders. These results from the National Assessment of Educational Progress would suggest that 37% of students in grade 4 in the U.S.A. are reading below a "basic level" of reading proficiency and that 68% of grade 4 students are not reading at the "proficient level", a level that the NAGB states should be reached by all students (and research in other English speaking countries tends to reveal that about 1/3 of students entering grade 4 are at least one grade level behind in reading comprehension). These results strongly show that there are a significant number of students entering Grade 5 (which is the beginning grade level of the focus for this book) who are behind in their reading skills. With almost every subject area requiring a specific degree of reading fluency, some of your students may encounter great frustration at school every day due to their lack of reading skills. While it is not the intent of this book to remediate reading skills, there is no doubt that structured and purposeful remedial reading programs could help a significant number of students to be more successful in school, and as a result lessen the stress, frustration and failure that some of these students experience, and as a result would help to reduce some misbehavior.

Similarly, within any subject discipline area there may be students who lack some basic readiness skills to be successful. In some cases students may have unidentified problems (such as lack of physical coordination that affects some students in physical education classes) which directly causes a lack of success.

As discussed further in Chapter 10, lack of success in any subject area can lead to misbehavior while achieving success can help to eliminate behavioral problems for some students.

> "People who fail to achieve their goals
> often get stopped by frustration."
> Anthony Robbins

iv) LACK OF ACCEPTANCE

Acceptance is a basic human need. For students who come to school, not being accepted by their peers, sometimes even their teachers, and sometimes even their parents, there can be a great deal of unresolved anger bubbling within. Similar to the other causes of anger being explored here, this anger can be expressed aggressively or even passively. In disciplining misbehavior it is important to still accept the student while focusing on the inappropriateness of the behavior.

The chapters at the beginning of this book provide activities that can help a student to feel accepted by both her teachers and peers. In addition to these kinds of activities, some schools have school goals that relate to "no student being invisible". In such schools, every student has some adult contact in the school to help the student feel more accepted and welcome. In addition, some schools offer peer helping/tutoring programs or student mentorship or ambassador programs that once again help students to feel connected and accepted.

> "The art of acceptance
> is the art of making someone
> who has just done a small favour for you
> wish that he might have done a greater one."
> Martin Luther King Jr.

v) HELPLESSNESS

Some students develop what might best be termed as learned helplessness. Repressed anger can play a role in students developing this helplessness that can be exhibited through apathy, not caring, easily giving up, not responding to constructive criticism, and a general lack of enthusiasm for learning. For example, a child who is prevented from ever making her own decisions because of a powerful, dominant (abusive?) parent may have learned long before entering school that decisions are to only be made by adults, or that failure is to be avoided at all costs.

In a sense students develop learned helplessness when they discover (even if this is only a perception in their mind) that nothing they do matters or will result in success. If somehow (and this can be an internal perception) a student learns this "helplessness", then from his standpoint there is no reason to try. It just makes more sense to give up rather than take action (especially if the action involves hard work and the risk of failure).

> "At the bottom of every one of your fears is simply the fear that you can't handle whatever life may bring you."
> Susan Jeffers in *Feel The Fear . . . And Do It Anyway*, 1987

vi) LEARNED RESPONSE

Students who grow up in a home where anger is either passively or aggressively exhibited may learn either of these responses even though the other causes of anger that were previously outlined in this chapter may not apply to the student. In other words a student may demonstrate an angry response in various situations even though the response itself is not rooted in what we might normally consider anger. While the other causes of anger that are listed here also lead to what we might identify as habitual learned responses from students, the difference here is that the habit may not have any external concrete cause. Similar to a student having learned to talk loudly because one of his parents also talks loudly (even though there may be no benefit for the student to talk loudly), a student may also learn to express anger even though there is no apparent benefit for this expression.

> "We are what we repeatedly do.
> Excellence, then, is not an act, but a habit."
> Aristotle

The expression of anger can result in both costs and benefits depending on the appropriateness of the actual expression.

In looking at the costs of anger, it is important to recognize that the inappropriate expression of anger can go beyond hurting others and/or making irrational decisions. Anger can often directly hurt the person who is angry. There is a physiological cost of anger that can be huge. Anger is generally associated with high blood pressure and this problem may be more significant if the anger is suppressed.

> "Higher blood pressure is significantly related to suppressed anger."
> Dimsdale, 1986

There are certainly many other studies that support this finding as well indicating that high blood pressure also results even when people outwardly express their anger. In a study by Crunnbaum (1997), a strong connection between anger and pathological changes in the arteries of even young school-age children was found. Chronic anger and hostility can cause serious damage to your heart and arteries.

In addition, anger affects relationships. Greenglass (1996) found that people with high scores on anger received less support from family members and had less trust in their closest relationships. Jones (1981) found a significant relationship between hostility and loneliness. In plain language, people don't enjoy being around others who are prone to anger.

> "Holding on to anger is like grasping a hot coal with the intent of throwing it at someone else, except you are the one who gets burned."
> Buddha

In considering the payoffs of outward anger, if the anger is expressed in an acceptable manner then there can be a reduction of stress. While an inappropriate anger discharge might result in a temporary absence of stress, this small break rarely lasts and unfortunately it is this immediate "release" that often reinforces the angry outbursts which helps to directly develop inappropriate habits of expression. It then becomes easier to lash out at others in inappropriate ways because there is this brief release of stress that feeds the habit. Unfortunately, there is a tendency for the outbursts to become more frequent and stronger in intensity resulting in others becoming both defensive and hardened to the angry responses.

From the list of causes of anger that were explained earlier in this chapter, it should be evident that many of these causes are related to hiding emotional pain. An angry outburst may seem to be a short term solution but in the end the cause of the anger remains unresolved. Not resolving the source of the anger can sometimes increase the inner pain that was at the root of the anger which then leads to more frequent outbursts of increased intensity.

Another apparent payoff of anger is that it generally gets everyone's attention, especially in the early stages of expression before it becomes an unwelcome, but anticipated habit. In the classroom, some teachers feel that anger gets results, but in the end students can become hardened and lose respect for the teacher, not to mention the creation of stress, tension and fear in what we would like to be a positive, accepting, learning environment.

While the activities in this chapter are aimed at helping all your students to better understand how the inappropriate expression or suppression of anger can be harmful to them and also to help your students to better understand some appropriate ways to manage and express their anger, the reality in most classes is that there are few students who have serious anger management issues. Although the activities in this chapter may be beneficial to such students (and may also be useful to other students in your class as they interact with students with anger management concerns), it is important to note that additional strategies and tips that can assist you in working with angry students will be found in Chapter 9.

It should also be noted that this chapter talks a little about relaxation techniques without going into great detail. There are a wealth of relaxation exercises and techniques available in the form of books or DVD's. These resources could help you to teach relaxation exercises to your students. In addition, guest speakers who are specialists in teaching relaxation techniques could help your students to learn more about relaxing. Relaxation techniques can help to reduce stress and also reduce anger. In addition to the calming physical effects from relaxation techniques, studies also confirm that relaxation helps to increase energy and focus, helps to combat illness and even increases problem-solving abilities.

The activities in this chapter begin with a look at helping students to identify things that make them angry. As students complete Activity #118, helping them to identify what makes them angry can help them to begin to understand that everyone gets angry and that there are certain "triggers" that affect different people in different ways. Identifying and understanding these triggers can help individual students to avoid situations that make them angry or be better prepared to resolve such situations in more positive ways.

Activity #119 focuses on what students do when they get angry. Activity #120 looks at the cost of anger and Activity #121 explores more appropriate ways to express anger.

Relaxation techniques can play an important role in dealing with stress and preventing inappropriate anger responses. Activities #122 + 123 provide a beginning look at helping your students to understand the importance of relaxation techniques and what they are. As mentioned above, this is an area that you can expand depending on your own level of skills, awareness, and availability of related resources.

An important aspect of learning anger management skills is to practice them. A good way to do this is through role-playing which is the focus of Activity #124. The chapter ends with a review to help students (and you) assess the learning that has occurred.

ACTIVITY 118

WHAT MAKES YOU ANGRY

1. Students identify situations at school that lead to them being angry (such as failing a test, losing their homework, being bullied, etc.). Keep a list of the responses.

2. After choosing ten of the most typical responses provided in #1 by your students, read each of these ten responses one at a time with your students, as individuals, giving a ranking from #1 to 10 for each response in terms of how angry it makes them (#1 being not very angry with 10 being extremely angry).

3. After you have read all ten responses and your students have written a personal ranking score for each response, tell your students to each add their scores. Students with high scores (this is out of 100) tend to be the students who are prone to anger. It would be interesting to collect each student's rankings and compare their self-assessments to your own perceptions of their tendency to become angry. For any students with very high scores, it is recommended that you share this information with a school counselor.

> "For every minute that you are angry you lose sixty seconds of happiness."
> Ralph Waldo Emerson

ACTIVITY 119

WHAT DO YOU DO WHEN YOU GET ANGRY?

1. Using the anger causing situations identified in Activity #118, tell your students to identify various ways they express their anger. It would be useful to keep a list of the results.

2. Discuss how some of the responses in #1 might be considered positive ways to express anger while others might be considered to be negative.

3. In small groups, students create a list of positive ways to express their anger and also a list of negative ways to express their anger.

4. Share and discuss the results from #3.

ACTIVITY 120

THE COST OF ANGER

1. Begin this activity by referring to the list of negative ways to express anger that was formed in Activity #119.

2. Each student completes page 241.

3. Share and discuss the results from #2. It would also be useful to share some of the health problems that can arise from anger.

THE COST OF ANGER

1. Describe some of the things you normally do when you get angry . . .

2. In what ways does your response to anger lead to possible problems with other people . . .

3. Describe an example where the way you expressed your anger hurt another person . . .

4. Describe an example where the way you expressed your anger hurt yourself . . .

5. Describe an example where the way someone else expressed their anger hurt you . . .

ACTIVITY 121

APPROPRIATE WAYS TO EXPRESS YOUR ANGER

1. With reference to Activity #119, once again discuss some positive and appropriate ways to both express and control anger. It is important to stress that feeling angry is "okay" but expressing it in a manner that hurts others or yourself is not okay.

2. In small groups, students prepare a list of suggestions for appropriately dealing with and expressing anger. These suggestions can come from #1 and from the quotes and tips on page 243 + 244.

3. Share the results from #2 and post a list of these suggestions somewhere in your room.

ACTIVITY 122

RELAXATION TECHNIQUES

When people feel tense or overly stressed, it is easier to get angry and to express it in inappropriate ways. Teaching your students some breathing and relaxation techniques could be a valuable exercise for individual students and your class as a whole. As there are so many possibilities of things to do in this regard, there is no specific plan given here although there are some relaxation tips on page 245.

Once you have taught your students some relaxation techniques, it would be useful to have them practice these techniques before writing a test, or during any times when stress and/or conflict has occurred in your classroom.

ANGER MANAGEMENT QUOTES

"Don't hold on to anger, hurt or pain. They steal your energy and keep you from love."
Leo Buscaglia

"I will permit no man to degrade my soul by hating him."
Booker T. Washington

"Anger is like a stone thrown into a wasp's nest."
Anonymous

"When you are angry count to 10 before you speak.
If you are very angry, count to 100."
Thomas Jefferson

"If you are patient in one moment of anger, you will escape a 100 days of sorrow."
Chinese Proverb

"Anger makes you smaller,
while forgiveness forces you to grow beyond what you were."
Cherie Carter-Scott

"Speak when you are angry
and you will make the best speech that you will ever regret."
Dr. L. J. Peter

"For every minute that you are angry you lose 60 seconds of happiness."
Emerson

"The more anger towards the past you carry in your heart,
the less capable you are of loving in the present."
Barbara De Angelis

"If you are angry, remember this.
This best cure for a short temper is a long walk."
Anonymous

"What I've learned about being angry with others
is that it generally hurts you more than it hurts them."
Oprah

ANGER MANAGEMENT TIPS

1. Learn to recognize the things that result in you becoming angry.

2. There are both healthy and unhealthy ways to express your anger.

3. Remember that how you express your anger is your choice.

4. Going for a walk or exercising can be a healthy way to deal with some of your anger.

5. Keeping your anger inside can be an unhealthy way to deal with your anger.

6. When you have choices, if you decide not to decide, then others will be making your choices for you and this can result in anger.

7. Talking about your anger with a trusted friend, a counselor or a teacher can be a healthy way to deal with anger.

8. If you say something inappropriate in a moment of anger, apologize.

9. Focus on remaining calm.

10. Take deep breaths.

11. Learn some relaxation techniques.

12. Be cool.

13. Count to ten or even one-hundred.

14. It's not worth the hassle to get angry.

15. You can always walk away rather than losing control.

16. It's better to listen than to say something without thinking.

17. You can state how you feel without yelling or screaming.

18. Even though you are angry you can choose to respond in a calm voice.

19. You can handle this without it turning into an argument or fight.

20. Try to understand the other person's point of view before you present what you think or feel.

RELAXATION TECHNIQUES

1. Listen to music that helps you to relax.

2. Focus on a calming picture (perhaps a beautiful scene) and learn to recall this picture in your mind when you need a quiet moment.

3. Go for a walk or engage in some other form of exercise.

4. Breath slowly and deeply for a few minutes.

5. Picture yourself doing something that brings you happiness and contentment, or actually do this thing.

6. Focus on tightening any muscles that are tense and then relax them. Repeat this several times.

7. Talk to someone who listens extremely well and who you trust about anything that is bothering you.

8. Get more sleep each night.

9. Organize your school work in a manner so that you know exactly when assignments are due. Set up a step-by-step schedule for working on major projects so that you don't leave these to the last minute which increases stress for you.

10. Set aside a few times throughout the day when you pause and relax.

11. Improve your posture. Smile.

12. Avoid eating junk food with artificial ingredients and high sugar content.

13. Eat slowly and avoid watching TV as you are eating.

14. Use all your senses to experience the best of the world around you.

15. Read books, articles, or watch videos related to learning relaxation techniques.

ACTIVITY 123

RELAXATION QUOTES

Using the quotes on page 247 or having the students research related quotes, each student should select a quote related to relaxation that is meaningful to them. It is recommended that your students create a poster that focuses on their quote. Posters could be shared and displayed in a prominent place in the classroom. Another option would be for students to create a business card sized copy of the quote that they could carry with them.

ACTIVITY 124

ANGER ROLE-PLAYING

1. An effective way for your students to demonstrate their learning in this chapter would be for them to role-play typical situations that generally provoke anger (such as those identified in Activity #118). It is recommended that your students form small groups with each group preparing a skit that demonstrates an inappropriate way to express anger and then a second skit showing an appropriate way to express anger in the same situation.

2. Students present their skits and the results are discussed.

RELAXATION QUOTES

"No matter how much pressure you feel, if you could find ways to relax
for five minutes every hour, you would be more productive."
Dr. Joyce Brothers

"To have less stress, take time to relax."
Catherine Pulsifer

"The time to relax is when you don't have time for it."
Sydney J. Harris

"Learning to ignore things is one of the great paths to inner peace."
Robert J. Sawyer

"For fast-acting relief, try slowing down."
Lily Tomlin

"How beautiful it is to do nothing and then to rest afterward."
Spanish Proverb

"Sometimes the most important thing in a day
is the rest we take between two deep breaths."
Etty Hillesum

"Relaxation means releasing all concerns and tension
and letting the natural order of life flow through one's being."
Donald Curtis

"Don't hurry, don't worry.
You're only here for a short visit so be sure to stop and smell the flowers."
Walter Hagen

"The real beauty of realizing your true nature is in the freshness,
peace and deep bodily relaxation which touches to the core of
your being, flows into your everyday life and bursts forth naturally
into blossoming from within itself.
Without you 'doing' a thing about any of it."
Julie Sarah Powell

ACTIVITY 125

ANGER MANAGEMENT REVIEW

1. Students complete page 249. It is recommended that you collect the results and provide individual feedback to students.

2. Another way to review the content of this chapter would be to refer back to Activity #118, once again having students identify some of the things that make them angry. Taking the 4 - 5 major things that students identify, divide your class into 4 - 5 groups with each group being formed by students who have identified a common thing that makes them angry.

3. Each group then develops a list of recommended appropriate ways to deal with their anger. Share the results.

> "We cannot make children think, feel, or be a certain way, but we can be firm, consistent, and clear about what behavior we will and will not tolerate, and what the consequences are for misbehaviour."
> Dr. Harriet Lerner in *The Dance of Anger,* 2002

ANGER MANAGEMENT REVIEW

Three things that generally make me angry are . . .

    1)

    2)

    3)

Three things I can do to relax more when I am beginning to feel some stress are . . .

    1)

    2)

    3)

Two positive ways for me to express my anger when I am upset are . . .

    1)

    2)

"When we are no longer able
to change a situation,
we are challenged
to change ourselves."
Victor Frankl

CHAPTER 9

SPECIFIC DISCIPLINE STRATEGIES

So far, this book has presented many tips and strategies that can be used to create a classroom environment that is more conducive to learning and to respond in a positive manner to conflicts that might occur. This chapter continues in an attempt to help you with behavioral problems that might occur in your classroom. While this theme has already been the focus of much of this book, the emphasis in this chapter will be on helping you to establish a plan that you can use on a regular basis to respond to behavioral problems. Although there may be many times when a non-verbal look that tells a student his behavior is inappropriate or a few words expressed assertively might stop the misbehavior, a question you might have wondered about is what do you do next when your first intervention with a student doesn't stop the misbehavior.

> "In general, discipline interventions resulted in a decrease of almost 80% in disruptive behavior."
> Scott Stage, David Quiroz (1997)
> from a meta-analysis that included 99 studies,
> 200 experimental comparisons, and more than 5,000 students

This chapter will first of all look at a model you can implement with four action steps. This model gives you a framework to use in working with students. Once you have mastered such a model, it can become a less stressful and more effective experience for you in correcting classroom misbehavior. Next, an overview will be provided of some programs that have proven to be effective in schools in reducing misbehavior (and often increasing student success). Some of these strategies can be used by individual teachers while others are better employed as part of a school-wide program.

1. A DISCIPLINE MODEL

In observing other teachers, I have sometimes witnessed a classroom scenario that plays out something like this. A teacher tells a student to "stop talking". The student nods as though he understands the request, but then he continues to talk to his friends. The teacher once again speaks to the student who may momentarily stop whatever he is doing that is inappropriate but then quickly resumes his misbehavior. The teacher once again tells the student to stop talking, this time raising her voice. Once again the student initially appears to respond to the request but then quickly continues his behavior, this time groaning sarcastically at the teacher as though she is being unfair. The teacher continues to tell the student to stop, at which time the student responds saying that she is being unfair as other students are also talking. An argument ensues between the teacher and the student. Their voices grow in intensity. The rest of the class stops working and begins to watch in earnest to see how this confrontation will play out. The teacher shouts louder. The student swears at the teacher. The teacher gives the student a detention. The student swears again and says he doesn't care. The student shoves his books on the floor and looks at the teacher in a completely non-respectful manner. The teacher responds by sending the student to the office. Does any of this sound familiar to you?

Discipline needs to be consistent, fair and follow a process that you are comfortable with and that your students understand. The above description of a conflict between a student and a teacher is disruptive to teaching and creates stress (most often for the teacher and for some students who are completely uninvolved in the conflict). It is also important to recognize that in the above example, and you may have experienced similar situations, whatever the teacher is doing is not working. An important aspect of being effective in the classroom is self-evaluating what you are doing and asking yourself what worked and what didn't work (and whatever didn't work, don't repeat this again and whatever worked, build on this strategy in the future). Unfortunately some teachers use the same discipline approach day after day and week after week even though the approach only ends in arguments, increased stress and time taken away from actually teaching. Albert Einstein defined insanity as doing the same thing over and over and expecting a different result. If you want a different result, then you have to change whatever it is that you are doing.

A four-step discipline model that many teachers have found effective, and that you can modify to suit your teaching style, is as follows:

i) Use non-verbal cues to stop misbehavior or reinforce appropriate behavior.

ii) Verbally remind your student(s) of the expected behavior.

iii) State an appropriate consequence if the misbehavior continues.

iv) Take action.

The following provides a further description of each of these steps. One of the keys here is that you consistently follow these four steps. When there is a specific pattern to your discipline approach your students will learn this and understand that you will apply some form of consequence if the behavior does not improve. It is this consistent structure paired with action and consequences that provides a framework for effective discipline.

i) Use non-verbal cues to stop misbehavior or reinforce appropriate behavior

One of the problems in verbally confronting a student on her inappropriate behavior is that every other student in the class is instantly aware of your request. Unfortunately, the misbehaving student in an attempt to "save face" with her peers may go to great lengths to defend herself (and even verbally attack you). One of the best solutions to this is to begin with a non-verbal approach. Non-verbal cues include things such as eye-contact, a frown of disapproval, a smile of approval (to encourage appropriate behavior), or even physical proximity. The advantage of all these non-verbal approaches is that other students are not disturbed and many times the other students do not even know that you have used them. In these situations the student being disciplined does not have the same immediate need to react negatively to you because there is no audience to "feed" her reaction.

To help you be more effective in using non-verbal cues, it is important to consider your physical location in the classroom. If your desk is at the back of the room you have taken away this wonderful approach whenever you are seated at your desk. If your students sit in groups in a manner that it is awkward for some of them to face you when you are teaching, once again you have put yourself at a disadvantage in using this approach. As you teach, and as you move around the classroom, keep in mind that being able to see the greatest number of students face to face is an important consideration in using non-verbal cues to either stop misbehavior or reinforce appropriate behavior.

While the "teacher stare" is something that every student is familiar with by grade 5, and this non-verbal technique can be very effective in correcting misbehavior, it is also important to remember that a smile of approval can also be a very important non-verbal cue to use in the classroom. Smiling often is likely a much more pleasant, and less stressful, manner to all in the classroom (including yourself) than is constantly staring daggers and frowning at your students.

In thinking about non-verbal cues, remember that you are always communicating whether you are speaking or not. As such, you might ask whether you are non-verbally tending to encourage your students or are you creating an environment, perhaps without even realizing it, that stifles risk-taking, creativity and the resulting learning? Similarly, as you become more aware of your own non-verbal communications (which might even require you to have someone visually record what you do are doing as a teacher or provide some feedback to you on what you are doing), you will also find it helpful to learn to pay close attention to the non-verbal behavior of your students. There may be times in which some of your students may be expressing anxiety or discomfort in understanding what you are teaching (even if they are reluctant to state it verbally) through their non-verbal behavior. This could include lack of eye contact, slouching in his seat, putting his head on his desk, some form of nervous twitching, tapping his feet, and so on. In fact, misbehavior itself can even be a form of a non-verbal response that is the result of frustration in understanding what you are teaching.

When you are disciplining your students, paying attention to their non-verbal cues (such as the crossing of arms, looking away, frowning, hanging head, etc.) may all indicate something the student is feeling but not verbally expressing. Paying attention to non-verbal cues can help you to be more effective in teaching and in your classroom management.

Keep in mind as well that the effectiveness of your non-verbal cues (as will also be explained in steps #2 + 3 of this model) is directly dependent on actually taking action (step #4 in this process) and applying some consequences for inappropriate behavior (or rewarding appropriate behavior). Without the application of appropriate consequences at some point, steps #1 - 3 in this process become meaningless. The consistent and fair application of consequences early in the school year can help to enhance the impact of the use of your non-verbal cues throughout the remainder of the year (as well as enhancing what you do related to both steps #2 + 3 in this process).

ii) **Verbally remind your student(s) of the expected behavior.**

If your non-verbal cues are not effective in stopping misbehavior then you proceed on to the next step which is verbally reminding your students of the expected behavior. In most cases, this verbal reminder should refer to a classroom rule or procedure. Research has shown that when you add the "because" to your demands you will be more successful in getting what you want. In other words when you say something like "Stop talking because this will help everyone in our class to focus on their work", this is more effective than simply saying "Stop talking". In stating the because it is important that your reason for your demand makes sense and is fair.

> "Adding 'because' (to your requests) increases the likelihood of cooperation from 60 - 90%."
> Ellen Langer, social psychologist

In reminding your students of the appropriate behavior, some students might better respond when you state something along the lines of "Stop talking because you are preventing others from listening to me," while other students might better respond by saying "By listening more carefully to what I am saying, you and others in our class will increase your learning". Both messages are aimed at telling the student to stop talking but their approach is slightly different (one a little more negatively focused while the other is a little more positively focused). Either message can be effective, but the key here is that their effectiveness may vary from student to student. As you observe what works and what doesn't work in your verbal reminders to students this can help you to apply the most effective responses to individual students. An important aspect of being perceived as being fair by your students in this regard is to remain calm, but be firm and assertive, in whichever approach you are using.

In any step in disciplining your students, you want to avoid getting into an argument with your students. This is particularly important during this step. You are simply reminding a student of your expectations. This is not open to discussion or debate. In most situations you are simply reminding a student of a class rule that was at some earlier time introduced into your class along with its rationale. The exception to this might be if it is early in the school year and the student in a calm manner is expressing a desire to better understand the rule.

iii) State an appropriate consequence if the misbehavior continues.

In the early weeks of a school year, this might be the most important step in disciplining students. Very quickly your students will learn whether you are simply going to keep "talking" or whether you are actually going to take "action" whenever you face misbehavior in the classroom. Action occurs in the form of consequences. Without fair, consistent consequences, most teachers find that discipline problems become overwhelming in their room (unless of course the whole class is motivated to learn and/or the teacher has a teaching style that is exceptional in engaging students in learning, and either or both of these things can happen).

While most teachers believe that consequences are important in correcting misbehavior, the real question becomes which consequences are most effective and also which consequences are most manageable. For example, a detention after school might work very well in one school, while in another school if the students have to take a bus to get home, then this option becomes impractical. Just like there is appropriate and inappropriate behavior, there are also appropriate and inappropriate consequences.

> "Interventions that do not include consequences (either positive or negative) have the lowest effect."
> Stage and Quiroz, 1997

In looking at consequences, it is important to remember that consequences can be categorized as either positive or negative, and that both forms have a place in disciplining students. Some forms of positive consequences might include things like praise, marks, token rewards, fun activities, games and any other type of recognition. Some forms of negative consequences might include detentions, calling the parents, time-out, separation from others involved in this misbehavior, loss of token rewards, missing the opportunity to engage in fun activities or games, etc. Interestingly what works for one student may be different for another (which can present a very real challenge for you in being perceived as "fair" when you enforce consequences).

The following provides an example of a list that shows how students rank negative consequences for their behavior. The important thing here is that consequences can be perceived differently although the top ranked consequences have all been chosen by the greatest number of students. It would be a useful activity to provide this list of consequences to your students (and any other consequences that you employ) and have each student rank them. Collect the results and you will then have a very quick way of knowing which consequences would be most effective to use with each of your students.

NEGATIVE CONSEQUENCES RANKED BY STUDENTS
(Grade 7 + 8 students, Brian Harris, 1998)

1. Teacher telephones their parents.
2. Having a lunch-time detention.
3. Teacher tells them what they are doing wrong in front of their peers.
4. Being sent to the office.
5. Having to work in an alternate location.

I think it would be useful to provide some further thoughts on these results. First of all, keep in mind that one of the key points that is being made here is not necessarily how these research results apply to your students, but rather that there are some types of negative consequences that will work better for your class as a whole than others and that there are also some types of negative consequences that will work better for some individuals than others. In one grade seven class that I taught, and in a small school situation where I taught this class almost all their subjects, every Friday afternoon for the last ninety minutes we first played some quiz-related games based on the content of our curriculum throughout the week. Then we spent some time playing various games in the gym. This ninety minute period of fun (although the first forty-five minutes was strongly curriculum based and the second forty-five minutes tied in with some aspects of the physical education curriculum) became such an important time for the students that it quickly became the most powerful form of either positive or negative consequence for the students. Whenever a student misbehaved, and as a result was taking time away from learning, this student was penalized an appropriate period of time (minimum five minutes) for our Friday end of day fun time. This student would then watch, but not participate, for a specific period of time. Once my students realized this consequence was going to be enforced, a simple warning that misbehavior would result in a time penalty for our Friday afternoon time of fun was almost always enough of a deterrent to immediately correct the inappropriate behavior. This form of consequence doesn't appear in the list of page 257 simply because the classes that were surveyed did not have some similar system used by any of their teachers.

In looking at the results on pages 257, there are a few other comments I would like to make as well. First of all, you will note two of the standard negative forms of consequences that are frequently used by teachers on this list. They are telephoning the student's parents and sending a student to the office. There are a few things to consider here. While these tend to be negative consequences that can assist in the discipline of some students, their effectiveness is also related to the reaction (and support) of either the parents and your principal (or vice-principal). For some kids, a telephone call to a parent is a joke and for some kids (in some schools) being sent to the office is actually an attention-getting reward rather than a punishment. The point here is that you need to know (through observation) whether these consequences really make a difference for the student whose behavior you are trying to correct. Secondly, there are only so many times you can continue to telephone the student's parents or send him to the office before the parent and/or the administrator become weary of being your negative consequence. In other words, even though these techniques can certainly work (and having a student's parents support you in what you are trying to do in a classroom can be very important), these are two consequences that should be used sparingly and my experience would strongly suggest that there are other consequences that you should look at first.

We are then left with three areas of negative consequences: one related to detentions, one related to some public form of discipline, and the final one (from the list on page 257) being related to some form of time-out. Let's look at each of these techniques and add another one to the list. First, let's consider the technique I would add. This strategy is a face-to-face interview with a student, at the end of a class (when almost everyone else has left the room), to assertively present your concerns. This meeting should focus on why the behavior is inappropriate (and should not be a personal attack on the student). During this talk you should provide a clear statement of what you expect and what the consequence will be if this misbehavior continues. This form of intervention is not included on the list on page 257 simply because it was a technique that was rarely used by any of the teachers whose classes were involved in this survey. My experience is that this one-to-one interview is often very effective. First of all, the other students are aware that you have told the student to "remain behind" for a few minutes. This lets everyone know that you are serious about your expectations and that there will be consequences when expectations are not met. Secondly, this form of intervention does not take away from class learning time and in a sense the mystery of what is going to happen can often decrease any further forms of misbehavior for the remainder of the class. Another advantage of this approach is that you have demonstrated respect for the student (which often results in your class have greater respect for you).

Next, let's look at the use of detentions. A detention can be seen as a logical consequence for a student who is wasting class time. For example, a student comes in ten minutes late and as a result will need to make up this ten minutes of time missed. Or, a student's inappropriate behavior takes ten minutes away from a lesson therefore the student will make up this time. There a few aspects of detentions that I would like to comment on further. In a very real sense here, the consequence is related to time. In my experience, this "time" form of consequence works best when the detention time is directly related to the time wasted. In other words, if a student is ten minutes late to class, a one hour detention often generates anger that fuels further conflict. For most students, a ten minute detention can be just as effective as some longer arbitrary figure and it has the advantage of being easy to enforce (remember, you are also giving up your time when you have to supervise students you have given detentions to). In addition, if you decide to use detentions as a form of a negative consequence, it is important for you to be aware of practical realities such as busing, noon-hour or after school meetings for you or activities for the student. A detention needs to be practical. Like any other negative consequence, you need to think it through before you take action. In some schools, detentions can be very effective in helping to correct inappropriate behavior while in other schools they can become a nightmare to enforce. Related to detentions, you should also look at my comments on "detention rooms" on page 276.

Another form of negative consequence from page 257 is the "time-out" or working in another location. As this is discussed in more detail on page 276, for now let me reiterate some of my comments that were suggested when you consider detentions as a form of discipline. Lengthy time-outs can be counter-productive if students return from the time-out seething with anger. As much as possible, keep the length of a time-out appropriate to the length of time wasted by the student. Similar to detentions, there is a practical reality component of a time-out. You need to know where the student will go for the time-out (this is often simply a seat that is away from others in the room although this is obviously limited by the size of your classroom and the number of students that you have). As well, if your student is actually leaving your room to spend the time-out in some other room, supervision for the student is paramount. The last thing you ever want to do is to send an angry student unsupervised into another area of the school. Some schools have established specific protocols for time-outs.

Finally, from the list of negative consequences on page 257, is telling your students what they are doing wrong, in front of their peers. This is probably the most common form of discipline that occurs in many classes. While this can certainly be an effective form of discipline (and one that most students will frequently identify as an effective form of discipline), there are a few dangers as well as benefits. Telling a student what is expected (in terms of behavior) is one of the most immediate forms of discipline and there is something to be said about consequences being immediate. Another benefit is that this form of consequence can be applied quickly and your class can move on with their lesson. And most teachers who use this type of negative consequence would argue that it is effective because it serves to remind everyone in your class that there are expectations and standards that need to be followed.

On the negative side of this approach is the reality that a student may feel embarrassed in front of his peers (which is one of the reasons this approach may work). The problem with this is that embarrassing students can undermine your efforts to establish a positive classroom environment where students feel comfortable (and safe). Without this comfort, students will tend to resist doing anything that may result in making a "mistake". When students avoid taking chances, this can stifle their learning. In addition, while this approach can work with most students, there are some students who thrive on gaining attention by being involved in the drama of conflicts. A public reprimand for misbehavior with these students may lead to a confrontation that becomes a major distraction to your teaching, sometimes leaving you and some of your students anxious, and sometimes escalating to the point where for all intensive purposes your lesson is finished for the period (and you may be finished for the day). Having said this, the reality is that it would be very difficult to discipline students without this ever occurring in front of their peers. Most of the time it would simply be impractical to always be waiting to find an appropriate time and place to talk to a student further about his misbehavior. It is therefore important to consider a few guidelines that can help you to be effective in disciplining your students while lowering the risk of either embarrassing them or causing a situation where they feel compelled to fight back.

Some important aspects of telling a student what he is doing wrong are being calm, assertive and factual. The moment you become emotional and/or you are perceived as attacking the student rather than the problem, you may be setting the stage for a conflict that will escalate. If you sense this is beginning to happen, you may have to "bite your tongue" for the moment and find an alternate way to deal with the inappropriate behavior (remember the strategies provided in Chapter 7 on conflict resolution). If your approach in disciplining your students is consistent then you will likely be perceived as being fair which is important to your students. There is a huge difference between personally attacking a student in a manner that degrades him and calmly, but directly telling him that a specific aspect of his behavior is not in keeping with classroom expectations. It is also important to remember that your non-verbal language may be conveying a message that is quite different than your words. If you think you are approaching your students in a calm, assertive manner, but you seem to be constantly finding that these situations turn into unacceptable responses from your students, it may be that the tone of your voice or body language or even the message conveyed through your facial expressions is sending a different message than you are intending. It this is the case, it might be useful to have another colleague observe your interactions with students and give you some feedback.

Another aspect of verbally disciplining your students in front of their peers is that this often becomes both steps #3 and 4 in the action process. Your verbal response may in itself become both the warning and the negative consequence. This may be especially true when your students learn that your verbal warning (step #3) will be followed with a specific consequence for misbehavior (step #4). For many students, it will not take very long before your verbal disciplining will be all that is required to keep these students on-task. These students have learned that even though you may not have stated the consequence that will result for misbehavior, it is implied because your students are familiar with you following through on your warnings from previous occasions. A polite, firm, calm, assertive verbal correction may be one of the most effective forms of classroom management. Essential for this to work is your consistency in using this method, your respectful manner in applying it, and your demonstrated willingness to apply appropriate consequences (step #4) if need be.

> "The presence of disruptive students can have negative effects on their own and all other students' achievement outcomes. Thus, reducing disruptive behaviors needs to be a core competency of any successful teacher."
> John Hattie in *Visible Learning - A Synthesis of over 800 Meta-Analyses Relating To Achievement*, 2009

> "The two biggest discipline mistakes are
> too much talking and too much emotion."
> Thomas Phelan, Ph.D., and Sarah Jane Schonour, M.A. in *1-2-3 Magic,* 2004

In disciplining your students you need to make your expectations clear and state them only once. If you continually state the same expectations over and over without any immediate consequences, your students will quickly learn that you are a "talker" rather than a "doer". Students tend to disregard talkers because they realize that the only consequence to what is being said is simply a continuation of what is being said. In fact, there are some students who love to "bait" teachers who are talkers for amusement and attention. Critical to effective classroom management are appropriate consequences. Taking too long or being too "wordy" before applying the consequences permits misbehavior to continue for longer than need be.

> "Remember that 7% of your impact comes
> from the words that you say,
> 38% from your tonal quality while saying it, and
> 55% from what your body is doing while you say it."
> Frances Cole Jones in *How To Wow,* 2008

Discipline, which has been previously defined in this book as a form of correcting, a way of helping students to learn appropriate behavior, can also employ positive consequences in order to be effective. The following provides an example of a list that shows how students rank positive consequences for their behavior. Similar to the previous thoughts on negative consequences, it is important to recognize that consequences can be perceived differently by each of your students although the top ranked consequences have all been chosen by the greatest number of students in this survey. Also, similar to the previous suggestion on negative consequences it would be a useful activity to provide this list of consequences to your students and have them rank the consequences in order of importance to them (and also add any other possible consequences to the list).

POSITIVE CONSEQUENCES RANKED BY STUDENTS
(Grade 7 + 8 students, Brian Harris, 1998)

1. Good marks
2. Telephone call home to parents
3. Praise in front of peers
4. Positive feedback written on assignments
5. Public recognition outside the classroom

Before proceeding to provide some additional thoughts on each of these consequences, it is important to recognize that these are a reflection of what occurred in one school. While they may be an indication of what might happen in other schools, there are definitely other forms of positive consequences that could be on this list. In reading on, consider how the intent of some of these consequences may also apply to some of the unique positive consequences that may occur in your classroom or school. For example, I previously shared (see page 257) how a Friday afternoon fun activity session could be used as a negative consequence (by taking time away from this fun time for any students who had "wasted" time during the week). The flip side of this example is that it could also be argued that this fun activity could be considered a positive consequence as it is a reward for students who behave appropriately during the week. Similarly, some other forms of negative consequences (poor marks as an example) often have a positive counterpart (good marks as an example). An important consideration related to classroom management (with the ultimate goal of establishing a welcoming positive learning environment) is the amount of time you may focus on negative consequences for inappropriate behavior compared to positive consequences for appropriate behavior. While some students might respond better to negative consequences (forms of punishment) while others might respond better to positive consequences (rewards), you would likely agree that your classroom would be more a more pleasurable and comfortable place to be if the emphasis was more reward focused than punishment focused. If it seems that you are generally disciplining your students with the use of negative consequences (which can be stressful), it might be useful for you to consider how you might shift towards the use of more positive consequences in helping your students to learn and demonstrate appropriate behavior.

In looking once again at the list of positive consequences that is provided on page 263, you will note that the students identified good marks as the number one form of a positive consequence for appropriate behavior (in this particular school). This is a result that could likely be replicated in many schools as students frequently identify doing well in school as a number one source of feeling good about themselves (which generally translates into better behavior). In addition, it makes logical sense that if a class is well behaved then more learning should be occurring as a result of more time on-task, and more learning should be contributing to better marks. There will be additional information provided on this in Chapter 10, but for now you might simply ask yourself how your misbehaving students are doing in terms of their learning in your subject area as measured by their marks. Your answer to this question might direct you to Chapter 10 for further help and understanding in this area.

> "Be an encourager. A lift-up brings students to life; a put-down destroys spirit."
> George M. Gazda in *Human Relations Development, A Manual For Educators*, 2005

During a recent school year one of my daughters who was in grade 5 did some particularly good work which was recognized by her teacher. The teacher then asked her what other form of recognition she would enjoy receiving. Her answer was a telephone call home to her parents. As previously mentioned, sometimes the flip-side of a negative consequence can become a positive consequence. While telephoning parents to inform them of inappropriate behavior can be effective, similarly telephoning parents to report appropriate behavior (or other forms of excellence) can also be effective. Back in Chapter 1, I mentioned the importance of making contact early in the school year with parents. Keep in mind that some parents may have never received a positive telephone call from a teacher so this can be an effective way of encouraging more positive behavior in your class. In addition, when you telephone a student's parents to report appropriate behavior (and/or excellence), you are sending a clear message to all your students that you are a fair person who considers and makes use of both positive and negative consequences for classroom behavior. I have witnessed some dramatic changes to the good in classroom behavior from students as the result of a positive telephone call home to their parents, and for students like my daughter who were already conscientious, the call becomes the icing on the cake.

Next, in looking at the list of positive consequences on page 263, you will see that the students identified praise in front of their peers as something desired. As noted in the previous examples, once again the opposite of a negative consequence (verbally correcting their behavior in front of their peers) can become a positive consequence. There is a saying that when you pay attention to something you tend to get more of the same thing. If you pay most of your attention to inappropriate behavior you will tend to get more of the same. If you pay most of you attention to appropriate behavior you will also tend to get more of the same. Doesn't it make more sense and wouldn't it be more welcoming in your classroom to go out of your way to recognize and praise appropriate behavior to get more of the same?

An important aspect of praising students (which is also important if you are verbally correcting their behavior) is to focus on using specific feedback. Simply telling a student that he is good or his behavior is good is vague. Feedback is much more effective when you are specific. Instead of just saying that your behavior is good, it is far more effective to say something like "I really like how you immediately started to get your work done", or "I think it's terrific when you have all your materials out and ready as I am beginning my lesson." Note the use of "I" in these sentences and to make them even stronger, consider adding the "because". When you add the because to the previous two sentences they would become "I really like how you immediately started to get your work done because this helps everyone to focus on getting their work done as well," or "I think it's terrific when you have all your materials out and ready as I am beginning my lesson because this makes it easier for me to teach you."

> "Feedback is the breakfast of champions."
> Ken Blanchard

On page 266 are some tips related to giving effective feedback to your students. Keep in mind that reinforcement (for example, praise) is more effective when it is random, when it is deserved, and when it is specific. Kids will very quickly "tune out" a teacher who is constantly saying "good, terrific, wonderful, awesome," etc. even though the praise may be unwarranted. Recognizing your students for excellence helps to breed further excellence; recognizing your students for mediocrity will only inspire more of the same.

TIPS FOR GIVING EFFECTIVE FEEDBACK

1. For feedback to be effective, it must be specific rather than general.

2. Effective feedback focuses on specific behavior rather than some aspect of the person.

3. Feedback is more effective when it is immediate. This includes marking student work. It is unfair to expect students to submit their work on time and then you take an inappropriate amount of time to mark it.

4. Feedback is more effective when it is genuine. Students know when you really care about them.

5. Effective feedback provides your observations, not your advice.

6. Effective feedback begins with "I" and somewhere in the middle has the word "because".

7. Effective feedback includes the how, when, where, and why.

8. Feedback is for everyone, not just those who beg you for it.

9. Be consistent in your emotional tone in giving feedback.

10. Feedback is more effective when the person receiving it is actually capable of doing something about it.

Fourth on the list of positive consequences was positive feedback written on assignments. The intent here is exactly the same as the comments on pages 265 + 266 related to feedback. Simply giving a student a mark or a word comment on any assignment does not reinforce what they have done well or help them to improve what they have failed to master. Effective written feedback on any assignment is one of the most important steps in a learning process. Some teachers require students to have major tests or assignments signed by their parents/guardians. Detailed feedback on such assignments helps parents to better understand your expectations on how their child is doing in meeting these expectations. When students do not receive this specific feedback, they can experience frustration and sometimes even harbor anger at a teacher for being indifferent to an assignment they worked so hard on completing. This frustration and anger can lead to behavioral problems in your classroom as well as discouraging students from doing their best. What is the value of striving for excellence when the teacher as the classroom leader fails to support and recognize such excellence? Similarly, how can students improve if they don't know exactly what they have to improve? Effective teaching, as explained further in Chapter 10, includes modeling excellence, and feedback on assignments is an opportunity to demonstrate what excellence looks like.

> "In most situations, praise and criticism may refer to routine, almost mechanical pronouncements of "good" or "no, you're wrong".
> This kind of feedback is not informative to the student; consequently, it may have no impact on the child beyond the realization that he or she got the answer right or wrong."
> Harris and Rosenthal, 1985

In looking at the above research finding, Harris and Rosenthal after examining 135 studies related to the effects of expectations on behavior also noted that the content of feedback might be more important than its frequency, timing, or simple positive versus negative nature.

Finally, from the list on page 263 (and once again it is important to recognize that these are not the only forms of positive consequences that can be used within a classroom), the students identified public recognition as another form of a positive consequence. For these students, public recognition included the posting of excellent work on a classroom or hallway bulletin board, recognition by the principal, a certificate of some sort presented at an assembly or parent evening, a listing in a school newsletter or on a school website, inclusion in a morning or afternoon school wide announcement, etc. In providing any of these forms of public recognition, once again it is important to apply the guidelines on the previous three pages related to providing effective feedback.

> "The first time a student misbehaves he or she should be warned. The second time, his or her parents should be called by the teacher. The third time, the student should be sent to the principal's office.
> Grade 7 Student

In the above quote from a grade 7 student, you can see that even students understand that there should be some progression of steps and consequences for misbehavior. So far, this chapter has been presenting a four-step model that you can apply when it is necessary to discipline your students. First, you looked at using non-verbal cues to stop the misbehavior or to encourage the appropriate behavior. Second, the model recommended that as a next step you verbally remind your student(s) of the appropriate consequence if the misbehavior continues. The third step, that you have just looked at, considers the need to state an appropriate consequences (either positive or negative). Finally, the step that underscores all the others is to take action. Without action to enforce your consequences your efforts at classroom management will be ineffective.

iv) Take action

Recently, as I stood in the line at a local grocery store, I heard a desperate mother tell her two young children that if they didn't stop misbehaving they would not be going to Disneyworld during their spring break. The mother repeated her warning at least ten times to no avail. I told this story recently as I was conducting a workshop for a group of teachers and everyone very quickly identified the flaws in what the mother was doing. "Her demands were unreasonable," one teacher said. "There was no way the mother was going to cancel this trip because her kids were out-of-control in a grocery store." Another teacher stated "It will never work to keep warning kids of a consequence if you are not actually prepared to take it." And another replied "All talk, no action, no results."

Throughout this book you have been looking at strategies and techniques for improving classroom management. One of the most important elements of effective classroom management relates to your use of consequences. Like the grocery store example provided above, unless you take action and follow through on your warnings, your students will be like the out-of-control kids in the store. Without action on your part, there will be no listening on their part. And unless your consequences are appropriate and enforceable, then they will become as meaningless as the threat to take away a trip to Disneyworld (which everyone in the grocery store knew was never going to happen).

There are four factors to consider in applying consequences as part of your discipline approach in classroom management. The four factors are as follows:

a) consequences need to be appropriate
b) consequences need to be consistent
c) consequences need to be enforceable
d) consequences need to be applied

Let's look briefly at each of these factors

a) Consequences need to be appropriate

It is likely that you have heard the term "logical consequences" before. A logical consequence is directly related to the behavior you are trying to either correct or reinforce. Another way to state that a consequence is logical is to say that it is appropriate. For example, a student comes in late or wastes time in class. An appropriate consequence in such a situation would be for the student to "make up" the time that was missed. On the other hand another student uses his time in a very meaningful manner. A consequence for such behavior might be to give this student a reward of some "free time" to do some fun activity. Similarly, a student involved in fighting might receive some form of "community service" within the school to help others. Along the same lines, a student who writes graffiti on a desk might have an appropriate consequence of cleaning the desk (and perhaps another one as well). These are examples of consequences that are appropriate to the behavior.

There has been some previous discussion (and examples) in this chapter related to both positive and negative consequences. In addition, there will be additional examples of consequences provided in the next section of this chapter. These examples of consequences can give you some clues as to what you might use with your students. Having a ready-to-use list of consequences related to your classroom rules makes a lot of sense. The rationale for this will be explained further in the next few points.

b) Consequences need to be consistent

If one student comes ten minutes late to class and is given a ten minute detention while another student comes to class ten minutes late and is given a thirty minute detention, this is an example of inconsistent consequences. The result of inconsistency is that you will be perceived as being unfair. The student who received the more severe consequence for the same infraction will likely harbor anger towards you which may result in your discipline being ineffective with this student. Fairness is important to students and being unfair may undermine your efforts to be an effective classroom manager.

c) Consequences need to be enforceable

In the discussion above, it was stated that it makes sense to have a ready-to-use list of consequences related to your classroom rules. A major reason for doing this is that sometimes in the heat of an emotional moment with a student, you might threaten a consequence that is very difficult to enforce. Having a list of possible consequences to choose from can help you to be more realistic when you talk about consequences with any of your students. For example, in a confrontation with a student a teacher might say, "If you don't start behaving, you won't be going on our field trip in three weeks". Unless the teacher is prepared to follow through on this consequence, it can become like the mother warning her children about the Disneyworld trip. In addition, even if you are determined to follow through on your warning, in a sense it is left "hanging" between you and the student for the next three weeks. This creates stress for you and it creates stress for the student, and it can also create stress within the class as other students begin to wonder if they will be added to your "can't go" list. Consequences are more effective when they are enforceable now, not at some later time.

As you consider your ready-to-use list of consequences, choose the ones that both work and are easy for you to implement. Applying consequences, if you are not careful, can sometimes punish you as much as the student. Lunch time detentions, as an example, can require you to be there to supervise the student. Missing your lunch can contribute to you being worn out at the end of the day (more on this in Chapter 11). Don't punish yourself as you attempt to punish a misbehaving student.

d) Consequences need to be applied

In other words, as the Nike slogan states, "just do it". In order to be effective, consequences require action (and this action is not based on "talking more"). It is often very easy to spot a teacher who is an ineffective classroom manager as this person continues to give "warnings" without ever taking action. In this chapter, you have been looking at a four-step discipline process. Remember the saying "three strikes and you're out". In this model, it's three strikes and take action.

You began with a non-verbal warning. You then stated what is expected. Next, you told the student what consequence was going to result if their behavior didn't change (in the case of inappropriate behavior). These are your three warnings. There is no need to repeat any of these steps. At the end of the third step (your third warning), take action. Apply the consequence you talked about in step #3 as calmly and assertively as you can. There is no further discussion or argument.

Once your students learn that you are prepared to move on to step #4 (taking action), you will soon find that the first three steps are far more effective. You will find with many students that the non-verbal cues in step #1 will suddenly be very effective (because students have learned that you are prepared to quickly move to the consequence and action stage of this approach if they do not pay attention to your expectations). Even with the chronically more disruptive students, they will generally be ready to listen to you by the time you reach step #3 because they know that you are quite willing to move on to step #4.

At the moment when you apply a consequence, there may be a further outburst from some students as they express their anger at you (although if you have followed all four steps and you take this approach consistently there will be less anger because your students will be more familiar with the process and there won't be any surprises for them). It is important that this "outburst" doesn't suck you into an argument with a student that escalates the conflict and sometimes even escalates the severity of the consequences. A silent response from you is often your best approach here to let the student "cool" down. At the end of class, you can talk to the student further about what has happened (having taken away his audience and hopefully after his anger has subsided).

In considering consequences, it is an unfortunate reality that you might have some students who simply won't respond to whatever form of consequence you might normally use. The following section in this chapter can provide some further ideas and even more formal programs that some teachers and schools use effectively that may help you with some of these "hard to reach" students. In addition, I can't stress strongly enough that one of the best ways to better understand the use of consequences as they apply to effective classroom management is to talk to experienced teachers in your school concerning what works for them. Learn from those who have been there before.

2. SPECIFIC APPROACHES/PROGRAMS

The following provide some specific approaches, programs and related thoughts that have been used within classrooms and schools to improve student behavior. They are listed in alphabetical order.

i) CASE CONFERENCE
While there are a variety of names that describe this approach, the basic idea is to bring together a student's teachers with other school staff (including but not limited to someone from administration, school social worker or youth counselor, school counselor, sometimes a psychologist, special education teacher, sometimes the parents, etc.) to discuss how to best help this student learn and behave more appropriately. Helping this student then becomes a "team" approach. Any recommended course of action needs to be followed by everyone involved.

As will be discussed further in Chapter 10, it is critical at such meetings that things like the student's reading level and learning style be discussed. Considering one of out every three students entering grade five is behind in expected reading skills, and considering reading is a fundamental contributor to school success, it is no wonder that some students in every class express their academic frustrations through misbehavior.

> "38% of all 4th graders in the U.S.A. read at the 'below basic' level."
> Mike Schmoker in *Results Now: How We Can Achieve Unprecedented Improvements in Learning and Teaching,* 2006

For some misbehaving students the most appropriate consequence that might change their behavior could very well be a remedial program in reading. For others, the most appropriate consequence might be to teach more appropriately to their unique learning style. While it is not within the scope of this book to provide information on remedial reading programs or to identify learning styles, there are experts within most schools and school jurisdictions. Workshops on these topics could be a very wise use of professional development days for school staffs.

In addition to discussing a child's reading ability and learning style, there are some other practical questions to consider such as :

Is there an adult in the building who has a good relationship with this student who could be a mentor for the student?

Is there some extra-curricular activity the student could be involved in to gain some acceptance and pride of being a student in the school?

Is there some form of responsibility that could be given to the student to help him/her gain positive recognition with others?

How can the student's parents be involved in a manner to support what you are trying to do to help this student?

What counseling resources exist that could help the student deal with any personal issues that he or she is carrying into school?

What works?

What is a consistent course of action that all this student's teachers could take when the student is not responding to the usual approaches to behave appropriately?

What are this student's interests and strengths and how could these be used as a foundation for success?

What has already been tried and what were the specific results?

Are there any alternate placements or programs that would better meet the needs of this student?

ii) CHARTING

To help understand the behavior of a student that is frequently inappropriate, it might be helpful to "chart" or keep a record of the inappropriate behavior. Although this may at first seem to be a time-consuming process, if it helps to provide some solutions then in the end it can be well worth it.

The basic premise of charting is that you will record every instance of a student's misbehavior over the period of a week or two. You can do this in some type of table format that shows the time, date, subject content that you were teaching, what the student did, your response, etc.

At the end of the period of time, you then look at your charting for trends. For example, it may be that the student's misbehavior increases near lunch (perhaps the student is hungry and acts out because of this), or the misbehavior occurs during seatwork times (perhaps the student is unsure what to do or is frustrated by the inability to do what is expected), or the misbehavior occurs whenever another student has just been praised for good work, and so on. If you find some trends, this might help you to resolve the behavioral issues with the student.

Another approach is to sit down one-to-one (in private) with the student at the end of the period of time and show her the results. Perhaps the student might be able to help you to understand the trends. If you are unable to come to some firm conclusions, then you can tell the student you will continue this for another week or two. Keep your recording sheet on a clip board or in a binder that the student recognizes. As she sees you recording any examples of her inappropriate behavior this can also help her to be more aware of her behavior which can lead to change.

If you then bring your concerns to a case conference, you will have some very specific documented information that may help you to find some solutions. As said earlier, this can be time consuming but if doing this for a few weeks might change the student's behavior in more positive ways for the remainder of the year, then wouldn't it be worth it?

Another variation of this approach would be for a student to chart her behavior and your responses (both positive and negative) to both appropriate and inappropriate behavior. In other words the student writes down the time, date, and her perception of what happened that led to a reaction from you. This information might also note some revealing trends as well as helping you to better understand the student and her reaction to the various forms of intervention and the related consequences that you use with her.

iii) CONTRACTS

In some situations, a contract between a student and teacher can have a positive effect on changing behavior. Although contracts may often be one of the recommendations that comes from a case conference or part of an approach that results when a student has been sent to the office, there is no reason why a teacher couldn't also implement this approach with a student. In many ways a contract is similar to step #3 in the discipline model previously discussed in this chapter with the exception that it is a written expectation along with a specific consequence.

Generally, a contract comes from a discussion with a student. Unless a student has had some direct input into the wording of the contract, then it is unlikely the student will be willing to participate in fulfilling its terms. Most of the time, as the teacher you will state the acceptable behavior that is outlined in the contract. In addition, you will likely identify the negative consequences that will be applied if the contract is not fulfilled (although this is one time where it would also be interesting and useful to get the student's input into what he thinks is appropriate). The area where most students enjoy participating is identifying a positive consequence if they fulfill the terms of the contract.

The contract then has a few basic parts. First, you want to identify the required behavior you want to encourage. Second, there is a need to identify both a negative consequence if the contract is not fulfilled and a positive consequence if it is fulfilled. Next, and very important, you need to identify a specific period of time covered by this contract (and the shorter the better). Strive for immediate success and build on this rather than having the contract cover a lengthy period of time where it becomes difficult for the student to be successful and a chore for you to monitor. Finally, the contract is signed by both you and the student with each of you having a copy. In most cases, you should involve the parents which would then require their signatures as well (and the parents might add consequences that will be applied at home).

Like any other discipline approach, contracts are only effective if action is taken to support the consequences that were identified. In situations where a student carries some form of contract from class to class, these contracts only produce results if every teacher is well informed of the purpose of the contract and is committed to monitoring its terms.

Inappropriate behavior, as previously mentioned in this book, can take years to become a habit. It is rare that more appropriate behavior will occur overnight. Time, patience and a serious commitment to helping the student change are part of the requirements for the change to occur.

iv) DETENTION ROOMS

Most teachers find it difficult to list consequences that are appropriate, enforceable and actually work. Detentions are one form of a negative consequence that are identified as a possibility. Most students do not like having to give up part of their lunch or after school time. The message here is very clear, "Time on-task is important to learning. If you fail to use class time effectively to learn, here is an alternate time to make up what you missed or wasted."

The difficulty that some teachers (and schools) face related to detentions is that busing concerns (and even walking home alone concerns) may prevent you from giving a detention after school. It is even possible that in some schools, there are reasons that prevent you from giving noon hour detentions (such as you want to eat your lunch alone, or you have to supervise some noon hour activity, or perhaps it is a reality that your students need a nutritious lunch and as such, detentions during this time are not permitted in your school). In any event, what would appear to be a logical consequence for many forms of misbehavior might become difficult to actually implement.

Some schools have found a solution to this by establishing a "time out" place or "detention room" or even a "study hall" that exists in a specific location throughout the school day. For this approach to work, it is important to have an available room each period and it is also important that the complete school staff supports this approach because it is generally necessary for each teacher to supervise the room during "preparation" periods. This then becomes a quiet room where students are expected to work (and where they will not be disturbing their classmates or preventing the teacher from teaching).

For these rooms to be effective, there is a need for some written process for sending a student to the room. In addition, there is a need for a teacher to also send some written outline of work to be done so that the receiving teacher who is supervising the room knows what the student should be doing. Some schools, where busing is not an issue, may set up detention rooms for before and after school as well.

A variation of this approach is "think time" where students are once again sent to a designated room when students don't respond to teacher interventions for more appropriate behavior in the classroom. In this case, the receiving teacher works with the student to identify the behavior that was considered inappropriate and what he would need to do differently when he gets back to the classroom so that the inappropriate behavior doesn't repeat itself. When the "think time" teacher feels that the student is ready to return to class, the student will then be sent back.

> "Think Time is a highly structured program that has been shown to decrease disruptive behavior in students as well as increase student engagement."
> Sugai and Colvin, 1996

Another variation of the detention room is "Saturday School" (think the movie "Breakfast Club"). Although this is a logical approach for time misused in class or for inappropriate tardiness or absences, this approach may be unworkable due to busing or other issues that might exist for students to actually attend a Saturday morning class. And another variation is "Recess Academy" which is self-explanatory.

v) FOCUS

It is common to hear teachers say that some misbehaving students lack focus. It isn't necessarily that they lack focus, it is rather that they lack focus on your behavioral expectations. A question you might ask yourself whenever a student misbehaves (this could be added to your "charting" on page 274) is what is the "payoff" for the student? In other words, what does the student gain, or in what way does he benefit from his misbehavior? This could include gaining attention from other students (or even from you, even though it may be negative in nature). For some students a negative emotional response might be preferable to none at all. For some students this might be exactly the kind of response they have learned to elicit at home so they are simply continuing this pattern at school. Other reasons for misbehavior might include peer recognition, interfering with the learning of subject matter that is too difficult for him, breaking the boredom, lack of sleep, lack of nutrition, and so on.

Understanding the payoff helps you to better understand a student's focus and often the reason for his misbehavior. If you can find a more appropriate way to deliver the same payoff then you can change the focus of the student and help him to adapt more appropriate behavior.

As previously mentioned in this chapter, if your misbehaving student is focusing on gaining attention or peer acceptance through his misbehavior, there are other more positive ways to do this. Belonging to a school team or club as examples can foster recognition and acceptance in positive ways. Similarly being given more responsibility in the classroom can also decrease student misbehavior. Back in Chapters 3 + 4 were some other suggestions that could help your student to gain attention and acceptance in a more positive manner.

> "There are two things that people want
> more than anything else - - recognition and praise."
> Mary Kay Ash

vi) LEADERSHIP PROGRAMS FOR STUDENTS

Leadership programs (also see further thoughts on peer mentoring and mediation on page 281 - 283) can make a very positive contribution to the learning atmosphere in any school. While it is natural that the students who are chosen to be in these programs are the most-deserving students, it is also important to consider some of your misbehaving students (and the well-behaving silent majority), who might have inappropriately expressed leadership skills. Including a few normally disruptive students in your student leadership programs can result in these students learning more appropriate ways to gain recognition and attention.

> "If you pick the right people
> and give them the opportunity to spread their wings,
> you almost don't have to manage them."
> Jack Welch

vii) NUTRITION PROGRAMS

Common sense would tell us that a hungry student is likely to have difficulty focusing on learning when his body is craving food. The relationship of nutrition to learning has been explored for some time. There now appears to be a growing body of evidence that nutrition does play a role in contributing to learning. As has been stated previously in this book, students who are encountering difficulties in learning, for whatever reason, are more likely to exhibit inappropriate behavior in the classroom due to their frustration and the lack of recognition that accompanies failure. In addition, kids who lack the appropriate nutrition tend to get sick more often, missing school, and falling behind in class.

The Community Childhood Hunger Identification Project (CCHIP) estimates that 12% of U.S. families with children under age 12 experience some forms of hunger.

> "Children in families who reported hunger were more likely to suffer from infections, have trouble concentrating, and miss more school than non-hungry children."
> Wehler et al, 1991

While there are a broad range of programs helping to contribute to solutions related to the problems of hunger and nutrition, the National Health/Education Consortium recommends that nutrition education in schools is most effective when it is coordinated with meals that may be served in the school.

It should also be noted that skipping breakfast, even among healthy, well-nourished students, can adversely affect performance (E. Pollitt, 1991). In considering solutions to classroom misbehavior that might be resulting in poor achievement, it would be wise to also consider the impact that nutrition and hunger may play in contributing to this. There may be times when there needs to be an emphasis on feeding the body before we can effectively feed the mind. Fitness, as discussed on page 284) can also have a correlation to achievement and behavior.

> "Studies demonstrate that when children's basic nutritional and fitness needs are met, they attain higher academic levels."
> J.F. Bogden, 2000 in *Fit, Healthy and Ready to Learn: A School Health Policy Guide*, 2000

viii) PARENTAL INVOLVEMENT

Looking back at pages 257 and 263 you will see once again that contact with parents, for most students, is a powerful consequence (both in a positive and negative sense). When schools and parents work together in areas of student behavior, the results are generally stronger than if the teacher is working in isolation although we also have to remember that there is a culture and language often used within schools that not all parents fully understand. When parents are to be involved in supporting a school's attempt to correct a student's behavior, it is important the parents understand all aspects of whatever approach is being used. It is also important to remember that most parents are not trained teachers, and as such may sometimes unkowingly create negative attitudes towards schoolwork because of their lack of training in helping their child in an appropriate manner. Some research has actually shown a negative correlation with school success when parents are overly involved with monitoring homework (Hong and Ho, 2005). On the other hand an emphasis at home on being responsible and respecting others can transfer in a positive manner to appropriate behavior at school. Ellen Slicker (1998) found that the effective use of rules and procedures at home is associated with a decrease in disruptive behavior at school. Helping parents to understand that their expectations significantly contribute to the success of their child is also important.

> "Parent aspirations were the most important influence on their children's achievement."
> Hong and Ho (2005)

ix) PEER HELPING

Excellent teachers understand the value of peers helping peers. As an example, an important aspect of learning relates to guided practice after a lesson has been taught. In many classrooms, this guided practice might occur with one teacher attempting to monitor and help twenty-four students. In many classrooms this is precisely the time when misbehavior occurs because some students don't understand what they are to do and there is simply not enough teacher to go around to all students at the same time. If one peer helper was involved in this room, the ratio of helper to helpee during guided practice drops to 1 to 12. If two peer helpers were involved, this ratio is then reduced to 1 to 8. The lower the ratio, the greater the assistance that each student receives. This helps to not only increase learning but to also decrease misbehavior.

Some schools have formal programs that select students to be trained as peer tutors. While there is certainly a positive value to such programs contributing to improved classroom achievement as well as contributing to an overall positive atmosphere in the school, effective teachers are also aware that peer helpers can be chosen within the ranks of any of his/her classes at any time. Consider a teacher who assigns ten math. questions to follow up the teaching of a lesson. This teacher might then state something along the lines of the first ten students who finish questions #1, 3, 5, 7 and 9 can then choose to be peer helpers or choose to complete the remaining questions. The teacher has now provided an incentive for students to complete this work and will likely very soon end up with ten "helpers" who can assist other students. This approach helps students to become more responsible and it also helps all students to get the attention and help they may require to complete their work. Using this approach in different subjects also provides an opportunity for a more diverse group of students to get involved as helpers because of their varying strengths in different subject areas.

> "The overall effect of the use of peers as co-teachers in classes is, overall, quite powerful. If the aim is to teach students self-regulation and control over their own learning then they must move from being students to being teachers of themselves."
> John Hattie in *Visible Learning - A Synthesis of over 800 Meta-Analyses Relating To Achievement*, 2009

Peer tutoring not only benefits the student being tutored but provides benefits to the tutor as well. Learning for the tutor is reinforced when this student helps to teach another student. Socially such students can gain both recognition and acceptance throughout the room. A review of the research related to tutoring supports the reality that those tutoring experience both social and academic benefits (Cook, Scruggs, Mastropieri, and Casto, 1985).

Peer helping programs in schools can also go beyond classroom tutoring. Some schools use student tutors in lunch hour study halls or after school help sessions. In some schools, peer helpers may even be employed by parents wishing to provide additional help for their child. Some schools have found success with programs that ensure that no student is "invisible". Peer helping programs can help to satisfy such a goal.

In addition to tutoring, peer helping programs may also focus on providing personal support and contact for students who could benefit from this type of acceptance. Some schools even name such programs as "Big Brothers" or "Big Sisters" although there are a wide range of other names as well. Regardless of the name given to the program, the intent is the same. Peer helpers can help other students to feel welcome and accepted. This can help to reduce behavioral issues that might be related to attention seeking and the need for acceptance. Peer helping programs can also help to reduce bullying. One of the results of a Peer Support Program that was developed in Australia and researched over a three year period at the University of Western Sydney was that the program changed students' perceptions of bullying. Students explained that the program encouraged them not to bully others and informed them of who to turn to for assistance if bullying occurs. One student even identified that the program had resulted in him establishing rapport with a person who had previously bullied him.

> "The program (peer support) enhanced student self-confidence and sense of worth. It gave them the confidence to be themselves and not be negatively influenced by others and submit to peer pressure. The program was proven to enhancing students' problem solving and decision making skills."
> University of Western Sydney, 2003

x) PEER MEDIATION

A basic goal of peer mediation programs is to train student leaders to assist in resolving conflicts among students. An objective within peer mediation is to help students move from blaming towards finding cooperative solutions. While I believe there should be some strong parameters set as to the type of situations that these students are involved in, these students can never-the-less provide some assistance in resolving minor conflicts before they escalate. The presence of such students within the school and within the classroom can help reassure some students that they are in a safer environment and that help is nearby, factors that can assist in both increasing student achievement and decreasing inappropriate behavior.

While it is not the intent of this book to provide a course outline in establishing a peer mediation program, it is important that students chosen to be peer mediators reflect the school's diversity including cultures, gender, academic, social and race. It is also recommended that the selection process be well advertised and that students can self-refer. It is important that a well-trained core group of staff members provide systematic monitoring of the program and regularly oversee the selection, training, actual mediation engagement and debriefing. It is also critical that peer mediators fully understand their limits and have immediate access to an appropriate staff member who can assist in resolving a problem beyond the training of the student. Peer mediation programs should be carefully explained to all students and adults in the building in order that everyone has a clear expectation of what can and cannot be accomplished through peer mediation. An example of a program that has been used in more than 100 school districts in the United States and worldwide is Working Together To Resolve Conflict (see http://education.ufl.edu/conflict-resolution/ for further information on this program). There are certainly other programs available as well so you would be advised to start with an internet search on peer mediation to expand the possibilities.

> "Perhaps most importantly, as a result of peer mediation programs many schools have seen a reduction in overall suspensions and a reduction in suspensions specifically for fighting."
> Joel Fredrickson, Bethal College and Geoffrey Maruyama, University of Minnesota
> in *Peer Mediation Programs: Benefits and Key Elements*, 1996

xi) PHYSICAL ACTIVITY

Physical activity is essential for the healthy growth and development of children. In a study of fifteen classes in North Carolina, it was found that participation in an in-class physical activity of one ten minute physical break involving no equipment per day (called Energizers) resulted in an improvement of on-task behavior (East Carolina University, 2006). From this (and from personal experience), we might conclude that a brief physical break for a few minutes every hour where your students simply stand and stretch could help with students maintaining a greater time on-task.

Previously in this book (particularly in Chapter 8) it was noted that stress and the inappropriate expression of anger can lead to conflicts and misbehavior. At that time it was suggested that physical activity can assist with the healthy reduction of stress and also be an appropriate healthy way to express anger. In one of the few research studies involving children, exercise, and anger, it was found that for healthy, but overweight, sedentary children an aerobic exercise program might be an effective strategy to reduce anger expression including aggressive behavior. In the abstract for this study, it is stated that physical activity has been shown to improve anxiety and depression in adults, adolescents and children. This study concluded that a healthy dose of organized, vigorous physical activity in childrens' daily lives may be beneficial not only for the maintenance of appropriate weight and cardiovascular health, but also for the development of appropriate social behavior (Joseph Tkacz, M.S., Deborah Young Hyman, Ph.D., Colleen A. Boyle, M.S., and Catherine L. Davis, Ph.D., 2008)

> "One of the benefits of outdoor play for children is improved mental health."
> The Canadian Fitness and Lifestyle Research Institute, 2011

xii) THE PRINCIPAL

One of the most frequent methods of disciplining students by some teachers is to send the misbehaving student to the principal (or vice-principal in a larger school). There are several potential problems with this approach although it can also have some merit. First of all, not every student views being sent to the principal as a negative consequence. Having worked in several schools in guidance departments (which have been located adjacent to the main office), I have seen groups of students in an office foyer having a great time. Sometimes administrators are too busy to immediately see a student so the "misbehaving" students gather for a socially entertaining time before they finally meet with the principal. In some schools, if there is no protocol for a staff member to accompany the misbehaving student to the office, the student may very well create further disturbances along the route and even stop in the cafeteria for a treat before his unscheduled and unannounced meeting with the principal. In other words unless there is a clear procedure in a school that provides some way of monitoring a student (and this should not be a secretarial job) who is sent to the office, then being sent to the principal may in fact be a reward rather than a punishment for the misbehaving student.

> "From a student's point of view,
> the office can actually be
> an 'interesting' place to be sent,
> a place of live 'soap opera' entertainment.
> For attention-seeking students,
> being sent to the office might be a reward."
> Robert J. MacKenzie and Lisa E. Stanzione
> in *Setting Limits in the Classroom*, 2010

In addition, unless there is once again some very clear procedure that explains (in detail) why the student has been sent to the office, the principal in many cases does not have enough information to take action and even if he/she has all the details, it may still be difficult to apply consequences that are fair and appropriate and that will make a difference (a little more on this on the next page). Unfortunately, as a result of this, a principal may give a student "the talk" to which most students will readily support and agree to change (their behavior). The student then returns to the class, as the "smiling hero", to the chagrin of the teacher. In such situations it doesn't take very long for students to realize that going to the office is not a punishment, and as such it becomes a consequence that does little to correct the behavior of the students who were sent there.

In some schools, on the other hand, there is a process that teachers and the administration have worked closely together to establish a meaningful approach to the involvement of the administration in supporting teachers who experience students with behavioral problems in the classroom. This procedure generally involves a progression of steps that the teacher first employs to correct the misbehavior (such as the different strategies and techniques that have already been presented in this chapter). The exception to this expectation would be if the misbehaving student presented a physical danger to other students, himself, the teacher, or school property, at which time the student might be sent directly to the office (and be accompanied along the way). Each school might formulate their own guidelines that would help a teacher to understand the circumstances when a student should be taken directly to the office (and how this should be done).

It would also be helpful to teachers to understand some of the consequences a principal might employ with students who have been sent to the office. To do this, it would make a lot of sense for a school staff to discuss school discipline as a school-wide initiative. When every staff member commits to maintaining a standard of discipline throughout the school and is willing to intervene when these expectations are not being followed (even if this occurs outside the teacher's classroom), then improved student behavior can occur throughout the school. Appropriate student behavior in the hallways and cafeteria can lead to improved behavior in the classroom.

In some circumstances a trip to the office for a student might result in a suspension (such as in schools that have a zero tolerance policy related to fighting or illegal drug involvement as examples). Unfortunately there are some teachers who see suspensions as the perfect measure of discipline. Unfortunately for some students, suspensions only serve to give the freedom (from school) to wreck havoc in the community. In addition, when students then return back to school from their suspensions, they are further behind in their academic work as well as sometimes harboring anger towards any teachers involved in the suspension (and sometimes now having that "delinquent" label, they feel compelled to live up to it). While there are times when an administrator must follow guidelines established in his/her school jurisdiction there is a body of research evidence that shows that suspensions are not always effective.

> **"Suspension is ineffective."**
> Dupper, D.R., Theriot, M.T., and Cruan, S.W.
> in *Reducing Out-of-School Suspensions:*
> *Practice Guidelines for School Social Workers*, 2009

While suspensions may not always be effective, and while in many school jurisdictions the number of suspensions is a rising, ongoing concern, the reality is that there is a need to address serious forms of student misbehavior. While suspensions do not always correct the receiving student's behavior, it is often argued that the suspension may help to improve school safety. Once again this is not necessarily true. While there is definitely a need to take disciplinary action of some sort when students jeopardize the safety of others (and this is generally stated as part of zero-tolerance policies), it has been found that once again suspensions are not necessarily creating the anticipated results.

> "It has been shown that suspensions do not improve overall school safety and are associated with lower academic performance, higher rates of dropout, failures to graduate on time, increased academic disengagement, and subsequent disciplinary exclusion."
> Achilles, G.M., Mclaughlin, M.J., Croninger, R.G., in *Sociocultural Correlates of Disciplinary Exclusion Among Students With Emotional, Behavioral, and Learning Disabilities in the SEELSDataset. Journal of Emotional and Behavioral Disorders*, 2007

As was stated previously, suspensions often result in students being left unsupervised in the community (and aren't these generally students who need adult supervision rather than being left on their own?). This can result in students getting into further trouble in the community and it can also result in some students further associating with other "undesirable" people which sometimes results in them coming back to school with a new set of inappropriate behavior.

Although suspensions may not be the answer to serious forms of student behavior, a reality in some situations is that there are few options. As has been previously been mentioned, where zero-tolerance policies exist suspensions may be part of an expected protocol rather than a choice. The real point I would like to make here though is that suspensions should be a consequence (if there are no other alternatives) for serious student misconduct, rather than a disciplinary consequence that is applied to all kinds of minor forms of misbehavior. While some teachers may need a "break" from some misbehaving students, the out-of-school suspension may very well result in some students returning back to the classroom with even more serious behavior problems. There is nothing wrong with a teacher (and other students in the class) needing a "break" from misbehaving students; it is just that there are more often more appropriate ways of doing this. Throughout this book have been many ideas related to establishing a positive classroom environment and for improving classroom behavior. The consistent application of these techniques and strategies can result in a classroom and a school where there is less need for suspending students.

> "Schools with low suspension rates have more favorable ratings of overall school appearance (e.g., cleanliness, condition, order, ambiance)."
> R. Skiba and J. Sprague, *Safety Without Suspensions. Educational Leadership*, 2008

What then for students with serious misconduct issues? First of all, let me state that these students are generally a school-wide concern, rather than just a discipline problem in one or two classes. As such, there is a need for a school approach (with administration leadership addressing both the problem and solution) to help in improving the behavior of such students. Although some of the other approaches outlined in this chapter could be viable alternatives, the following discussion will explore in-school-suspensions (ISS) as an option.

First of all, with some research questioning the value of suspensions, an alternate has been the in-school suspension. An in-school suspension is exactly what the term implies - a seriously misbehaving student is withdrawn from class and placed under some form of supervision within the school for a period of time. The advantage of this approach is that the student has been taken out of the classroom but instead of being turned loose unsupervised in the community, the student can continue to do his work under the supervision of some other staff member. The obvious disadvantage of this approach is that someone has to supervise the student and that some coordination of the assignments that the student should be focusing on needs to be done. To simply have the student sit in the office area, and as I have witnessed in some schools then become an assistant to one of the secretaries, helping to staple newsletters or some other similar task, can become a reward for misbehavior rather than a deterrent. If a student is going to have an in-school suspension it is very important that this time be used to help the student to continue his related school work. If this is not done, the student then returns back to the class in a day or two, frustrated by now being a little further behind, and prone as a result to very quickly once again becoming a behavior problem. For an in-school suspension to be effective there is a need for the student to be engaged in his school work in a supervised manner by a staff member who is qualified to provide academic assistance.

> "The fundamental purpose of discipline is to provide remedial treatment that identifies the underlying problem and eventually improves or corrects misbehaviour, and not simply to inflict a penalty that temporarily extinguishes the undesirable behavior."
> Sullivan, 1989

One of the keys to using in-school suspensions in an effective manner is to have a room and a staff member available to supervise such students. While this might be a practical approach in a school where there are frequent in-school suspensions, this approach may prove to be impractical in schools where in-school suspensions are much less frequent. To be effective, ISS require planning, coordination and a commitment from the staff involved. Having said this, if the implementation of an ISS program can improve student behavior then the time invested may pay later dividends.

There are a few key components in establishing an effective ISS program. As already mentioned there is a need for a room for such students and the availability of a staff member to supervise (and teach) in such a room. Some schools find it meaningful to have a teacher with either special education or some form of remedial teaching training to staff such a room. Some school jurisdictions are even employing "student success" teachers who are experts in the field of remediation and resolving inappropriate student behavior. As in any other form of escalating misbehavior it is important that parents are involved as well as a school counselor. Serious misbehavior is rooted in some need and unless an expert can help to uncover and remediate this need, the misbehavior will likely continue regardless of how many times the student might be suspended. In addition, any suspension, to be more effective, should also have a routine follow-up by your school counselor, social worker, or ISS teacher, once the student has returned back to his regular classroom (s). Like any other consequence applied to misbehavior, an in-school suspension needs to be fair and consistently enforced. One aspect of fairness relates to the amount of time a student is given in an ISS. This amount of time should be well identified and appropriate to the level of misconduct (and appropriate to what actually works).

Schools involved in using ISS programs report that students dislike such programs because they can't sleep or avoid continuing their academic work and they don't generally have access to their friends. In many ways, an ISS program in itself can become a form of behavioral modification because it is an effective consequence for misbehavior. Unlike out-of-school suspensions where students essentially gain a holiday for themselves, an ISS program ensures that students continue to follow school rules, procedures and academic expectations.

> "Out-of-school suspensions are counter-productive and alternatives like in-school-suspensions work best. The literature supports ISS if qualified counselling support is provided, parents are involved, a philosophy is established through shared decision-making, and continued academics are part of the program."
> Guindon, 1992

xiii) TECHNOLOGY

Some forms of misconduct are directly related to tardiness, attendance issues and failure to complete work on time. While these kinds of issues have been addressed in other areas of this book, it is useful to recognize that the appropriate use of technology can be advantageous in assisting with these concerns. For example, some schools have automatic attendance communication systems whereby a parent/guardian is instantly informed by an automatic voice mail or email if their son/daughter is absent. Such instant feedback can be helpful in ensuring that students attend their classes. In addition, this technology can save a tremendous amount of secretarial (or other staff) time that is sometimes spent in trying to reach a parent personally by telephone.

Similarly, some teachers post a weekly or monthly calendar of upcoming assignments and tests on school websites. Once again, parents (and students) can quickly see the course expectations which can then help to reduce the number of assignments that are not handed in at the designated time. Similar to the above example, this can be a great timesaver as teachers simply need to make one entry that is then immediately available to every parent and student. A variation of this is an email to parents once again providing a calendar of upcoming due dates for tests and assignments. Some teachers also make effective use of emails to inform parents of test and assignment results. Obviously, there may be some schools where not every parent has internet access but this is becoming less of a concern each year.

As well, online courses are of growing importance in many school areas and these are proving to be effective alternate forms of learning for some students who are unsuccessful in the traditional classroom. In the previous discussion on ISS programs, some schools use online courses very effectively with students who are serving in-school suspensions and even more so in situations where it is necessary to remove a student from a regular classroom for a more extended period of time.

xiv) TOKEN REWARDS

Token rewards are generally considered to be concrete rewards for appropriate behavior. These can include verbal forms of recognition but are more often thought of as things like some form of reward point system where students can trade their "earned points" at some future point for prizes or gaining some form of classroom privilege such as listening to music, no homework for the weekend, watching a video, etc. It is important that if you are using some form of token reward system in your classroom that you ensure that your rewards don't conflict with any school policies. In addition, token recognition can also be as simple as the use of something concrete like stickers which reward good work or behavior. While most teachers feel that these kinds of token reward systems are best for younger students and have lost their usefulness by the time students reach grade 5, the reality is that many students will still benefit from this kind of approach throughout middle school and even into junior high school.

One of the keys to this approach, like any other form of reward or punishment, is that it is consistent and fair. A common complaint already expressed by the "silent majority" in most classrooms is that those who misbehave get too much attention and take up too much of a teacher's time, so going out of your way to reward a normally misbehaving student at the smallest sign of appropriate behavior may create resentment from the remainder of your class unless you are actively involved in rewarding their appropriate behavior as well. An important aspect of this approach is to be genuine. By grade five most students clearly understand when they are being "bribed" to which they may not respond well.

> "When rewards are used they should support students' engagements and self-management rather than emphasize teacher control over student behavior."
> Reeve, 2006

Although it would be fairly easy to find research that demonstrates the use of token rewards is not the best option for increasing student learning and reinforcing student behavior (for example, Deci, Koestner and Ryan caution that "the use of extrinsic rewards, especially tangible rewards, can reduce under some circumstances students' intrinsic motivation to engage in the rewarded activity", 2000), remember in this chapter we are talking about students who are "already unmotivated" and who exhibit serious forms of inappropriate behavior. If token rewards are helping to increase appropriate behavior, then by all means keep using them. Similarly if everything else has been tried to no avail, then why not consider some form of token rewards?

A common example of a token rewards is when a teacher establishes a "point" system of some sort where students "earn" points (or even paper money) for appropriate behavior (and in such systems students can also have their points taken away for inappropriate behavior). At the end of the week students can trade their points (or use their paper money) for small prizes (purchased by the teacher at a "dollar" store) or for other privileges such as no homework for the weekend, an hour of playing games, and so on. As previously mentioned it is important that your prizes do not conflict with any school policies because other classes (both students and teachers) may complain if they see your class watching a movie and eating popcorn last period on a Friday afternoon. At the beginning of the school year you can offer the "prize and privilege" sessions at the end of each week. After a month or two, it is recommended that the frequency for the action rewards becomes once every two weeks and eventually once a month, and in the end may even disappear.

While in most of these token reward systems each student in a sense competes for points (and as has already been stated it is critical that you are fair and consistent with every student), some teachers also make effective use of token rewards to motivate appropriate behavior for an entire class. For example, while students might be able to "purchase" small prizes once a week from your "store" with the points they have earned, you might add a class-wide prize (such as popcorn and a movie) which is based on a larger number of points that could only be attained by every class member contributing his/her points to reach this total. This way, the complete class is aiming for a goal and there is increased peer pressure to achieve this reward.

As students, by grade 5, may have already experienced some form of a token reward system, it might be advantageous to explain some possibilities here (with the underlying rationale that you are trying to gain an increase in time on-task that can increase student learning) and then let your students design the basics of a system you could implement. Using this approach your students will be more likely committed to the program and also be less likely to view the system as outright bribery. Whichever system you decide to use, keep it simple. After all, you don't want your token reward system to suddenly take away time from your actual teaching.

One of the drawbacks to most negative forms of discipline is that students are generally told what they are doing wrong but they don't always fully understand (and certainly don't practice) what they should be doing. One of the advantages of a token rewards system (and any other form of positive consequences) is that you are constantly recognizing what students are doing right. This helps them to form better habits which can eventually be exhibited without the continual need for a concrete reward.

> "A teacher affects eternity."
> Carl Jung

PART C

COMMON TRAITS
OF HIGHLY EFFECTIVE TEACHERS

In conducting workshops for teachers, one of the most frequently mentioned reasons I hear teachers state for choosing their career is "to make a difference". The focus of this book is classroom management and how this can help you to make a positive difference with your students. In looking at classroom management and the goal of making a difference, there are a few final areas to consider.

A major focus of many of the activities and the content that is presented in this book is to help you establish a positive classroom learning environment. Now that you have a better idea on how to establish a classroom environment that allows you

> "We live in an era when research tells us that the teacher is probably the single most important factor affecting student achievement - at least the single most important factor that we can do much about."
> Robert J. Marzano in *Classroom Management That Works Research-Based Strategies For Every Teacher*, 2003

to teach with less disruptions, an obvious next question might be - as you seek to make a positive difference with your students - "Are there some teaching approaches or methods that work better than others?" Chapter 10 will help to provide some thoughts on this question as well as exploring the direct impact that your subject area curriculum can have on classroom behavior (and student success).

Finally, Chapter 11 will help to consider how you take care of yourself. After all, if you are the most important factor in helping your students to be successful, then your health and well-being are critical to effective teaching.

"To thine own self be true."
Shakespeare

CHAPTER 10

HOW YOUR TEACHING METHODS IMPACT CLASSROOM MANAGEMENT

A basic premise of this book is that it is the classroom teacher who can make a significance difference in student success. As well, a common theme throughout this book is that time on-task contributes in a very positive way to student learning and that time on-task is directly affected by your classroom management skills. A relevant question at this point may very well be "How does a teacher's teaching style, technique, or methods affect classroom management and the resulting learning? Is it possible that one style of teaching is more conducive to learning than another and as such, is it possible that one style of teaching is also more appropriate to improved classroom management?"

The reality is that most kids respond in different ways to dissimilar teacher personalities and approaches. I was reminded of this on one occasion when I was conducting a workshop for summer recreational leaders in the city where I live. My role in this workshop was to help give the teenagers (who would be summer camp counselors) some thoughts on discipline and management techniques. I began by asking the question, "Based on your experience at school, what are some traits of effective teachers?" The young people (about one-hundred of them) worked in groups of 5 - 6 students to answer this question. As the students chose their own groups, I noticed immediately that they tended to divide into groups according to their ages (which generally ranged from 15 - 19). When the task was completed it was very interesting to hear the responses from groups of 15 year-old students in comparison to the 19 year-olds. The younger groups identified factors such as "warm, caring, fun to be with, and approachable" as key factors that contributed to teachers being effective. The older groups, on the other hand, identified factors such as "high expectations, well organized, subject expertise, and fairness" as the key factors that contributed to their teachers being effective. And the groups in the middle, the 16 to 18 year-olds, generally had a combination of the factors mentioned by the other two groups although most 16 year-olds were closer to the thoughts of the 15 year-olds while most 18 year-olds were closer to the thoughts of the 19 year-olds.

Based on the example I gave above, one might conclude that a teacher's style has a direct impact on effective teaching (and classroom management) and that her approach (to be considered effective) might vary according to age groups and also individual students. While there is certainly some truth in this, the reality is not as clear cut as the example that I gave above. In this example concerning the training of teenage camp counselors, after each group shared their thoughts on the key factors that contributed to teachers being effective, in the ensuing discussion the younger students quickly acknowledged that a teacher who actually teaches is preferable to even the "coolest" teacher in the school. While most students prefer having a teacher who they like and who also likes them and accepts them, in the end kids want to learn. Students want a teacher who teaches and helps them to be successful. Any teacher who forgoes the curriculum in an attempt to be "popular" is doing her students a great disservice. On the other hand, many outstanding teachers understand the importance of taking some time here and there to listen to students even if this occasionally takes away from the immediate task (although many of these teachers also understand the best place for such informal dialogue is often in the hallway or cafeteria).

The students who fall into the age group, intended for the teachers of this book, are those who appreciate and respond better to teachers who are positive and who accept them for who they are (and is this really any different for any age group?). The first four chapters of this book provided a framework for establishing a positive classroom environment that was conducive to teaching. It is critical to remember that once this atmosphere is established, it is then time to help your students learn the curriculum for your subject area.

In one informal bit of research in this area, I asked six Grade 7 + 8 classes (164 students) to prioritize the following sentences:

- I learn best from a teacher who takes an interest in me.
- I learn best from a teacher who actually teaches.
- I learn best from a teacher who is strict.
- I learn best from a teacher who is fun to be with.
- I learn best from actually being involved in activities in the classroom.
- I learn best from a teacher who carefully explains things.
- I learn best from a teacher who is informal and relaxed.
- I learn best from a teacher who has high expectations.
- I learn best from a teacher who is a subject expert.
- I learn best from a teacher who understands me.

Based on the results from the six classes, overall the students ranked the sentences as follows (with #1 being most important to their learning while #10 was the least important):

1. I learn best from a teacher who actually teaches.
2. I learn best from a teacher who has high expectations.
3. I learn best from a teacher who carefully explains things.
4. I learn best from actually being involved in activities in the classroom.
5. I learn best from a teacher who takes an interest in me.
6. I learn best from a teacher who is a subject expert.
7. I learn best from a teacher who is strict.
8. I learn best from a teacher who understands me.
9. I learn best from a teacher who is informal and relaxed.
10. I learn best from a teacher who is fun to be with.

While it can certainly be said that these questions might be better worded or even more specific, my follow-up discussions with each of the six classes revealed a common concern (which supports their #1 ranking in this informal survey). This concern focused on the need for teachers to "actually teach". When I asked students for further clarification on this, they expressed their frustration with teachers who spend most of their time attempting to manage student behavior, or who constantly assign readings and questions from texts without ever teaching a lesson, or who easily get off topic (often sharing completely unrelated personal stories), or teachers who sit at their desks and mark (instead of coming around the room to help them), or who sit at their desk and text on their cell phones among other tasks totally unrelated to teaching. Students also frequently mentioned that the teachers they learned the best from were well organized, well prepared, and could effectively communicate the content of their lessons in a variety of interesting ways. While students acknowledged that they might initially state that they liked teachers who were fun to be with (or who were perceived as being "one of them"), in the end they were fully aware that a teacher with high expectations (even if there was clearly a distinction in the classroom roles of the "teacher" and the "student") was the preferred choice for helping them to learn. And perhaps most directly related to the theme of this chapter, there was no single teaching style or approach that emerged as being the most preferred. The desires of the students could be summarized in two words: "Just teach!"

The remainder of this chapter will take a closer look at both the research and the "common sense" realities of learning to explore the question of how teaching methods impact classroom management and the eventual learning by students of the curriculum. As a counselor of more than two decades in many educational environments and as a teacher for even a longer period of time, I have seen curriculum success help students develop a healthy mindset. On the other hand I have also observed a lack of success in the curriculum result in a myriad of problems for the student (and often for the teachers who had to find ways to cope with the resulting by-product of inappropriate behavior). It is not the intent of this book to be an exhaustive look at teaching approaches. While outstanding teachers often employ a variety of methods (and both research and student evaluations supports this), it is difficult to find a research study that clearly identified any one particular teaching style as the most effective approach to helping kids learn. Having said this though, there are some commonalities that could be applied to almost any teaching method that could help to make the approach more successful. This chapter will focus more on such universal factors that contribute to effective teaching, rather than evaluating the wide range of approaches that could be employed by teachers.

Before taking a more detailed look at some of the factors that contribute to effective teaching - which in turn, can dramatically lower the incidence of inappropriate behavior in the classroom - I would like to first of all share a few thoughts on the curriculum itself.

1) CURRICULUM

Regardless of what subject area you are teaching, students who are successful in learning the content of your curriculum will generally exhibit more appropriate behavior in your class.

> "I want to be as emphatic as possible:
> the impact of the actual taught curriculum
> on school quality and student learning
> is indescribably important."
> Mike Schmoker in *Results Now: How We Can Achieve Unprecedented Improvements in Learning and Teaching*, 2006

Although it may appear overly simplistic, a basic question any teacher might ask is "How can I help students to be more successful in the subject area I am teaching?" It is often this very success that has an immediate and direct correlation with student behavior in your class. In general, most students like to learn and as my previous thoughts in this chapter have already indicated, students encounter great frustration with teachers who do not teach (and this generally results in increased inappropriate classroom behaviour). I have sometimes heard teachers say something along the lines of "I can't teach because all my students are misbehaving." This rationalization often results in teachers trying to develop a more positive relationship with their students by "playing games" or engaging in "informal chats" which will eventually frustrate the students because inherently they know they should be learning the curriculum. Teachers who focus on the curriculum instead of getting sidetracked for whatever reason will generally encounter fewer student behavioral problems. This is not to say that you shouldn't take some time at the beginning of a semester to better understand your students and to build some class cohension, but the sooner your students begin to learn the content of your curriculum in a meaningful, engaging manner, the sooner you can say goodbye to most forms of inappropriate behavior.

In considering curriculum, many teachers struggle with balancing curriculum expectations with the actual ability and needs of individual students. What is appropriate for one student may be overwhelming for another. What is challenging for one student may be boring to another. In my experience, effective teachers are sensitive to student needs while maintaining curriculum expectations. This is not an easy task and it is often one that can dramatically increase preparation time and distract from teaching the class as a whole. As suggested elsewhere in this book, strategies that involve peer helpers, as an example, can be a tremendous help in meeting the unique needs of individual students while maintaining an appropriate "pace" to complete the expected curriculum. This is also an area where experienced teachers can be mentors for beginning teachers to help them understand how to meet the needs of individual students while maintaining a focus on curriculum expectations.

I have been often asked whether it is subject area success that results in improved student behavior, or whether it is improved student behavior that results in subject success? While these two factors are closely linked and one obviously impacts the other, if I had to decide which of the two to first focus on, I would go with subject area success as my number one priority. As an example to support my thoughts here, Ken was a fourteen year old boy who was a constant disruption in most of his classes, other than mathematics. Although mathematics was by no means Ken's best or most favorite subject, Ken's teacher employed an almost methodical step-by-step teaching approach with lots of student practice and high expectations for students. The success that Ken enjoyed in mathematics resulted in him behaving appropriately every day in this class even though in his other classes, he was often involved in arguments with his teachers and on many occasions sent to the office. In talking to Ken's other teachers some of them went to great lengths to build a relationship with Ken. One teacher even gave him a wide range of activities (apart from the subject area curriculum) that were supposedly designed to increase self-esteem. While some of these approaches may work for some students, they did not work for Ken. It seems quite clear that the most direct influence on him exhibiting appropriate classroom behavior came in a subject area where he was successful in learning the curriculum in spite of the fact that he didn't even really like the subject. From my teaching and counseling experience I could give many other examples to further support my thoughts here. Yes, as I outlined at the beginning of this book, there can be significant value in knowing more about each student on a personal level, but having said this, it is even more important to "teach" your curriculum and to find some way to help every student experience success in your subject area. You may have wonderful personal rapport with all your students, but unless these students are successful in learning the expectations within your subject area, the frustration they encounter will quickly exhibit itself in inappropriate behavior even though they may genuinely like you as a person.

In considering curriculum, there is one other factor that I think is important to mention. While it is natural for most students to have their unique subject area strengths and weaknesses, there is one skill area that can either enhance success or contribute to failure in almost all other subject areas. That skill set is reading.

I have seen a number of research studies that demonstrate that by the end of Grade 4 (see pages 233 + 272), somewhere between 30 - 40% of students are at least one grade level behind in their reading skills. As the scope of this book focuses on helping students in Grades 5 - 9, this research shows fairly clearly that approximately one in three students will enter grade 5 at least one level behind in their reading ability. As specific instruction in developing both reading speed and comprehension has vanished in some schools by grade 5, these students who are behind in their reading skills are often left to fend for themselves. To read slower than others and to have more difficulties than others in understanding what has been read can be tremendously frustrating and discouraging to affected students. It is this frustration and sense of discouragement that can translate into inappropriate behavior, whether exhibited by unacceptable attention seeking or by a general sense of apathy towards completing any school work. It is my belief that schools (at the grade 5 - 9 levels) need to develop reading programs offered by reading specialist teachers to help these students. Regardless of how many times these students might be disciplined with whatever strategies are employed in classrooms or schools, unless the reading problems are resolved, inappropriate student behavior will go on and on.

Sally was a Grade 8 student who one day began to have serious seizures at school. Although a few staff members were trained to deal with such medical emergencies, on at least half-a-dozen occasions an ambulance was called into the school because of the intensity and duration of the seizures. Sally was a cooperative student in all her classes who was also conscientious in completing her work. As a local children's hospital was involved in helping to diagnose the sudden cause of Sally's seizures, the school tended to adjust to the problem rather than thinking there might be some school related cause to the problem. During one severe seizure that occurred on a stairway in the school, a teacher walking by stated (out of frustration), "Not again, how many tests is she going to miss?" A nearby guidance counselor, overhearing the teacher's comments, did some follow-up exploration once the girl's current seizure had ended. To make a long story short, Sally was found to be more than three grade levels behind in her reading comprehension which was causing enormous stress for her as she attempted to keep abreast of the work in each of her classes. Sally was placed in a remedial reading program for part of her day and the schedule for her classes was modified to accommodate this program. From the first day that Sally started the remedial reading program, her seizures vanished and never returned. It is my experience and belief that a lack of reading skills can have a powerful and often very negative effect on student behavior which can be expressed in a multitude of inappropriate ways.

> "If students do not develop sufficient reading acumen by the middle of elementary school, they are handicapped from learning other curriculum as it does not take too long in schooling to move from learning to read to reading to learn."
> John Hattie in *Visible Learning - A Synthesis of over 800 Meta-Analyses Relating To Achievement*, 2009

> "Reading is essential for school success."
> Cunningham and Stanovich, 1998

2. TEACHING METHODS

There are a multitude of strategies, models and approaches that can be used in teaching. Some of the methods include (but are not limited to) the following:

- Direct Teaching
- Cooperative Learning
- Team Teaching
- Lecture
- Lecture with Discussion
- Panel and Discussion
- Labs
- Brainstorming
- Computer Assisted
- Discussion
- Learning Centers
- Video/Film
- Role Playing
- Worksheets
- Guest Speakers
- Online Teaching

In looking at a multitude of research related to effective teaching, I have been unable to find a credible research study that clearly identifies any single teaching method as the number one strategy that should be employed by teachers the majority of the time. After a study of public school teachers by researchers at Harvard University in 2001, School Superintendent Dr. Peter C. Gorman concluded from the results that "Highly effective teachers come in all shapes and sizes." Even though there may not be a single teaching method that contributes to the greatest learning, there are two factors that are important to consider. First of all, research clearly shows that it is the teacher who has the greatest impact on student achievement (and who also has the greatest impact on classroom management).

> "Improved classroom instruction is the prime factor to produce student achievement gains."
> Odden and Wallace, 2003

> "The best teachers in a school have as much as six times as much impact as the bottom third of teachers."
> Haycock and Huang, 2001

> "Effective teaching is the best preventative discipline strategy."
> Thomas Phelan, Ph. D., and Sarah June Schonour, M.A., in *1-2-3 Magic*, 2004

Secondly, although there might not be a single teaching method that is considered to be the most effective, there are none-the-less elements that are common to many strategies that contribute the most to effective teaching. I have summarized four of these key components as follows:

i) Clear Expectations

ii) Purposeful Teaching

iii) Guided Practice Including Specific Feedback

iv) Independent Practice

The following discussion will take a brief look at each of these components.

i) Clear Expectations

Whether it is rubrics, some form of goal setting, or simply modeling what the end result will look like, effective teaching begins with giving your students clear expectations of what they are going to be learning or achieving. Being able to clearly visualize the end result of what is being learned is very helpful to students, otherwise they don't know what they are trying to accomplish. For example, some effective teachers keep copies of past student work that is outstanding. This work is shown to students before instruction begins in order that students can clearly see and understand the learning outcomes for the current topic. Some effective teachers hand out sample copies of outstanding work and have students, in small groups, evaluate the work according to the rubrics or expectations that have been outlined. Plain and simple, an effective teacher generally begins by informing the students what they are going to be learning.

> "When you provide rubrics at the outset of a unit of instruction, you give students clear academic targets."
> Robert J. Marzano in
> *Classroom Management That Works*, 2003

ii) Purposeful Teaching

Earlier in this chapter I stated that students prefer to have teachers who "actually teach". In talking to many students further about this (over many years), students often add three factors that tranform what they mean by "actually teaching" to the more desirable category of "effective teaching". Many of the informal comments that students have made to me relating to effective teachers often fall directly into the area of what is considered "purposeful teaching". The three factors often suggested by students that relate to effective teaching are: being organized, being interesting, and providing individual assistance. As the first two of these factors directly relate to the concept of "purposeful teaching", I will comment a little further on them here. The third factor of "providing individual assistance" will be explored further under the heading of "Guided Practice" beginning on page 309.

First of all, students appreciate and respect teachers who are well organized and who have actually planned a lesson as opposed to teachers who repeatedly tell students to read specific pages from a text and then answer the questions, or who constantly give self-directed activity sheets/handouts, or who regular use videos to do their teaching. The realities of time management in teaching would dictate that every lesson cannot be a world-class performance. Unfortunately with the fast paced entertainment available on television and the internet, it has become increasingly difficult for teachers to provide instruction that is anywhere close to the Hollywood fast-paced editing that students have become accustomed to. None-the-less, students recognize and appreciate teachers who are organized. And this most definitely includes teachers who place a priority on marking assignments and tests as quickly as possible. It is very frustrating for students to hand assignments in on time and then wait for a significant time before receiving the assignments back. Research with students of all ages would stress the important of the timely return of assignments with constructive feedback.

Evidence of being organized begins immediately when a class starts on time instead of ten or fifteen minutes into the period after the teacher has fumbled around trying to locate his lesson materials. As previously mentioned under the heading of "Clear Expectations", an outline of what is going to be covered during the period and approximate timelines for the various steps in the outline provide evidence to students of a teacher being organized. A lack of organization can be a root cause of classroom misbehavior.

In addition to being organized, students often state that effective teachers are those who present interesting lessons at a pace that is understandable.

Teaching an "understandable lesson" requires an awareness by the teacher of the sequential nature of what is being taught and having the ability to break the skills down into manageable steps. Students learn best (and inappropriate behavior decreases) when they are involved in a step-by-step process of learning, with a mastery of each step before progressing to the next step.

> "The secret of getting ahead is getting started.
> The secret of getting started is breaking your complex,
> overwhelming tasks into small manageable tasks,
> and then starting on the first one."
> Mark Twain

While there are a wide range of techniques for making a lesson interesting, one of the fundamental strategies is to involve students in the learning process - whether answering questions, discussing concepts, or role-playing as examples. Most people learn significantly more when they participate in the actual learning, rather than being a passive spectator.

In a research study conducted by Yair (2000), the findings stated that "the more students felt challenged and the greater the academic demand - the more students are engaged with instruction and less prone to external preoccupations." The unfortunate reality in many classrooms is that the range of student abilities (and motivation) may be so great that what is challenging to some students may be boring to others. Effective teachers recognize student differences and find ways to address unique needs through individualized instruction and often by teaching to the recognized learning styles of individuals. A common complaint by students of ineffective teachers is that the lessons are boring. While this concern is often the result of a teacher who does all the talking and fails to involve the students in the lesson, it can also be a result of teaching to the "lower end" of the abilities within the class (or in some cases, teaching only to the higher end or even the middle).

When a teacher is organized and presents an interesting lesson, there is a flow to what is happening. It is this flow, like a good story, that holds the attention of most students and keeps them focused on learning instead of drifting into inappropriate behavior.

> "A central theme in managing activities well is the idea of activity flow, the degree to which a lesson proceeds smoothly without digressions, diversions, or interruptions. Lessons with a good flow keep student attention and are less likely to offer opportunities for deviance because most of the cues for students are directed towards behaviors appropriate for the lesson."
> Edmund T. Emmer and Carolyn M. Evertson
> in *Classroom Management for Middle and High School Teachers*, 2009

Another aspect of purposeful teaching is teaching with enthusiasm. If you love what you are teaching there is a much better chance that this will engage your students more than if you dislike what you are doing. Enthusiasm is contagious and your love of what you are teaching can inspire your students to learn. Enthusiasm in often identified in research studies as an important trait of effective teachers.

Another factor that students express related to effective teaching is "assisted practice". This is explained next under the heading of "Guided Practice".

iii) Guided Practice

In my conversations with students over many years, they have emphasized the importance of teachers helping them as individuals with their work based on whatever lesson has been taught. Students stressed that this help was more beneficial when the teacher (and peer helpers) actually move around the room to assist them with the work being done. A major complaint by students is that too many teachers, after assigning the work based on their lesson, quickly retreat to their desks and mark or do something else, making themselves unavailable to students during this critical learning time. Some students even expressed their concern that they hesitated (feared) to ask certain teachers for help during this time because the teacher's non-verbal cues and sometimes even words stated very clearly "leave me alone". Experts in the teaching field have labelled this time as "guided practice", noting the importance of teachers being accessible to help individual students. Without this help, some students will give up while some others might complete the work but do it incorrectly.

Guided practice is an important time when feedback is given to students. Effective teachers recognize that feedback is more than just giving praise or rewards. Effective feedback provides information related to the skills/content that is being learned. Sometimes too much feedback is given related to the "self" rather than the content of what is being learned. Constructive feedback assists a student with learning what has been taught.

> "Practicing without feedback is like bowling through a curtain that hangs down to knee level. You can work on technique all you like, but if you can't see the effects, two things will happen:
> You won't get any better, and you'll stop caring."
> Steve Kerr, former chief learning officer of Goldman Sachs

Guided practice also offers an opportunity for a teacher to evaluate how effective his teaching is. Working with individual students, a teacher should be able to quickly ascertain whether his lesson actually worked, and if not, what might be done during tomorrow's class to better assist students with the mastery of the goals for this particular aspect of the curriculum. In the same way that a "unit test" can be a measure of how well your students have learned a specific unit of work, guided practice, either after or even during a lesson, can provide you with feedback as to how effectively you are helping your students to master the identified learning outcomes. Following guided practice comes independent practice which I will explore next.

iv) Independent Practice

A fourth common trait of effective teaching is the use of independent practice. In contrast to guided practice (outlined on the previous page), independent practice is the time during which students attempt to solve problems or complete assignments without the direct, ongoing supervision of their teacher (although there may certainly be a need for teachers to sometimes assist with this process). Independent practice is often the "homework" part of a lesson although it may also occur in the classroom, provided that "guided practice" has first occurred.

> "Of the thousands of pieces of advice, inspiration and encouragement I've received over the years, the most powerful one - the one that has played a central role in my life, both as a child and as an adult - boils down to a single word - practice."
> Itzhak Perlman, Musician

A key component of guided practice is giving students feedback on what they have done. Similarly, even though independent practice may occur outside the classroom, it remains equally important to provide feedback. Students encounter a great deal of frustration when they spend significant time to complete a homework assignment (independent practice), only to have a teacher completely ignore this work. Independent practice is given for the reason of solidifying the mastery of learning outcomes. Unless students are given some constructive feedback on their independent practice, there might be some students who spent significant time doing things the wrong way that will negatively impact further learning in the skill area, concept or topic being presented.

While the previous few pages provide some thoughts on four common factors that are part of effective teaching, there may be times in which you unexpectedly hit a "home run" with one of your lessons. At times like this, it is worthwhile taking some time afterwards to ask yourself what you did that worked so well. In the Apollo 13 movie, the first question that was asked after a problem occurred was "What's working?" Sometimes we put too much focus on what is wrong instead of on what is working. Not only is it important to ask yourself what is working, but it is also valuable to ask your students for feedback in this area. Many effective teachers ask their students, from time to time, what is working for them. This keeps the emphasis on the positive and it can also help to empower your students to be more active in taking some ownership for what is happening in the classroom, especially if you take the time to build further on the responses that your students provide.

TRAITS OF HIGHLY EFFECTIVE TEACHERS

- Student work could be found everywhere, inside the classroom, out the door and, in some cases, down the hall.

- The teachers did not stand still and lecture; they covered every part of the room and monitored every activity that took place.

- Multiple small group activities were often found in their classrooms, with the traditional arrangement of desks in rows practically non-existent.

- Students in their classes were at ease asking questions and commenting on statements made by teachers and other students.

- Expectations for the students were clearly stated and exemplars of previous years' assignments were shown to students as models of what to produce.

- The organization of the rooms and the lessons was clearly evident. Materials were easily accessible when needed and no class time was wasted from lack of preparation.

Research results from a study
by the Public Education Foundation, 2002

"Respect yourself
and others
will respect you".
Confucius

CHAPTER 11

LOOKING AFTER YOURSELF

It has sometimes been said that the best way to approach teaching is to consider each day as part of a marathon, rather than a sprint. Unfortunately there are days when the marathon turns into a sprint and another reality is that running a marathon over some two-hundred days can wear down even the most prepared people.

When you enter a classroom feeling exhausted, sick, or emotionally drained, classroom management and effective teaching can suffer. It is sometimes on days when you should be at home in bed that you say and do things that might be contrary to your normal teaching approach. In addition, by pushing yourself on such days you sometimes increase whatever illness is affecting you which then results in missing more than just a day or two.

Mike was an outstanding teacher who was often the first person to enter the school each day and the last to leave. He rarely took time to actually sit down and eat lunch as he was involved in coaching or running clubs during noon hours or after school. At the beginning of the school year, Mike launched himself like a rocket into every aspect of his teaching and his involvement in extracurricular activities. During September and into the first part of October, Mike was one of the most productive, energized and positive teachers in the school. Like clockwork, by mid-October Mike began to suffer headaches and flu-like symptoms. Throughout November, year after year, Mike began to drag himself into school, sometimes late. Throughout the day, the once highly effective teacher assigned more and more "readings" for students and did less and less actual teaching. His patience with students evaporated, and classroom management problems, that were once non-existent, became more and more pronounced. By December, it was predictable that Mike would miss much of the month because of illness. This pattern then repeated itself to a less extreme degree during the second part of the school year.

Mike illustrates the obvious concerns that can occur when a person does not look after himself and/or find appropriate ways to pace himself. Unfortunately, Mike's story is not unusual although it can play itself out in different ways. Some teachers, unable to prioritize their time, or unable to say "no" to just about any request, or too tired to obtain some appropriate exercise and time outside, or setting unrealistic personal time demands may eventually leave teaching because it is just too overwhelming for them. Other teachers, in similar situations, may "survive" several years in the profession before they "crash", suffering various forms of illnesses throughout the school year.

Although time management has already been explored in this book, it would be useful for you to revisit the tips provided in Chapter 3 and give some thought as to how they relate to your own time management skills. Most teachers understand the importance of exercise or having relaxing hobbies or personally satisfying interests outside of school, but are often "too busy" or "too exhausted" to pursue them. Improved time management skills can help you to have the time to "have a life" outside of teaching, which can be a very positive contributor to remaining healthy and "balanced", two important ingredients that can contribute in a very positive manner to being an effective teacher. For many years as an educator, I found a way to get a fifteen minute walk at lunch. It is my belief that this walk each day made a very positive contribution to my effectiveness within the school. Over and over again I heard other teachers say how much they wished they could find fifteen minutes during the course of a day for a walk. In the end it's all about priorities and time management, although it's also about understanding that looking after yourself can play a direct role in being a more effective teacher. I have known some teachers who built their "fifteen minute" walk at the beginning or even the end of their day. The important thing here is the simple reminder that we all need to do something to look after ourselves each day, and for most people some simple form of physical activity can make a significant difference.

Another consideration related to looking after yourself is to consider how you respond to "change". In a rapidly changing world, employers often identify "being adaptable", or "being flexible", as key factors in being successful in a job. Teaching is no different in this regard. Being able to positively deal with change can be an asset helping you to be a more effective teacher as well as reducing stress. Resisting change often results in greater self-imposed stress and anxiety. There will be some tips provided in this chapter that relate to being flexible and approaching change with a positive mindset.

A final area in this chapter related to looking after yourself is giving some thought as to what you can do in advance of being ill so that when the day comes - and it will for most teachers - you will feel more comfortable staying home because you know you have left a framework in place that will assist whoever is taking your class for a day or two. Many teachers acknowledge that they know when they should stay home, but they fail to do this because they know when they return back to school their classroom and students will sometimes be in upheaval. Another comment often heard by teachers who are suffering some form of illness is that it is easier to come into school then it is to prepare the lessons for a "substitute" teacher. This chapter can provide some ideas to ensure that some plans are in place long before you ever get sick.

Similarly, there may times when you miss some classes due to your involvement in extra-curricular activities and/or professional development activities. Whatever your reason for missing a class, the teacher who will be replacing you will benefit from some pre-planning on your part. It is suggested that some of the activities in this chapter that relate to helping "substitute teachers" be placed in an envelope in a convenient desk drawer where it is easy for someone to locate when you are going to be away, even if your absence is "last minute" and unplanned.

> "For every minute
> that is spent in organizing,
> an hour is earned."
> Anonymous

CHANGE QUOTES

"If you don't like something, change it;
if you can't change it, change the way you think about it."
Mary Engelbreit

"When we are no longer able to change a situation,
we are challenged to change ourselves."
Victor Frankl

"Without accepting the fact that everything changes,
we cannot find perfect composure."
Shunryu Suzuki

"God grant me the serenity to accept the people I cannot change,
the courage to change the one I can, and the wisdom to know it's me."
Anonymous

"The world hates change,
yet it is the only thing that has brought progress."
Charles Kettering

"Change is the law of life. And those who look only to the past
or present are certain to miss the future."
J. F. Kennedy

""The truth is that our finest moments are more likely to occur when
we are feeling deeply uncomfortable, unhappy, or unfilled. For it is only
in such moments, propelled by our discomfort, that we are likely
to step out of our rut and start seeking a different way or truer answers."
M. Scott Peck

"Our universe is transformation; our life is what our thoughts make of it."
Marcus Aurellius

"Growth itself contains the germ of happiness."
Pearl S. Buck

"Life is progress, and not a station."
Ralph Waldo Emerson

TIPS FOR DEALING WITH CHANGE

1. Look for the opportunities and benefits
that the change can bring to you.

2. Don't waste energy on resisting change
if it's going to happen anyway.

3. Decide how to react to change rather than letting others
tell you how they think you should react.

4. Take responsibility for changing yourself,
not others.

5. Keep things in perspective.
We allow most things to become much worse
in our mind than they actually become.

6. Focus on what you can control,
not what you cannot.

7. Learn how to deal with the stress of change
by employing techniques such as exercise or meditation.

8. Explore the different choices you have related to the change.

9. Get all the information related to the change
and attempt to understand it before you react.

10. Identify the emotions you are feeling
and deal with them
before you attempt to work through the change.

SOME THOUGHTS ON HOW TO PREPARE BEFOREHAND FOR POSSIBLE FUTURE ABSENCES

EMERGENCY LESSON PLANS

The format on page 319 provides you with a sample plan outline that can be adapted to various lessons. You could also design your own outline for this activity. The basic idea here is to complete a few generic lesson plans that could be substituted at any time in your program. The plans should be specifically set up for a substitute teacher who might not necessarily be an expert in your subject area. If you are absent, the substitute teacher can be directed to these lesson plans that are stored in a convenient place in your classroom.

TIPS FOR TEACHING MY CLASS

Being a substitute teacher can be a difficult teaching role. Simple things like not knowing the names of the students or where they sit, or being unaware of classroom procedures and expectations can create havoc for a substitute teacher and often provide the rationale for a substitute teacher failing to complete whatever you have left to be done by your students.

Earlier in this book, it was suggested that classroom rules or expectations (as well as any procedures) be posted in your room. This information can be very helpful to substitute teachers. It was also suggested that you establish a program where students engage in the role of being classroom monitors. When you are absent, these students can be leaders to assist the substitute teacher.

Page 320 provides a framework that you can use to record some thoughts that can be provided to help substitute teachers better understand the rules and routines that are expected in your class.

Lesson Objectives:

Steps involved in this lesson and approximate timelines:

Students, peer helpers or other classroom assistants who could assist you in teaching this lesson:

Reference Materials used in this lesson and where they are located:

Homework/assignments related to the lesson:

Other:

TIPS FOR TEACHING MY CLASS

Seating plans, emergency lesson plans, class times, etc. can be found . . .

A list of our classroom rules and/or procedures can be found . . .

Classroom management strategies that work well with my students are . . .

Classroom management strategies that are not effective with my students are . . .

Other . . .

ACTIVITIES THAT WORK WELL WITH MY CLASS

Throughout the year there are often activities that you find work very well with your students. These activities might include games or even silent reading times. As a teacher you may find that these are the activities that give you a "breather". These activities may become part of your classroom routines and may even be used as a reward for your students when they have achieved specific learning objectives. Such activities can be very helpful as well to "substitute teachers" as they often provide a routine that students enjoy which can reduce potential classroom management problems. When the students are involved in activities they enjoy and recognize as part of their normal routines, they will respond in a more natural and positive manner to substitute teachers which can result in less work for you when you return from your absence. The information on page 322 can be completed and left in an appropriate place for substitute teachers.

CLASSROOM ROUTINES

Although the previous three suggestions relate in some ways to classroom routines, this activity specifically looks at the normal procedures that occur in your classroom. Once again, helping both the substitute teacher and your students to sense that the normal ways of doing things are being followed can reduce classroom management problems that sometimes occur with substitute teachers. And reducing classroom management problems can help the substitute teacher to actually teach the lesson content that you left for them. Page 323 can assist you with identifying some classroom routines that could be beneficial to any substitute teacher who is filling in for you when you are absent.

> "Although predictability can be tedious for adults, children thrive on sameness and repetition."
> Liza Asher, *The Importance of Routines,*
> keepkidshealthy.com

SUGGESTED ACTIVITIES

Seating plans, emergency lesson plans, class times, etc. can be found . . .

A list of our classroom rules and/or procedures can be found . . .

Classroom management strategies that work well with my students are . . .

Classroom management strategies that are not effective with my students are . . .

Other . . .

SUGGESTED ROUTINES

Some students who can assist in taking attendance are . . .

Attendance reports are sent to the office at . . .

If a student is late for class you should . . .

The normal routine for a student going to the washroom is . . .

The normal routine for going to the library is . . .

Some routines that need to be completed at the end of the day (such as stacking chairs or locking the classroom door) are . . .

Students are not generally permitted to . . .

Other . . .

QUOTES RELATED TO LOOKING AFTER YOURSELF

"He who trims himself to please everybody will soon whittle himself away."
Raymond Hull

"Always be a first-rate version of yourself,
instead of a second-rate version of someone else."
Judy Garland

"The great majority of us are required to live a life of constant duplicity.
Your health is bound to be affected, if day after day, you say the opposite
of what you feel, if you grovel before what you dislike, and rejoice
at what brings you nothing but misfortune."
Boris Pasternak

"There is just one life for each of us: our own."
Euripides

"Every time you don't follow your inner guidance,
you feel a loss of energy, loss of power,
a sense of spiritual deadness."
Shakti Gawain

"Be who you are and say what you feel,
because those who mind don't matter and those who matter don't mind."
Dr. Seuss

"Like the sky after a rainy day we must open to ourselves.
Learn to love yourself for who you are and open so the world can see you shine."
James Poland

"Take care of your body. It is the only place you have to live."
Jim Rohn

"A friend is a present you give to yourself."
Robert Louis Stevenson

"No one is in control of your happiness but you; therefore you have the power
to change anything about yourself or your life that you want to change."
Barbara De Angelis

"Most teachers have little control
over school policy or curriculum
or choice of texts or special placement
of students, but have a great deal
of autonomy inside the classroom.
To a degree shared by few other occupations,
public education rests precariously on
the skill and virtue of the people
at the bottom of the institutional pyramid."
Tracy Kidder

NOTES

BIBLIOGRAPHY + SUGGESTED READINGS

Adair, J. *How to grow leaders: The seven key principles of effective leadership development.* London: Kogan Page Publishing, 2005.

Akin-Little, K. A., Eckett, T. L., and Little, S.G. *Extrinsic reinforcement in the classroom: Bribery or best practice.* School Psychology Review, 33, 344-362, 2004.

Beck, A. *Prisoners of Hate: The Cognitive Basis of Anger, Hostility and Violence.* New York: HarperCollins, 1999.

Bicard, D. F. *Using classroom rules to construct behavior.* Middle School Journal, 31(5), 37-45, 2000.

Bossidy, Larry, and Ram Charan. *Execution: The Discipline of Getting Things Done.* New York: Crown Business, 2002.

Brophy, J. E. *Motivating students to learn – 2nd Edition.* Hillsdale, NJ: Erlbaum, 2004.

Brophy, J. E. *Teaching problem students.* New York: Guilford, 1996.

Buckingham, Marcus. *Go - Put Your Strengths To Work.* New York: Free Press, 2007

Canfield, Jack. *The Success Principles.* New York: HarperCollins, 2005.

Canfield, Jack, Mark Victor Hansen, and Les Hewitt. *The Power of Focus.* Deerfield Beach, Fla.: Health Communications, 2000.

Carlson, Richard. *Don't Sweat the Small Stuff...and It's All Small Stuff: Simple Ways to Keep the Little Things from Taking Over Your Life.* New York: Hyperion, 1997

Carolan, J., and Guinn, A. *Differentiation: Lessons from master teachers.* Educational Leadership, 64(5), 44-47, 2006.

Carter, Les, and Frank Minirth. *The Anger Workbook.* Nashville, TN: Thomas Nelson, Inc., 1993.

Charan, Ram. *Know-How: The 8 Skills That Separate People Who Perform From Those Who Don't.* New York: Crown Publishing, 2007.

Collins Jim and Hansen, Morten T. *Great By Choice: Uncertainty, chaos and luck - Why some thrive despite them all.* HarperCollins: New York, NY., 2011.

Colvin, Geoff. *Talent Is Overrated. What Really Separates World-Class Performers From Every-*

body Else. New York: Penguin, 2008.

Cote, James E., and Anton L. Allahar. *Ivory Tower Blues. A University System In Crisis*. Toronto, ON: University of Toronto Press, 2007.

Covey, Stephen, A. Roger Merrill, and Rebecca R. Merrill. *First Things First.* New York: Fireside, 1995.

Cunningham, A. J. *The contribution of computer-generated instructional graphics on measured achievement gains: A meta-analysis.* East Texas State University, TX, 1998

Damiani, V. B. *Crisis prevention and intervention in the classroom: What teachers should know.* Lanham, MD: Rowman & Littlefield, 2006.

Dickinson, Arlene. *Persuasion - A New Approach to Changing Minds.* Toronto. ON: HarperCollins, 2011.

Dweck, Carol, Ph. D. *Mindset: The New Psychology of Success.* Random House: New York, NY., 2006.

Ellis, A. *How to Control Your Anger Before It Controls You.* Secaucus, NJ: Carol Publishing Group, 1998.

Emmer, Edmund T. and Evertson, Carolyn M. *Classroom Management For Middle and High School Teachers.* Upper Saddle River, NJ: Pearson Education, Inc., 2009.

Emmett, Rita. *The Procrastinator's Handbook: Mastering the Art of Doing It Now.* New York: Walker Publishing, 2000.

Fenwick, D. T. *Managing space, energy, and self: Junior high teachers' experiences of classroom management. Teaching and Teacher Education, 14*, 619-631, 1998.

Gazda, George M. *Human Relations Development: A Manual for Educators.* Boston, MA: Allyn and Bacon, 2005.

Goldbert, Donna, with Jennifer Zwiebel. *The Organized Student.* New York: Fireside, 2005.

Good, T. L,, and Brophy, J. E. *Looking in classrooms (6th Edition).* New York: Harper Collins, 1994.

Harris, Brian. *The Student Success Handbook.* Burlington, ON: CGS Communications, 2011.

Harris, M. J., and Rosenthal, R. *Mediation of interpersonal expectancy effects: 31 meta-analysis. Psychological Bulletin, 97 (3),* 363 - 386, 1985.

Haycock, K. *Good Teaching Matters ... a lot. Thinking K-16, 3 (2)*, 1-14, 1998.

Hattie, John. *Visible Learning: A synthesis of over 800 Meta-analyses Related to Achievement.* New York, NY: Routledge, 2009.

Hill, Napoleon, and W. Clement Stone. *Success Through a Positive Mental Attitude.* Englewood Cliffs, NJ. Prentice-Hall, 1977.

Hong, S. and Ho, H. *Direct and indirect longitudinal effects of parental involvement on student achievement: Second-order latent growth modeling across ethnic groups. Journal of Educational Psychology, 97 (1)*, 32-42, 2005.

Hulley, W., and Dier, L. *Harbors of hope: The planning for school and student success process.* Bloomington, IN: Solution Tree, 2005.

James, Tad. *The Secret of Creating Your Future.* Honolulu, Hawaii: Advanced Neuro Dynamics, 1989.

Jensen, Eric. *Student Success Secrets.* Hauppauge, New York: Barron's, 2003.

Jones, V. F., and Jones, L. S. *Comprehensive classroom management: Creating communities of support and solving problems (8th edition).* Boston: Allyn and Bacon, 2007.

Kersey, Cynthia. Unstoppable: *45 Powerful Stories of Perseverance and Triumph From People Just Like You.* Naperville, IL.: Sourcebooks, Inc., 1998.

Kline, Peter, and Martel Laurence. *School Success.* Arlington, VA: Great Ocean Publishers, 1994.

Kottler, J. A. *Students who drive you crazy: Succeeding with resistant, unmotivated, and otherwise difficult young people.* Thousand Oaks, CA: Sage/Corwin Press, 2002.

Lerner, Harriet. *The Dance of Anger.* New York, NY: HarperCollins, 1997.

Lofland, Don. *Powerlearning.* Stamford, CT: Longmeadow Press, 1994.

Lowry, R., Sleet, D., Duncan, C., Powell, K., and Kolbe, L. *Adolescents at risk for violence. Educational Psychology Review, 7 (1)*, 7-39, 1995.

MacKenzie, Robert J., and Stanzione, Lisa. *Setting Limits in the Classroom. A Complete Guide to Effective Classroom Managment with a School-Wide Discipline Plan.* New York, NY: Three Rivers Press, 2010.

Malone, B.G., and Tietjens, C.L. *Re-examination of classroom rules: The need for clarity and specified behavior. Special Services in the School, 16, 159-170*, 2000.

Marzano, R. J. with Marzano J.S. and Pickering, D.J. *Classroom Management that Works – Research Based Strategies for Every Teacher.* Alexandria, VA: ASCD, 2003.

Marzano, R. J. *What works in schools: Translating research into action.* Alexandria, VA: Association for Supervision and Curriculum Development, 2003.

McClard, Stephen T. *The Superior Educator - A Calm and Assertive Approach to Classroom Management and Large Group Motivation.* Kindle, 2008.

McKay, Matthew, Ph.D., and Rogers, Peter, Ph.D. *The Anger Control Workbook – Simple, innovative techniques for managing anger and developing healthier ways of relating.* Oakland, CA: New Harbinger Publications Inc., 2000.

McGuinness, Diane. *Early Reading Instruction: What Science Really Tells Us About How To Teach Reading.* Cambridge, Massachusetts: MIT Press, 2004.

McGuinness, Diane. *Language Development and Learning to Read: The Scientific Study of How Language Development Affects Reading Skill.* Cambridge, Massachusetts: MIT Press, 2005.

McKay, Matthew, and Peter Rogers. *The Anger Control Workbook.* Oakland, CA: New Harbinger Publications, Inc., 2000.

Mighton, John. *The End Of Ignorance. Multiplying Our Human Potential.* Toronto, ON: Vintage Canada, 2007

Miller, Matt. *The Tyranny of Dead Ideas. Letting Go Of The Old Ways Of Thinking To Unleash A New Prosperity.* New York: Times Books, 2009.

Pace, J. L. *Revisiting classroom authority: Theory and ideology meets practice. Teachers' College Record, 105,* 1559-1585, 2003.

Peale, Norman Vincent. *The Power of Positive Thinking.* New York: Fireside, 2003.

Phelan, Thomas W., and Schonour, Sarah Jane. *1-2-3 Magic for Teachers - Effective Classroom Discipline Pre-K through Grade 8.* Glen Ellyn, IL: ParentMagic, Inc., 2004.

Race, Phil. *How To Study: Practical Tips for Students.* Malden, MA: Blackwell Publishing, 2003.

Reeve, J. *Extrinsic rewards and inner motivation. in C. Evertson & C. Weinstein, Handbook of classroom management.* Mahwah, NJ: Erlbaum, 2006

Robey, Dan. *The Power of Positive Habits.* Miami: Abritt Publishing Group, 2000.

Robinson, Adam. *What Smart Students Know.* New York: Three Rivers Press, 1993.

Rose, Colin and Malcolm J. Nicholl. *Accelerated Learning for the 21st Century.* New York: Dell Pub., 1998.

Rozakis, Laurie. *Super Study Skills.* New York: Scholastic, 2002.

Rubinstein, Gary. *Reluctant Disciplinarian – Advice on classroom management from a softy who became (eventually) a successful teacher.* Fort Collins. CO: Cottonwood Press, Inc., 2010.

Schmoker, Mike. *Results Now - How We Can Achieve Unprecedented Improvements in Teaching and Learning.* Alexandria, VA: ASCD, 2006.

Scott, Steven K. *Simple Steps To Impossible Dreams: The 15 Power Secrets of the World's Most Successful People.* New York: Fireside, 1998.

Seligman, Martin E. *Learned Optimism. How to Change Your Mind and Your Life.* New York: Random House, Inc., 2006.

Sheets, R. H., and Gay, G. *Student perceptions of disciplinary conflict in ethnically diverse classrooms. NASSP Bulletin,* 84-93, 1996.

Shukla-Mehta, S., and Albin, R. W. *Twelve practical strategies to prevent behavioural escalation in classroom settings. Preventing School Failure, 47*, 156-172, 2003

Silver, Larry B. *The Misunderstood Child: Understanding and Coping with Your Child's Learning Disabilities.* New York: Three Rivers Press, 1998.

Skiba, R. J., Peterson, R. L., and Williams, T. *Office referrals and suspensions: Disciplinary interventions in middle schools. Education and Treatment of Children, 20(3)*, 295-315, 1997.

Smith, Hyrum W. *The 10 Natural Laws of Successful Time and Life Management: Proven Strategies for Increased Productivity and Inner Peace.* New York: Warner Books, 1994.

Stage, S. A., and Quiroz, D. R., *A meta-analysis of interventions to decrease disruptive classroom behavior in public education settings. School Psychology Review, 26 (3)*, 333-368, 1997.

Syed, Matthew. *Bounce - Mozart, Federer, Picasso, Beckham, and the Science of Success.* New York, NY: HarperCollins, 2011.

Thomas Marlo. *Right Words at the Right Time.* New York, NY: Atria Books, 2002.

Thorson, S. A. *Listening to students: Reflections on secondary classroom management.* Boston: Allyn and Bacon, 2003.

Thurston, Cheryl Miller. *Attitude: Helping Students Want To Succeed In School And Then Setting Them Up For Success.* Fort Collins, Colorado: Cottonwood Press, Inc., 2003.

Tolle, Eckhart. *The Power of Now: A Guide to Spiritual Enlightenment.* New World Library: Novato, CA,1999.

Tracy, Brian. *Create Your Own Future.* New York: John Wiley & Sons, 2002.

Wang, M. C., Haertel, G. D., and Walberg, H. J. *Toward a knowledge base for school learning. Review of Educational Research, 63 (3),* 249-294, 1993.

Weiss, Brian. *Eliminating Stress, Finding Inner Peace.* Carlsbad, CA: Hay House: 2003.

Wright, S. P., Horn, S. P. and Sanders, W. L. *Teacher and classroom context effects on student achievement: Implications for teacher evaluation. Journal of Personnel Evaluation in Education, 11,* 57-67, 1997.

Young, Steve. *Great Failures of the Extremely Successful.* Los Angeles: Tallfellow Press, 2002.

OTHER BOOKS BY BRIAN HARRIS

THE STUDENT SUCCESS HANDBOOK
ISBN # 978-1460906323   -   soft cover - 204 pages

This book, written primarily for students in grades 8 - 10, provides 125 ready-to-use activities and related handouts to help students to be more successful. Chapter titles include: "Establishing Trust", "Be Your Success Attitude", "Conflict Resolution" (including anger management), "Organizing For Success", and more.

www.highlyeffectiveteaching.com

OTHER BOOKS BY BRIAN HARRIS

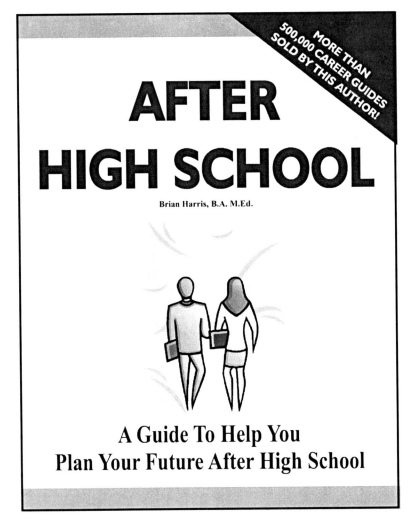

ISBN #9781460906293 - Soft Cover - 80 Pages

- includes a self-scoring interest survey
- includes a self-scoring abilities assessment
- includes a self-scoring values assessment
- includes an up-to-date list of more than 450 occupations

Specifically Written To Help High School Students Plan Their Future

www.highlyeffectiveteaching.com

OTHER BOOKS BY BRIAN HARRIS

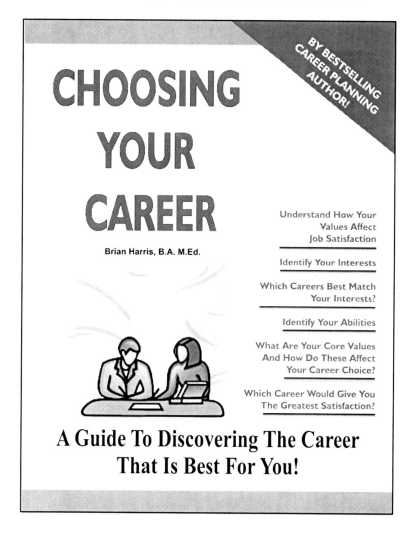

ISBN #978-1460930885   80 Pages

- includes a self-scoring interest survey
- includes a self-scoring abilities assessment
- includes a self-scoring values assessment
- includes an up-to-date list of more than 450 occupations

For College Students and Other Adults

www.highlyeffectiveteaching.com

OTHER BOOKS BY BRIAN HARRIS

ISBN #978-1460930908   90 Pages

- shows you the 6 major factors employers look for when they hire
- helps you to better understand what you should be writing in your resume and cover letters
- helps you to better understand how to answer interview questions
- helps you to better understand how to effectively market yourself

Can Be Used By High School Students and Adults

www.highlyeffectiveteaching.com

OTHER BOOKS BY BRIAN HARRIS

THE MILLIONAIRE LIFEGUARD
ISBN # 9781451509472
soft cover - 174 pages

Two young adults seek the help of a legendary lifeguard in Hawaii. As they attempt to discover his magic formula for financial success, their lives are changed forever as they encounter the wisdom of a master teacher.

www.millionairelifeguard.com

OTHER BOOKS BY BRIAN HARRIS

CHAPTER TITLES

1. What Are Employers Looking For
2. Identifying Your Future Goals
3. Developing A Positive Attitude
4. Identifying Your Skills
5. Developing Effective People Skills
6. Identifying Your Work Ethic
7. The Importance of Being Adaptable
8. Tips For Marketing Yourself
9. Writing Effective Cover Letters
10. Writing A Strong Resume
11. Successful Job Interviews

THE JOB SUCCESS HANDBOOK
ISBN # 9781460906316 - Soft Cover - 260 pages

    THE JOB SUCCESS HANDBOOK provides 201 classroom activities that teachers/career counselors can use with high school students. The activities include black-line masters for handouts that can be freely photocopied for your students. THE JOB SUCCESS HANDBOOK is based on the major factors that employers look for when they hire. In addition to helping your students to get hired into jobs (whether full-time as they leave school, or part-time to help support their future educational costs), these factors can also help your students to be more successful in school.
    This book can save teachers hours of preparation time.

www.highlyeffectiveteaching.com

CPSIA information can be obtained at www.ICGtesting.com
Printed in the USA
LVOW09s1823230813

349377LV00008B/1107/P